UNIVERSITY OF CAMBRIDGE
DEPARTMENT OF APPLIED ECONOMICS

MONOGRAPHS

This series consists of investigations conducted by members of the Department's staff and others working in direct collaboration with the Department.

The Department of Applied Economics assumes no responsibility for the views expressed in the Monographs published under its auspices.

The following monographs are still in print.

THE ANALYSIS OF FAMILY BUDGETS

BY

S. J. PRAIS

AND

H. S. HOUTHAKKER

SECOND IMPRESSION

ABRIDGED

WITH A NEW PREFACE DESCRIBING
DEVELOPMENTS IN METHODS OF
COLLECTION AND ANALYSIS OF DATA
IN THE PERIOD 1955–70

CAMBRIDGE
AT THE UNIVERSITY PRESS
1971

PUBLISHED BY
THE SYNDICS OF THE CAMBRIDGE UNIVERSITY PRESS
Bentley House, 200 Euston Road, London NW1 2DB
American Branch: 32 East 57th Street, New York, N.Y. 10022
Preface to Second Impression © Cambridge University Press 1971

ISBN: 0 521 08118 1

First published 1955

Reprinted with a new Preface and
omitting Tables C1—X13 1971

First printed in Great Britain at the University Printing House, Cambridge
Reprinted in Great Britain by Lewis Reprints Limited, London and Tonbridge

On y verra de ces sortes de demonstrations, qui ne produisent pas une certitude aussi grande que celles de Geometrie, et qui mesme en different beaucoup, puisque au lieu que les Geometres prouvent leurs Propositions par des Principes certains & incontestables, icy les Principes se verifient par les conclusions qu'on en tire; la nature de ces choses ne souffrant pas que cela se fasse autrement. Il est possible toutefois d'y arriver à un degré de vraisemblance, qui bien souvent ne cede guere à une evidence entiere.

HUYGENS, *Traité de la Lumière*

CONTENTS

PART II. THE ANALYSES

Chapter 7. THE ENGEL CURVE

Chapter 8. QUALITY VARIATIONS IN THE CONSUMPTION PATTERN

Chapter 9. HOUSEHOLD COMPOSITION AND UNIT-CONSUMER SCALES

Chapter 10. ECONOMIES OF SCALE IN CONSUMPTION

LIST OF TABLES IN PARTS I AND II

LIST OF FIGURES

FOREWORD

The analysis of consumers' behaviour is the branch of econometrics which has been most intensively investigated at the Department of Applied Economics since it came into being in 1946, and the work on this subject now being conducted there owes much to the researches of S. J. Prais and H. S. Houthakker reported in this monograph.

These inquiries relate to the analysis of family budgets, that is to say they are based exclusively on cross-section data. While the results of a number of budget inquiries have been used, the main body of material analysed is based on a special tabulation, undertaken by the authors, of information obtained in two similar collections of family budgets made in this country in 1937–8 and 1938–9 by the Ministry of Labour and the Civil Service Statistical and Research Bureau respectively. Since in the past this material has been available only in relatively summary form, the detailed tabulations used by the authors are set out in full in Part III of this monograph for the use of other investigators.

As is well known, the data on which the analysis of consumers' behaviour is usually based take the form either of family budgets or of time series or of a combination of both. The present study naturally concentrates on aspects of consumers' behaviour, such as the relationship between expenditure on individual commodities and total expenditure (or income), quality variations in the consumption pattern, household composition and unit-consumer scales, economies of scale in consumption, and social, occupational and regional factors in expenditure patterns which can be investigated on the basis of a single (as opposed to a continuous) family budget inquiry.

The essential ingredients of applied analysis, theory, observations and methods of inference, are discussed in Part I. The more general aspects of theory and method are covered by references to standard works and the treatment given in the text relates largely to special problems and to extensions of the usual forms of presentation. Their interplay in analysis is fully illustrated in Part II, which also shows the possibilities and limitations of special assumptions designed to restrict, for the time being, the complexity of the hypotheses to be tested. Thus it is shown that it is possible to make a satisfactory study of Engel curves without at the same time introducing a sophisticated treatment of unit-consumer scales; and also that the derivation of such scales involves a formulation of the problem which is essentially non-linear and cannot be handled satisfactorily by a linear approximation.

B

The investigations which were undertaken as a contribution to our knowledge of an important sector of the economic system did not have any specific practical aims in view. It is to be hoped, however, that some of the findings will be of interest to many whose concern with consumers' behaviour is not purely academic. Thus much of the material presented here, and especially the sections on the form of the Engel curve and the values of the total expenditure elasticities, should be of interest from the standpoint of market research, while the analysis of unit-consumer scales is important in connexion with any rational scheme of social security benefits and of tax reliefs in respect of dependents. For these latter purposes, however, it would be important to extend the derivation of unit-consumer scales to cover all commodities.

The work on the analysis of family budgets is being continued at the Department and extended in various ways. In particular, a detailed analysis of post-war food expenditure is now being made which permits a comparison with the pre-war position described in this volume.

RICHARD STONE

DEPARTMENT OF APPLIED ECONOMICS
CAMBRIDGE

December 1954

PREFACE TO THE FIRST IMPRESSION

THIS book is the work of many hands. It is the authors' duty and pleasure to acknowledge the advice and help that so many have given so generously at all stages of the inquiry: in preparing the basic data, in carrying out the computations, and in writing the text.

First, in preparing the data presented as Part III of this book, our thanks are due to the Ministry of Labour and National Service for releasing the records, and to them and to Mr P. Massey for answering various queries. For transferring the information to punched cards and tabulating the results, thanks are due to a number of government departments, especially to the Ministry of Food, the Ministry of Agriculture and Fisheries, and to the Social Survey. The Royal Aircraft Establishment at Farnborough and the College of Aeronautics at Cranfield kindly undertook extensive parts of the punched-card work and carried them out in a very helpful manner. Mrs A. E. Gill and Mrs M.V. Allnutt helped with tabulations at the University Mathematical Laboratory, Cambridge, and at the National Physical Laboratory, Teddington; we wish to thank them and these institutions for allowing the use of their equipment. The main work of turning the tabulated figures into orderly tables has been carried out at the Department of Applied Economics by Mrs A.V. Church with remarkable patience and our thanks are especially due to her.

Secondly, for carrying out the many laborious computations at the Department we are considerably indebted to Mrs E. M. Chambers, Mr R. A. Arnould, Mrs J. R. Bottle, Mrs Church and Mrs A. Pink. Mr Arnould also prepared the diagrams for this book. In addition, we have to thank Dr M.V. Wilkes, Director of the University Mathematical Laboratory in Cambridge, for permission to use the EDSAC.

Thirdly, our thanks are due to Richard Stone, Director of the Department of Applied Economics, for general guidance at all stages of this inquiry and for writing the foreword to this book; the present work is closely associated with that described in his recent *Measurement of Consumers' Expenditure and Behaviour in the United Kingdom, 1920–1938*, on the manuscript version of which we have been able to draw in preparing the text. Further, we have to thank J. Tobin for his part in the initial planning of this inquiry, and J. A. C. Brown, whose experience in survey work has constantly stood us in good stead. His advice and detailed comments on the manuscript have improved both the style and the argument of the text throughout.

Our thanks are due to the Editors of the *Economic Journal*, the *Journal of the Royal Statistical Society*, the *Journal of the American Statistical Association*, the *Review of Economic Studies* and *Économie Appliquée* for permission to reproduce some results which have already appeared in these journals.

The text has been read in page proof by Professor Margaret G. Reid of the University of Chicago, by D. A. Rowe of the National Institute of Economic and Social Research, London, and by J. Aitchison and the late Dr R. E. Brumberg of this Department. We are indebted to them for a number of improvements in the exposition.

As in all cooperative research projects of this nature, it is difficult to delineate the precise border between each of the main authors' activities. The approximate border is nevertheless best set on record. H.S.H. was mainly concerned with the organization of the tabulations and initiated some of the subsequent calculations; S.J.P. undertook the detailed analyses and the draft of the text, with the exceptions of §§ 2.2–2.4 which were drafted by H.S.H. H.S.H. left for the United States in December 1951, and the results of the inquiry as they then stood were set out in his paper, 'The Econometrics of Family Budgets', read to the Royal Statistical Society and subsequently published in their *Journal*. He visited the Department in November and December 1952 while on leave of absence from the Cowles Commission for Research in Economics for further discussions on the inquiry. Both authors accept responsibility for the text as it now stands.

S. J. P.
H. S. H.

DEPARTMENT OF APPLIED ECONOMICS
CAMBRIDGE

December 1954

PREFACE TO THE SECOND IMPRESSION

In the twenty years that have elapsed since we carried out the research reported in this book, there has been a tremendous growth in the collection and analysis of family budgets in all parts of the world. From time to time in the latter half of this period, colleagues and friends working in this field have kindly pressed on us the desirability of re-issuing this book (which has been out of print since 1961). Had time permitted, we should before now have presented a revised version incorporating a full survey of the advances in methods made in this period. However other work has intervened and a full-scale version has not proved possible; rather than further delay a reissue, the original text of the book has now been reprinted virtually as it stood in the original edition (some minor errors and misprints have been corrected); in addition a selection of the tables from Part III of the original impression is here reproduced.

The full set of tables, extending over some 200 pages, and giving the basic data of the two British inquiries, were included in the first impression mainly to serve as a basis for further research work; in the event, the book has had a broader circulation than anticipated and, we understand, has occasionally done duty as a post-graduate textbook. So that it may continue to serve the latter purpose we have thought it right to retain in Part III of this impression certain of the summary tables; but, for the sake of economy, these have been restricted to some twenty pages. It is hoped that these will prove adequate for exercise purposes and, perhaps, for further research into the shape of the Engel curve, etc. Research workers requiring the more detailed commodity tables will, we trust, find it possible to have access to the first impression at a reference library; alternatively, photographic copies of individual tables can be supplied by the Secretary of the Department of Applied Economics at cost.

Without wishing to go fully into all the developments in research during the past two decades, some words may be offered here to guide the reader on the now generally widened scope of family budget inquiries and recent analytical developments.

First, on *subject matter*: in the pre-war period information was generally collected on household expenditure only, while income was usually thought too difficult to obtain; but in post-war inquiries some information on income has almost always been collected, and without too much difficulty. This, no doubt, is a result of changes in deep-rooted social attitudes with regard to what information is private, and what may be discussed more or less publicly, and the result of corresponding changes in the public's attitudes to the role of the government and its information-gathering agencies. Though doubts remain on the reliability of the income-information collected, the availability of some information on income is better than none, and is of obvious importance for the analyst of expenditure patterns (see p. xxvi below). Certain surveys have gone further and have attempted to cover savings, derived either as a residual between income and expenditure, or as the difference between total family net assets at the beginning and end of the period. Progress has also been made in surveys of consumers' intentions to spend on major durable items in the coming months, or coming year, as an aid to forecasting demand.*

The second important widening in the scope of family expenditure surveys relates to their *frequency and accuracy;* in several countries surveys are no longer carried out as isolated investigations to meet particular needs, but increasingly form part of a routine programme of collecting information on the economy (the great increase in frequency can be judged from the immense ILO survey of family living studies, 1955, the ILO report, 1954 and the ILO symposium, 1961). Certain surveys are, in fact, now carried out on a continuous basis, with changes in the sample of households from time to time (in Britain, every two weeks), so providing a moving picture of changes in household expenditure.** There are substantial advantages in the operation of a continuous survey, analogous to economies of scale in production: work is organized on a continuous basis for those interviewing, editing, and punching and processing the records, etc. In addition, continuity over a longer period allows the central staff to introduce experimental variations in methods at very little cost, and improvements in methods can be put into practice step by step. This process is well exemplified in the British family expenditure survey where, following a series of research papers (mainly by Kemsley, see references at end of this Preface), a *Handbook* (1969) has now been produced—after twelve years' operation of the survey— summarizing the advances made in its sampling, fieldwork and coding procedures.†

* For descriptions and discussions of surveys covering savings, see Cole and Utting (1956), Lydall (1955), Hill (1955), Hill *et al.* (1955); the most notable survey of intentions to spend is the quarterly household survey of the US Bureau of the Census.
** Pearl (1968, p. 6) lists the following countries as having continuous surveys: United Kingdom, France, the Soviet Union, Hungary, Greece, Pakistan, Japan. He suggests that the United States should also adopt this practice.
† It is difficult to avoid commenting at this point that two continuous surveys—curiously enough—are carried out in Great Britain, one by the Ministry of Labour (now Department of Employment and Productivity) and the other by the Ministry of Agriculture, Fisheries and Food. The former covers all household expenditure; the latter covers only food expenditure, though in greater detail, including quantity information, and the publication contains much interesting econometric analysis. One would have thought that there would be obvious economies in co-ordinating sample design and selection, definition of commodities, expenditure categories, etc.; but, though both surveys have been running for many years, it appears that plans for their integration remain tentative. The outsider is hard put to find anything but a studied indifference with regard to each other in the publications associated with these surveys.
The machinery of government provides a control mechanism to catch inefficiencies of this type in the shape of the Estimates Committee which, from time to time, examines various topics in depth; a 500-page report on *Government Statistical Services* was produced in the 1966–7 Session (HMSO, 1966). The Ministry of Labour gave evidence before that Committee, including a description of its Family Expenditure Survey, but without referring to the competitors' product; the competitor, the Ministry of Agriculture, did not give evidence. There was consequently no discussion of the overlap between the surveys. (S.J.P.)

The techniques of collecting the information have thus gradually been improved to yield more accurate results, and scientific sampling methods—which have developed immensely in the last generation—have been put into practice to yield results with greater efficiency (that is, to obtain lower sampling variance for the costs incurred).

The scope of expenditure surveys has been widened in a third way, in that the *coverage of the population* has been extended. Before the war surveys were usually restricted to a particular social class, as was the 'working class' survey analysed in this book—which was intended to provide the basis for the revision of the working class cost-of-living index number. The recent trend has been to extend the coverage of such surveys to the whole population as far as possible; nevertheless the extremes of the distribution probably remain under-represented. Perhaps the omission of those living in hotels is of no great consequence; but the omission of those at the lower end of the economic scale—those living in various institutions (old-age homes, hospitals, prisons, etc.), those living in no fixed home, and the unemployed—means that we still do not have a correct picture of the proportion of the population that is living below any particular level of subsistence. There has been increasing interest in measuring this proportion (however arbitrarily defined), though in most surveys they are at present omitted (cf. the report by OECD, 1968).

Clearly, much more statistical information is now available in this field; the reader will next wish to know whether advances have also been made in our understanding of the laws governing consumers' expenditures or, if no new laws—forming part of a scientifically integrated body of knowledge—have been discovered, whether at least any new regularities have been observed in consumers' behaviour.

At this level, the progress to be reported is also not unsatisfactory, though of course much remains to be done. Perhaps the main advance has been in investigations of the shape of the Engel curve: the evidence for a non-linear relation between total expenditure and the expenditure on a particular item, and a tendency towards a saturation level in certain commodities, to which we drew attention in our original study, has also been suggested by subsequent studies. For example, Liviatan (1964, p. 30) also finds the semi-log formulation most satisfactory; on the other hand, Jorgensen (1965, p. 77) suggests that his Danish data are better described, on the whole, by a double-log function—perhaps because he is relatively more concerned with non-foods.

The implication for foodstuffs that there would be a declining elasticity of demand with rises in income, has also been confirmed in various investigations; the following elasticities for expenditure on all food calculated for *separate* samples in various recent years in Britain are of especial interest in this connexion (they come from the National Food Survey report for 1965, p. 136):

	Elasticity
1955	0·30
1958	0·28
1960	0·25
1962	0·27
1965	0·23
1966	0·23

Real total personal consumption per head over this period rose by some 25%, and a fall in elasticity was accordingly to be expected; further investigation is however necessary before one may conclude that non-linearity was the sole reason for the decline.

The idea that a single family of curves should be applicable to all commodities has been pursued further. One of the possibilities investigated in this period was the integral log-normal curve proposed by Aitchison and Brown (1957, see also Brown, 1963). This is a sigmoid curve, having application in biological assay work where it is used to represent the empirical relation between a stimulus and a response (in biology the relation would be, for example, between the dosage of a drug and the rate of cure; in our field it is between total expenditure and a particular expenditure).

The log-normal curve has three parameters in general, though it has usually been applied with one of the parameters fixed ($\sigma = 1$), so that it has two free parameters as have the curves originally studied in this book. It is not easy to fit, in that it requires iterative methods, and non-convergence is apparently possible (as Jorgensen, 1965, p. 55, found in his analysis of Danish budgets). Of course a three parameter curve has potentially greater flexibility and may seem better, in some sense, simply for that reason; but it is not yet clear whether it is always useful to go to such complexity—that may depend on the range of the observations in the sample studied (the broader the range, the greater the complexity). On the other hand, it may sometimes be necessary to go even further; as suggested in section 2.41 it is conceivable that a commodity may be a necessity or a luxury at lower income ranges and an inferior good at higher income ranges; the curvature of the log-normal function (or, indeed, of most other functions that have been proposed) would not be able to represent the demand for such a commodity.

The last word has clearly not been said on this subject! It may be argued that the search for a single family of curves is a chimera and that, in empirical work involving wide income ranges, we ought to be satisfied with a graduation or smoothing of the data using a flexible polynomial, or the like; and that if the elasticity at the mean income is the sole concern, then a linear (or log-linear) form is adequate.* In applied research work it is however extremely useful (one might

* The National Food Survey now regularly presents elasticities calculated for some 120 foodstuffs simply using the double-log form (see, for example, the very interesting table in the *Report* for 1965, pp. 137–43, which gives expenditure and quantity elasticities calculated for each commodity for each of five years in the period 1955–65).

even say, essential) to have a simple but realistic formula, such as the homogeneous semi-log and double-log forms used in this book, the properties of which incorporate the main regularities of consumer behaviour in relation to the majority of commodities (such as, in the case of foodstuffs, an initially high elasticity, declining as income rises, and the properties with respect to family size set out in section 9.21).

In our opinion, research for improvements over the simple forms proposed here should not be given up. In particular, the formal theory of consumers' choice, which had remained somewhat in the background of our earlier work, may yet yield fruit. By choosing particular forms of utility functions it is possible to find new shapes of Engel curves which necessarily satisfy the adding-up criterion. Thus two additive modifications of the double-log Engel curve, one of which was first suggested by Leser (1941, 1964), have been successfully applied to British data (Houthakker, 1960).

The effects on consumption of variations in family size and composition have been further studied, but without substantial progress. Forsyth (1960), in a critical but not entirely conclusive study based on the British budget inquiry of 1953-54, drew attention to the need for a set of restrictions on the specific and income equivalence scales if they are to be simultaneously determined from empirical data; otherwise, he argued, there would be a spare degree of freedom in the system in relation to each type of person distinguished. This difficulty can be met in principle by specifying in advance the coefficients for certain commodities; for example, in relation to tobacco the children's specific coefficients may be set equal to zero and, similarly, for women's clothing the coefficient for men can be set at zero, etc. It should not be difficult to find an adequate number of *a priori* restrictions and, in this way, the problem is overcome in principle.* But only further research can tell whether this device in practice is adequate to allow a simultaneous estimation of income and specific effects. It has been suggested (by Forsyth, *ibid.*, and Jorgenson, 1965, p. 92) that this line of research should be abandoned in view of its difficulties; we nevertheless retain the view that any analysis of consumption according to family size is virtually meaningless unless income effects are distinguished. We therefore hope that research will be continued in this field.

The route by which household composition effects the demand for consumer durables has been explored by M. H. David (1962), who drew attention to the role of family formation and the 'life cycle' in the timing of such purchases. This is an interesting additional scheme of factors which could be superimposed on the equivalent-scales approach, but no such attempt at integration has yet been made.**

---

* One is therefore forced back to the methods of Nicholson (1949) and Henderson (1949), see p. 132 below, but in terms of our broader framework. Compare also the comments of Cramer (1969, p. 169), and the study by Barten (1964).
** By way of a footnote to the survey of developments in the analysis of Engel curves, the reader is referred to a generalization of the adding-up theorem (see pp. 84–5 below) given by Nicholson (1957).

The derivation of price-elasticities is an important innovation, which has become possible following the collection of family budgets on a continuous basis for a lengthy period. The analysis, in principle, is no different from that classically applied to time series, but the results recently achieved using family budget records appear more successful. The consistency of the data is probably the main reason for greater success, in that both prices and quantities are collected simultaneously, using precisely the same commodity-definitions and methods of observation, and over a lengthy period. Seasonal co-variations in prices and quantities (which are of course marked in foodstuffs) can be closely examined and, more especially, the reaction of demand can be examined to shifts in supplies differing from the usual seasonal shift-pattern. The approach was developed by Brown (1958 a, b), and has since been applied by the National Food Survey on a broad front (see, for example, the extensive list of price elasticities in their *Reports* for 1958, p. 26 and 1963, p. 33).

We now turn to some *methodological issues*. Whether families are better classified by reported income or by reported total expenditure in a given period, in order to approximate to their true economic level of living, has long been debated in the literature, especially in connexion with the determining variable in Engel curve analysis (see section 7.12 below). The well-known work of Friedman (1957), while primarily directed to the reconciliation of time-series and cross-section evidence on the aggregate consumption function, had greatly clarified the conceptual problems involved.* In particular it may be inferred from this work that our use of total expenditure in lieu of income is not necessarily a defect from a theoretical point of view, especially when data for more than one year are not available. New light has also been thrown on this problem by Liviatan (1961 and 1964), based on the theory of instrumental variables. In its simplest form his suggestion is as follows: the families are first grouped according to the reported income of the household (or of the head of the household, if supplementary earnings are not available or, as is often the case, are not reliable); average *total expenditure* is then calculated for each *income group*, and those averages (that is, of total expenditure) are used as the explanatory variable in subsequent analyses.

The advantage of this method can be appreciated on considering a family that has bought, for example, an expensive refrigerator during the period of observation. On the older method of classifying families by their total expenditure, such a family would tend to be classified with the highest economic group, though the remainder of its expenditure pattern may correspond more closely (subject to some possible off-setting) to a more average level; any analysis of the relation between consumption of particular commodities and economic level is consequently biased. On the new method, the family will be thrown into

---

* It is worth noting that equation (7.32) of our book provided Friedman with an important piece of evidence in favour of his 'permanent income hypothesis'.

its correct economic group, and whether it buys a refrigerator or not merely contributes to the variance of the observations in that group but does not lead to bias;[*] if there are enough families in that group, the average total expenditure will be close to normal, and will be hardly affected by such exceptional items.

This method will probably be more widely adopted in the future. However, the difficulties of obtaining reasonably accurate income data, even if great care in collection is taken, argue for the use of total expenditure as both a classifying and an independent variable. Thus Houthakker and Taylor (1970, Section 6, IV) concluded from a principal component analysis of the 1960–1 US Survey (in which income data were emphasized) that observations on income do not contribute anything further to the explanation of particular expenditures; income appears to be useful only to the extent that it is correlated with total expenditure.

A number of investigations on the accuracy of the account-book method have been carried out, pointing to the conclusion that the first few days of record-keeping produce especially high expenditure figures. Two balanced samples of families in Israel keeping records for the same fortnight have been compared (Prais, 1958, p. 319), of which one had also kept records for the previous fortnight, while the other had not kept records during those two weeks; the latter sample returned higher expenditures which, for food as a whole, amounted to some 7% (this comparison, it may be emphasized, is confined to the common period of two weeks during which both samples kept records). Kemsley and Nicholson (1960, p. 326) have analysed the number of entries made each day by a sample of families who kept records over a four-week period in England; they found that the first day of the inquiry had 23% more entries than the average of the first week, and the average number of entries in the first week was 5–7% higher than the average for the subsequent three weeks. In another investigation Kemsley (1961, p. 118) showed that, in the three-week Ministry of Labour inquiry of 1953–4, total expenditures recorded in the first week were on average 8% higher then than those for the subsequent two weeks. It also appears that expenditures in the last day, or last few days, of an inquiry are high (Prais, 1958, p. 318).

These are examples of the kind of study recently carried out (further references will be found in Pearl, 1968) all pointing to certain margins of uncertainty in the basic records. Few entirely definite conclusions have been reached, but it seems likely that the first and last few days of record keeping are better omitted if unbiassed results are required. There is much scope for further research; for example, it would be interesting to know whether all families are equally prone to over-statement on these days, and whether those that are peculiar in this

---

[*] Apart from possible bias due to 'errors in variables', if ordinary least-squares is used; this bias would be small if the range of variations is large, as it usually is. If the technique of instrumental variables is used, this small bias also disappears, though sometimes at a considerable cost in efficiency.

respect have any other distinguishable peculiarities. Such research may lead to modifications of the questionnaire, or may suggest that for certain families other methods of inquiry are more appropriate. The reader is bound to feel that only the surface has been scratched so far, and a very ambitious research programme—in co-operation with governmental and private survey agencies—is called for.

We are conscious, more than ever, that there are passages in the book that follows breathing an air of optimism for which maturer years might have substituted an air of caution! Some passages (such as those dealing with electronic computation) may be somewhat dated though even these, we think, retain their validity. But we have let the words stand as we wrote them if only to serve as a reminder of the ebullient spirit that then permeated applied economics, not least at the Department in Cambridge bearing that name. If progress is to be made in economics as in the natural sciences, we remain convinced that it is essential for economists not only to work in teams, but more especially in teams that include mathematicians and statisticians; that idea was put into practice by Professor Richard Stone at the time we were fortunate enough to be engaged there on this project. In presenting the second impression of this book to the public, we are conscious of our debt to him for his stimulation and interest in our work and for providing such a congenial atmosphere in which to carry it out.

December 1970   S.J.P.
                                                                       H.S.H.

REFERENCES

AITCHISON, J. and BROWN, J. A. C. (1957) *The Lognormal Distribution*, Cambridge.

BARTEN, A. P. (1964). Family composition, prices and expenditure patterns. In *Econometric Analysis for National Economic Planning*, ed. by Hart, P. E., Mills, G., and Whitaker, J. K. Butterworth.

BROWN, J. A. C. (1958a). *On the Use of Covariance Techniques in Demand Analysis*. Rome, FAO/ECE.

BROWN, J. A. C. (1958b). Seasonality and the elasticity of demand for food in Great Britain since derationing. *J. Ag. Econ.*, **13**, 228.

BROWN, J. A. C. (1963). Economics, nutrition and family budgets. *Proc. Nutr. Soc.*, **14**, 1.

COLE, D. and UTTING, J. E. G. (1956). Estimating expenditure, saving and income from household budgets. *J. Roy. Statist. Soc.* A, **119**, 371.

CRAMER, J. S. (1969). *Applied Econometrics*. Amsterdam: North Holland.

DAVID, M. H. (1962). *Family Composition and Consumption*. Amsterdam: North Holland.

FORSYTH, F. G. (1960). The relationship between family size and family expenditure. *J. Roy. Statist. Soc.* A, **123**, 367.

FRIEDMAN, M. (1957). *A Theory of the Consumption Function*. Princeton.

HILL, T. P. (1955). Income, savings and net worth: the savings surveys of 1952-4. *Bull. Oxf. Univ. Inst. Statist.*, **17**, 129.

HILL, T. P., KLEIN, L. R. and STRAW, K. H. (1955). The savings survey 1953: response rates and the reliability of the data. *Bull. Oxf. Univ. Inst. Statist.*, **17**, 89.

HOUTHAKKER, H. S. (1960). Additive preferences. *Econometrica*, **28**, 244.

HOUTHAKKER, H. S. and TAYLOR, L. D. (1970). *Consumer Demand in the US* (2nd ed.). Harvard.

INTERNATIONAL LABOUR OFFICE (1959). *International Standardisation of Labour Statistics* (Studies and Reports, New Series, No. 53).

INTERNATIONAL LABOUR OFFICE (1961). *Family Living Studies: A Symposium* (Studies and Reports, New Series, No. 63).

JORGENSEN, E. (1965). *Income-Expenditure Relations of Danish Wage and Salary Earners.* Copenhagen.

KEMSLEY, W. F. F. (1959). Designing a budget survey. *Appl. Stats.*, **8**, 114.

KEMSLEY, W. F. F. (1960). Interviewer variability and budget survey. *Appl. Stats.*, **9**, 122.

KEMSLEY, W. F. F. (1961). The household expenditure enquiry of the Ministry of Labour—Variability in the 1953-4 Enquiry. *Appl. Stats.*, **10**, 117.

KEMSLEY, W. F. F. (1965). Interviewer variability in expenditure surveys. *J. Roy. Statist. Soc.* A, **128**, 118.

KEMSLEY, W. F. F. (1966). Sampling errors in family expenditure survey. *Appl. Stats.*, **15**, 1.

KEMSLEY, W. F. F. (1969). *Family Expenditure Survey: Handbook on the Sample, Fieldwork and Coding Procedures.* London: HMSO.

KEMSLEY, W. F. F. and NICHOLSON, J. L. (1960). Some experiments in methods of conducting family expenditure surveys. *J. Roy. Statist. Soc.* A, **123**, 307.

LESER, C. E. V. (1941). Family budget data and price-elasticities of demand. *Rev. Econ. Stud.*, **9**, 40.

LESER, C. E. V. (1964). Forms of Engel functions. *Econometrica*, **32**, 443.

LIVIATAN, N. (1961). Errors in variables and Engel curve analysis. *Econometrica*, **29**, 336.

LIVIATAN, N. (1964). *Consumption Pattern in Israel.* Jerusalem: Falk.

LYDALL, H. F. (1955). *British Incomes and Savings.* Oxford: Blackwell.

NICHOLSON, J. L. (1957). The general form of the adding-up criterion. *J. Roy. Statist. Soc.* A, **120**, 84.

O.E.C.D. (1968). *Measurement of Changes in National Levels of Living* (MS/S/68.156). Paris.

PEARL, R. B. (1968). *Methodology of Consumer Expenditure Surveys.* Washington: U.S. Department of Commerce.

PRAIS, S. J. (1958). Some problems in measurement of price changes with special reference to the cost of living. *J. Roy. Statist. Soc.* A, **121**, 312.

PART I

THE MATERIAL AND THE TOOLS

CHAPTER I

THE ANALYSIS OF FAMILY BUDGETS

1.1. ALTERNATIVE APPROACHES TO FAMILY-BUDGET STUDIES

The household is often regarded as the point of convergence of the various branches of the social sciences; in economics in particular, as the original meaning of the word testifies, it is impossible to go very far without a knowledge of the behaviour of the household in typical circumstances. The collection and analysis of the detailed records of a large number of households—records which are especially concerned with their expenditures and hence known as family budgets—are therefore of considerable interest from a number of points of view.

First, from the general point of view of social policy, these records may cast light on the conditions of life of the nation, showing how poverty may affect certain sections of it, what proportions of families live in various states of poverty, and how those proportions change through time. The desire to obtain this kind of information was undoubtedly the motive of the earlier collections of family budgets; thus Sir Frederic Morton Eden, one of the earliest investigators to collect records in a systematic manner for the whole country, published his results in a three-volume work entitled *The State of the Poor: or, an History of the Labouring Classes in England, . . . in which are particularly considered their Domestic Economy with respect to Diet, Dress, Fuel, and Habitation . . .* (London, 1797). Again, one of the principal conclusions to emerge from the studies by Ernst Engel of Belgian working-class households was that a smaller proportion of expenditure was devoted to food at the end of the nineteenth century than at its beginning, in consequence of the general rise in the standard of living. A similar approach is to be found in the studies by Rowntree, Orr and others, conducted in this century.†

Secondly, family budgets may be collected for the more specific purpose of providing weights for index numbers of the cost-of-living. From a more general point of view these weights can be derived from a set of entries in a system of social accounting; family budgets may therefore be regarded as providing estimates of consumers' expenditures, subdivided if desired according to various classes of consumers, for use within such a general framework. The more immediate requirements

† References to the literature on family budgets may be found in an excellent survey article by Dorothy W. Douglas in the *Encyclopaedia of the Social Sciences* under that head, and in the survey by Staehle (1935). A comprehensive and fairly detailed account of family budget studies up to the First World War has been given in a recent article by Stigler (1954).

of the cost-of-living index have led to the official sponsoring of very many thorough inquiries, but since the index numbers are generally intended to refer only to the working classes the inquiries have, in the pre-war period, been similarly restricted.

A third approach to family budgets is that related to econometric investigations of the determinants of consumers' expenditures; by examining households in different circumstances laws may be derived for the way in which those circumstances affect the behaviour of the household. The possibility of examining income variations in this way in order to derive estimates of income elasticities and of the marginal propensity to consume is no doubt one of the main reasons for the increased interest in family-budget investigations since Keynes directed attention to these concepts. One of the main features of the present analysis is to show how the econometric approach can be used in an analysis of the effects of household composition and thus lead to the possibility of comparing the standards of living of households of different composition in a more precise manner.†

The econometric approach in the main underlies the investigations presented in this book, and the table of income elasticities given in Chapter 7 may, perhaps, be regarded as our central result. It would, however, be mistaken to place too much emphasis on this table of estimates; the interest of the study, at any rate from the authors' point of view, lies rather in the development of the kind of model that has been suggested by the investigations as these have gradually become more complicated. The aim throughout has been to investigate the behaviour of consumers as far as the available information allowed or, conversely, to attempt to explain every significant regularity displayed by the information in terms of a theory of consumers' behaviour. Thus, while at the beginning the interest lay in the analysis of income variations, this very soon led to questions such as those concerned with scales of equivalent-adults and economies of scale in consumption.

The different approaches enumerated above are, of course, to be regarded as complementary rather than competitive. In particular, the summary measures of consumers' behaviour provided by an econometric investigation may be used subsequently in an analysis with a more immediate social intention; an example of this is when a deficiency in a certain nutritional element in the diet of certain classes of families is attributed to the high-income elasticity of demand for the commodities in which that element is to be found.

† There is, further, a fourth point of view, the importance of which we have no desire to diminish. This holds, with Mrs Beeton, that the careful study of the records of the expenditures of a great many households may be of help to those about to set up a household of their own and to those who are concerned with having to budget for an expected increase in the size of their families and the like.

1.2. THE STARTING POINT OF THIS INQUIRY AND ITS AIMS

On account of the way in which the interests of investigators vary, the scope of any two inquiries has rarely been the same. In general, the results of a survey are required as soon as possible after it has been carried out so that its lessons may be applied with the least delay. This has often the unfortunate consequence that insufficient attention is paid to the basic problems of the presentation and the analysis of the data, so that the survey is of limited value to other investigators.

The results of the two pre-war inquiries presented in this book have already appeared in a summary form some years ago. These inquiries are the working-class inquiry organized by the Ministry of Labour in 1937–8 in order to provide information for a revision of the cost-of-living index,† and that organized by the Civil Service Statistical and Research Bureau in 1938–9 in order to provide comparable information for a sample of middle-class households.‡ Both inquiries are described in detail in Chapter 3 below. When after the war the Department of Applied Economics in Cambridge under its director, Richard Stone, began its programme of research in demand analysis, it was thought desirable to undertake a more detailed analysis of these inquiries. The smaller degree of urgency which rightly surrounds an academic project made it possible to devote a greater amount of time than usual to the investigation of a number of new aspects of household expenditure and to the statistical analysis of the basic data. It is the results of these investigations which provide the justification for presenting the results of these pre-war inquiries at this late date.

It may be noted, however, that as far as concerns the analysis of demand in the post-war market it may well be that a survey conducted in 1938 is of greater relevance than one conducted in, say, 1950, when there were still a number of controls on consumers' expenditures. The gradual re-establishment of the pre-war pattern of expenditures as these controls are removed has been one of the interesting features of the post-war market; now that rationing is completely abolished it is to be hoped that a thorough comparison will in due course be made with the pre-war situation in which the present figures may be used.

Two main objects of this book may thus be distinguished. First, there are presented the detailed results of the two pre-war inquiries in a suitable form and in sufficient detail for further analysis; secondly, the results of a number of analyses of the data are presented together with a general survey of the problems encountered in analysing family budgets. The information conveyed by a family-budget survey can to a con-

---

† The earlier tabulations are given in a duplicated report issued by the Ministry of Labour and National Service in July 1949 entitled *Weekly Expenditure of Working-class Households in the United Kingdom in 1937–8*. This gives information additional to that published in the *Ministry of Labour Gazette* in December 1940, January and February 1941.

‡ The average expenditures according to four income groups have been given by Massey (1942).

siderable extent be summarized in a few fundamental measures, and the object of the analyses has been to derive those measures which are economically most meaningful. But it may be that further study of family budgets will yield better summary measures of consumers' be-haviour and the present approach should therefore be regarded only as indicative of the type of problem that may be solved by an econometric analysis of family-budget data.†

The results presented here are thus in the nature of a report on a piece of research which, building on the work of others, attempts to add a brick here and there, and ends with the hope that in so doing no weak points in the structure are concealed. As one of its main starting points it has taken the now classic work on *Family Expenditure* by Allen and Bowley (1935). The reader should not estimate its influence on our work merely by the number of explicit references to it in the following pages; there is hardly a chapter of this book which would have had the present form but for the work of these authors. Another main point of departure for this book is the recent work of Stone *et al.* (1954) which is closely connected with that presented here. In a number of places the reader may find it necessary to refer to Stone for the more general aspects of the problems discussed.

At several points in Part II of this book we should have liked to continue our researches before presenting them to the reader. It seems, however, that in this kind of work some loose strands must always be left and a more or less arbitrary decision taken to call a halt to research and to begin the writing. It has been our intention to indicate as clearly as possible at which points it is thought the argument requires extension in order that this may encourage further research along these lines.

1.3. THE ORDER OF DISCUSSION

This book falls into three parts which are here taken in the reverse order. In the third part there are presented the detailed results of the two surveys referred to above and these are given in, as far as possible, a comparable form. The second part of the book presents the special analyses that have been carried out, and these are concerned with three main problems.

The first of these, presented in Chapter 7, is concerned with the investigation of the effects of variations in income and household size on the expenditure pattern of the household. The results are summarized in the parameters of Engel curves which are estimated for all the items of expenditure distinguished in the surveys.

Secondly, in Chapter 8, it is shown that the prices paid by a household for physically similar items of expenditure vary systematically with the

---

† Some extensions of the approach developed in Part II are to be found in articles by Brown and by Brown and Aitchison to appear in *Econometrica* and the *Review of Economic Studies*. These are based on a more involved form of Engel curve not considered in the present investigations and make use of certain methods in probit analysis developed by biologists.

standard of living of the household. This leads to a difference between the Engel curve for the quantity bought of a commodity and the expenditure on it.

The third main problem, discussed in Chapter 9, is the method of measuring household size so as to allow comparisons of 'per capita' levels of consumption. A new method of analysis is applied to estimate unit-consumer scales for a number of items of expenditure which may be used for this and other purposes.

The above analyses are supplemented by a discussion in Chapter 10 of the possibility of economies of scale in consumption, and in Chapter 11 by a discussion of the effects of social, occupational and regional factors.

These are the main problems discussed in the second part of this book. Turning now to the first part, this attempts to give a systematic account of the tools and methods of analysis adopted. It begins in Chapter 2 by setting out some of the considerations suggested by economic theory which should influence the analysis. Chapter 3 then proceeds to consider the method of collecting information on consumers' expenditures by means of family-budget inquiries, and Chapter 4 discusses some of the imperfections of this kind of information. The statistical methods used in this type of analysis are for the most part well known but are subject to a number of limitations. In Chapter 5 some new results are derived which allow of a more precise treatment of some of the basic peculiarities of family-budget data; the results are given in a general form, and it is to be expected that they will be of use in other fields as well. Chapter 6 gives an account of the computational problems encountered in handling family budgets and, in particular, some of the uses that have been made of the Cambridge electronic computer are briefly discussed.

CHAPTER 2

THE THEORY OF CONSUMERS' DEMAND

2.1. THE BASIC ASSUMPTION OF FAMILY-BUDGET STUDIES

In an analysis of family-budget data designed to establish laws describing the behaviour of consumers the assumption has to be made that, by observing consumers in different circumstances at the same time, information may be obtained which is relevant in forecasting the behaviour of any particular consumer when his circumstances change through time. To take a particular example, it may be assumed that if there are observations on two households enjoying different incomes, and the income of the first household is next year changed to that of the second, then its expenditure pattern will tend to correspond with that of the second household as observed in the base year. In principle, the assumption made need not be so restrictive as in this example, but whenever a so-called cross-sectional study is made there must ultimately be some assumption which allows the results to be applied to changing situations. In general, it is assumed that the differences which are observed to exist are the result of the differences in circumstances acting on consumers who react in substantially the same manner.

The 'different circumstances' in which consumers are observed consist, as far as concerns this study, in different incomes, different household sizes, and different compositions of the household in terms of age and sex of the members. These are not the only variables which can conceivably be analysed with the help of family-budget investigations; for if the geographical regions covered were sufficiently diverse so that the prices charged for the same commodities varied between consumers it would be possible to analyse the effects of price changes. The same end may, of course, be achieved by comparing family budgets collected at different times.†

There are many reasons why the basic assumption will occasionally not be satisfied, but they may formally be reduced to two types of complications. First, there are dynamic factors which include: a resistance on the part of the consumer to immediate changes in his habits which may be demanded by changes in his circumstances; the effects of stocks of commodities held by the consumer (on which there is generally little information); and the fact that consumers take into account not only changes that have occurred but also those that they expect to occur. Secondly, there is the possibility of the interdependence of consumers' preferences which may lead to different responses according to whether

† As in the study by Duesenberry and Kistin (1953).

there is a change in the income of a particular household only or changes in the incomes of all households in the community. In beginning an analysis these complications may be ignored as they usually are in the static theory of consumers' behaviour. Accordingly, in the next section an outline is given of the theory of the single consumer, and this is followed in the third section of this chapter by a discussion of the theory of many consumers and the formation of market demand.

The style of exposition adopted in these and the other sections of this chapter differs somewhat from that in the rest of the book since the theory of consumption is well established. A number of systematic expositions are now available of the basic theory of demand in the works of Hicks (1939), Samuelson (1947), Schultz (1938), Stone *et al.* (1954) and Wold (1943–4, 1953), and it is assumed that the reader is familiar with one of these. This level of exposition allows some treatment of the dynamic complications *en passant*, but the effects of interdependence are considered separately.

The fourth section of this chapter considers the problem of the specification of commodities and the associated problem of the variations in the quality of commodities as bought by different consumers. The discussion here is at a theoretical level and is a development from the empirical investigations presented in later chapters. It is presented at this stage of the book in order that the reader may have a preview of some of the results presented in the second part, where many of the empirical implications of the arguments of this chapter are given at greater length.

Finally, in the fifth section of this chapter, the effects of interdependence are considered and a procedure is outlined which may be appropriate when it is thought that these may be of importance.

2.2. The Single Consumer

The theory of choice for a single consumer under static conditions is one of the best established parts of economic theory, many applications of which may be found in other branches of the subject. It is therefore important to investigate its relevance to empirical observations of consumers' behaviour such as the household budgets here analysed. There is, however, a gap between the assumptions of classical consumption theory and the conditions under which our observations are obtained, and this makes it difficult to test the empirical validity of the classical model directly. The purpose of this chapter is, accordingly, to see where the theory needs extension in order to make it more directly applicable to our observations.

Classical consumption theory deals with a consumer whose preferences for various sets of goods are given and who buys subject to the budget constraint that total expenditure is equal to income. Its theorems relate purchases to prices and income; they are usually expressed in infinitesimal terms, though occasionally statements about the effects of finite changes can be made.

The static character of the theory, which means that time does not enter explicitly, is evidently an abstraction from reality. The two typical phenomena of economic dynamics, lags and stocks are both present in consumers' behaviour. It will take the consumer some time to adjust his purchases to changes in prices and income, and usually the quantities which he buys will not be consumed instantaneously (though this does happen with services, gas and electricity, restaurant meals, etc.). In a cross-sectional study for a short period of time there is not much that can be done about lags, but this point will require further comment in connexion with the relative merits of income or total expenditure as an independent variable.

As regards stocks it must always be remembered that budgets provide information about purchases rather than consumption if no allowance is made for changes in stocks. This distinction is especially pertinent in the case of durable commodities which consumers buy at dates separated by lengthy intervals because of their indivisibility, so that it becomes a matter of chance whether any particular household will record an expenditure during the period of observation.

Even if we abstract from dynamic factors, the preferences of a consumer will not have the simple form assumed by the theory, since he will often be in doubt as to the satisfaction derived from certain commodities. Some purchases will therefore be of an experimental nature and may lead to a revision of preferences. This complication will arise most clearly if expenditures are specified in great detail (for instance, different brands of the same good); it will be less important if the expenditure categories are relatively broad.

The separate treatment of supply and demand which is fundamental in economic analysis raises some further questions notwithstanding the difficulty of dealing with them satisfactorily in empirical work. In the first place this separation presupposes that the spending habits of a consumer are independent of the sources of his income. This is not correct if, to take an example, the consumer's food or clothing needs are related to the nature of his work; in that case a change of employment may cause a change in expenditures even if preferences, prices and income remain unchanged. A second and rather different kind of supply-demand interrelation occurs in those rare cases where the price of an article is not a datum for the consumer but has to be determined by bargaining.

This last possibility should not be confused with a much more common one in which the price for one unit of an item of consumption depends on the 'quality' of that item, so that different consumers may record different unit prices for the same item. It is clear that this can only happen if expenditure categories are defined so as to include more than one variety or brand; in other words, if these categories could themselves be split up into sub-categories. In a sufficiently detailed list of goods there would of course be only one price for each item. This grouping together is of fundamental significance for consumption theory in general and for the analysis of family budgets in particular. We shall give a theoretical discussion in the fourth section of this chapter and some empirical results in Chapter 8.

2.3. THE THEORY OF MANY CONSUMERS

The real interest of the theory of the single consumer lies undoubtedly in its capability of generalization to the behaviour of many consumers. In order to relate the expenditures of different consumers to the theory of a single consumer assumptions have to be made about the determinants which these expenditures have in common.

For the sake of completeness it should be pointed out that there is already some difficulty in passing from a single consumer to a single household† because all purchases are not usually made by the same person. The point of view adopted in this analysis is that the household is the unit of decision as far as concerns the economics of consumption. This does not exclude the possibility of investigating the precise manner in which a household arrives at a decision, but such investigations are here regarded as belonging to the study of the psychology of family life.

If all households in a survey had the same preferences, were faced by the same prices, and reacted to income and price changes instantaneously, then observations of expenditure at different levels of income would all lie on the Engel curve which is common to all these families. None of these assumptions is entirely fulfilled in reality, and we must now examine how this affects the observed relation between the expenditures and incomes of particular households.

By 'preferences' is meant here 'the non-economic determinants of expenditures'; the only economic determinants usually considered are income, prices and, sometimes, the level of assets held. While in the pure theory of consumption preferences are regarded as given, in empirical research it is often necessary to study them in more detail, in order to specify in what manner they differ between households.

The first and probably the most obvious cause of variations in preferences is family composition, a subject that occupies a major place in this book. Secondly, there are differences in location which reflect external conditions and social habits; thus the demand for overcoats, at the same prices and income, will be larger in Stockholm than in Singapore. Social class may also influence the demand function; so may religion and various psychological characteristics of the members of the household. We cannot hope to isolate all these sources of variations, however, and must be content with introducing the more conspicuous ones explicitly and assume that the others, which are presumably numerous and unimportant individually, give rise to an error term conforming to some probability distribution. The demand, v_{ir}, of the rth household for the ith commodity may then be written

$$v_{ir} = f_i(v_{0r}; p_1, ..., p_n; t_{1r}, ..., t_{kr}; \epsilon_{ir}), \tag{2.1}$$

† Cf. Samuelson (1950), pp. 374–5.

where v_{0r} is the income of the rth family, $p_1, \ldots, p_n$ are the prices of the n commodities, $t_{1r}, \ldots, t_{kr}$ are the values of the taste factors $t_1, \ldots, t_k$ for the rth family (for example, the number of persons in a certain age-sex class), and ϵ_{ir} is a random variable; f_i does not depend on r.

The assumption that all families in the sample have to pay the same prices for identical commodities is invalidated to some extent by the existence of regional price differences. These will be found most distinctly in products sold by local monopolies such as gas and electricity; in fact, demand analyses for these goods are sometimes based on regional variations.[†] Smaller geographical price differences are present in most other commodities. In practice it may be difficult to separate them from differences in average prices per unit due to quality variations, to quantity discounts and to regional variations in preferences.

Reference has already been made to dynamic complications which were distinguished into lag and stock problems. Lags in the response to price changes may well be of small importance in investigating family budgets, for even if households face different prices the prices may move rather closely together. Income lags are a much more serious question and highly relevant to the interpretation of Engel curves. There is much evidence for their existence, for instance, in the paper by Tobin (1950), and also for the closely related phenomenon that expenditure is not much influenced by the less stable 'transitory' components of income.[‡]

From this argument it also follows that the income elasticities derived from family budgets cannot be used without qualification for estimating the effect on expenditures of short-term changes in income. The elasticities thus derived are of a long-term nature and may generally be expected to be larger than short-term coefficients; it will depend on the length of the time interval considered which elasticity is appropriate. This is one of the problems arising in the combined use of family budgets and time series in demand analysis.[§]

The existence of lags in the influence of income on expenditures already implies the emergence of one type of stock variable, namely, liquid assets (or liabilities) which are often held to be of great usefulness in forecasting consumers' demand. Stocks of durable commodities are a problem principally because of the indivisible nature of these items. It is here that the simultaneous observation of very many households is essential if any sufficient number of positive observations is to be obtained. But the mere examination of the average expenditures (that is, averages of households that have and have not recorded expenditures on the item) will not bring out the full complexity of the problem. Even if this simplification is adopted it is still necessary to make assumptions about

---

† See, for example, Houthakker (1951).

‡ Cf. Vickrey (1947) and Reid (1952). The observation by Tinbergen (1951, p. 96) that the marginal propensity to consume is much lower for people with fluctuating incomes (farmers and businessmen) than for people with stable incomes (wage and salary earners) points in the same direction.

§ See Stone (1954, pp. 409–10).

the age distribution of stocks in order to relate expenditure to consumption, and it seems clear that for the study of durable goods data on expenditures are of more limited value.

The final point to be considered in the relation between the theory of many consumers to that of the single consumer is the method by which income elasticities for the nation of consumers, that is, market elasticities, may be obtained from the income elasticities for the individual consumers.[†] If V_i is the aggregate demand for the ith commodity by consumers with an aggregate income V_0, so that

$$V_i = \sum_r v_{ir} \tag{2.2}$$

and

$$V_0 = \sum_r v_{0r}, \tag{2.3}$$

then the aggregate elasticity is

$$\frac{V_0}{V_i} \frac{\partial V_i}{\partial V_0} = \frac{1}{V_i} \sum_r \left\{ v_{ir} \left(\frac{v_{0r}}{v_{ir}} \frac{\partial v_{ir}}{\partial v_{0r}} \right) \left(\frac{V_0}{v_{0r}} \frac{\partial v_{0r}}{\partial V_0} \right) \right\}, \tag{2.4}$$

that is, it is a weighted average of the products of the individual income elasticities and the elasticities of individual incomes with respect to total income. The weights are the expenditures of the individual consumers. If the assumption is made that all incomes change in the same proportion so that $\dfrac{V_0}{v_{0r}} \dfrac{\partial v_{0r}}{\partial V_0} = 1$ for all r, then (2.4) simplifies to

$$\frac{V_0}{V_i} \frac{\partial V_i}{\partial V_0} = \frac{1}{V_i} \sum_r v_{ir} \left(\frac{v_{0r}}{v_{ir}} \frac{\partial v_{ir}}{\partial v_{0r}} \right), \tag{2.5}$$

that is, the market elasticity is a simple weighted average of the individual elasticities.

In order to analyse the effects of income redistribution rather more particularized assumptions are necessary. A possible model is as follows. Suppose, in consonance with the results of Chapter 7, that the Engel curve is given by

$$v_{ir} = \alpha_i + \beta_i \log v_{0r}, \tag{2.6}$$

and, further, that the distribution of incomes always follows the lognormal distribution.[‡] This distribution, as has been known for some time, gives a fair representation in the central income ranges as opposed to the Pareto distribution which is only valid for the upper income groups. For most analyses of demand the log-normal distribution is therefore to be preferred.

---

† The exposition follows that given by Stone (1954, p. 265).
‡ For an account of some of the properties of this distribution see Quensel (1945) or, more briefly, Cramer (1946, p. 220 and p. 258, Ex. 17). For the application to income distributions the classic work of Gibrat (1931) should be consulted. A general treatment of the log-normal distribution and its application to economic data is at present in preparation by Messrs J. A. C. Brown and J. Aitchison and will appear shortly in this series of monographs.

The principal mathematical property of this distribution required here is that the arithmetic mean of the incomes, say, $\bar{v}_0$, is related to the geometric mean, say v_0^*, by

$$\log v_0^* = \log \bar{v}_0 - \tfrac{1}{2}\sigma^2, \tag{2.7}$$

where σ^2 is the variance of the logarithms of income. A redistribution of incomes in these circumstances is equivalent to a change in the parameters of the log-normal distribution which are such as to leave the arithmetic mean income unchanged.

The mean, and hence the aggregate, demand for a commodity with the Engel curve (2.6) may then be found by inserting into the right-hand side of (2.6) the mean value of $\log v_0$, that is, $\log v_0^*$ as given by (2.7). There results.

$$\bar{v}_i = \alpha_i + \beta_i \, (\log \bar{v}_0 - \tfrac{1}{2}\sigma^2), \tag{2.8}$$

which provides a simple method of investigating the effects of income redistribution on aggregate consumption.†

The market elasticity under the above assumptions can be seen to be $\beta_i / (\alpha_i + \beta_i \log v_0^*)$.

2.4. THE SPECIFICATION OF COMMODITIES

There is no difficulty in defining 'expenditure on food', which is a sum of money, but it is a very different matter to say what is meant by the 'quantity of food', or the 'price of food'. In the latter case we are speaking of aggregates of heterogeneous entities and we have to consider how such aggregates can be formed and used; their introduction cannot be avoided in practice because the number of different goods that could be distinguished is virtually unlimited. This is not only a practical problem, however; it is also of theoretical importance, since it is intimately connected with the problem of non-negativity, that is, the impossibility, in general, of buying negative quantities of goods.

That the quantities bought by a consumer are by definition positive or zero is a proposition that could hardly be disputed; yet few consumption theorists have tried to set up their analysis accordingly.‡ The reasons for this are mainly technical. The customary methods in this field are diagrams of indifference curves for the two-good case and the application of the differential calculus for more general situations. On indifference diagrams one is not likely to draw negative quantities, but the two-good case becomes trivial if one of the two goods vanishes, and little can therefore be achieved by this method. Ordinary calculus techniques are perhaps even more misleading, for there is usually no

---

† The assumption has been implicitly made that all consumers are in the income range in which the commodity is bought. If this is not so, the above method may be extended by integrating only over the relevant portion of the Engel curve.

‡ This difficulty was not really recognized until the 1930's; in production theory it led recently to the development of 'linear programming' or more generally 'activity analysis'; cf. Koopmans (1951).

means of knowing the signs of the quantities that solve a constrained maximum problem, so that it is not possible to say whether the solution is economically meaningful.

2.41. COMPLETE ENUMERATION AND NON-NEGATIVITY

Two ways of dealing with this complication will be considered. The first and straightforward method is to specify commodities in the utmost detail, so that each has only one price for all consumers and no questions of aggregation arise. We then formulate the maximum problem:

maximize
$$u(q_1, ..., q_n) \tag{2.9}$$

subject to
$$\Sigma p_i q_i = v_0 \tag{2.10}$$

and
$$q_i \geqslant 0 \quad (i = 1, ..., n). \tag{2.11}$$

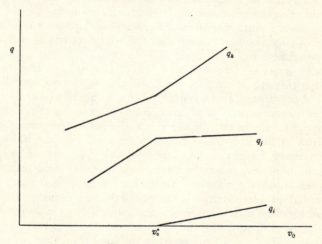

Fig. 1. Non-negativity.

This can be solved by determining for each set of values of the p_i and v_0, which of the q_i are positive and applying the ordinary Lagrangean multiplier technique to (2.9) and (2.10) for those q_i only, since (2.11) can then be ignored.[†]

For our present purpose we are only interested in the relation between the q_i and v_0. Clearly, as v_0 changes, the conditions (2.11) will cause certain of the q_i to disappear from the list of goods actually bought, while others will be introduced into it. This does not necessarily cause the Engel curves to become discontinuous, but there will certainly be kinks in the Engel curve for those goods that are already in the list at the values of v_0 where the list changes. Fig. 1 depicts what happens to

† A recursive method for finding the positive q_i in the case of a quadratic utility function is explained in Houthakker (1952b).

the Engel curves for q_j and q_k at v_0^*, where q_i enters the list (the curves drawn here consist of straight sections for convenience, but this is not essential to the argument). From (2.10) it follows that the sum of the slopes of all the Engel curves must equal unity for every value of v_0. Consequently if the q_i curve changes its slope from zero to a positive value (as happens at v_0^*) the slopes of the other Engel curves have to be adjusted. The signs and magnitudes of these adjustments can be analysed by an application of the theory of rationing,† for we may say that to the left of v_0^* the ith good is rationed at zero whereas it is free to the right. It follows that the introduction of q_i will reduce the slopes of the Engel curves of its substitutes (such as q_j in Fig. 1) and increase that slope for its complements (such as q_k); this holds also if these substitutes or complements are inferior goods whose slopes are negative. Similar conclusions apply if at v_0^* the ith good disappears from the list.

The first result to emerge from this argument is that, if rigorously considered, Engel curves for an individual consumer consist of continuous segments with a discontinuously varying slope because of changes in the list of goods bought; hence they cannot be represented exactly by an analytic function.‡

Secondly, since preferences vary between consumers it is to be expected that turning points such as v_0^* will not always occur at the same income. Accordingly, these points will be difficult to estimate statistically from observations of a large group of consumers which are at all heterogeneous. In fact, if there is sufficient heterogeneity the discontinuities in the individual Engel curves will become indiscernible and the average Engel curve will be smooth.

We can, however, advance some very tentative and approximate conjectures about the shape of Engel curves in typical cases. It has been pointed out already that the slopes of the curves have to add up to unity, and that the introduction of a new commodity causes the slopes of its substitutes to drop and those of its complements to rise. Hence the substitutes must be more important in the total than the complements, which is, of course, a well-known theorem of consumption theory.§

If it can also be assumed that as v_0 increases from zero the list of goods bought gradually expands, then, on the average, the slopes of Engel curves for commodities already on the list will tend to fall. If the commodity considered is a low or medium grade of some item this fall will ultimately make the commodity inferior until it disappears altogether as in Fig. 2.

Although the empirical evidence for the existence of saturation phenomena is extremely meagre it does not seem likely that any *specific* item of expenditure will have a positively sloped Engel curve at a very high level of income. On the other hand, if a number of commodities are

---

† See Tobin and Houthakker (1951, formula (4.10)).
‡ For a quadratic utility function the Engel curves are broken straight lines. Allen and Bowley (1935) obtained unbroken straight lines in this case, but this came from ignoring non-negativity.   § Hicks (1946, pp. 311–12).

aggregated it is quite possible that the composite Engel curve will have an upward curvature for a considerable range of incomes. These conjectures appear likely to maintain whatever validity they have if we consider a group of consumers rather than an individual.

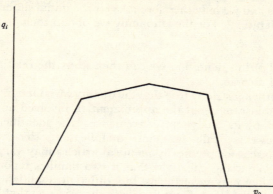

Fig. 2. The saturation phenomenon.

2.42. THE METHOD OF QUALITY VARIATIONS

The second approach to the problem of commodity specification is perhaps theoretically less satisfactory than the one just described but is more closely related to the information with which students of consumption are accustomed to work. It is also more accessible to orthodox mathematical techniques. Commodities are now no longer specified in complete detail, but, on the contrary, each is assumed to be available in a continuous range of varieties out of which the consumer selects one and only one. This definition of commodities requires therefore some degree of physical homogeneity (so that quantities can be expressed in the same unit); moreover, the consumer's purchases of exactly one variety, or quality, have to be positive.

For the purpose of this analysis a number z_k is associated with the kth variety, of which a quantity q_k is bought. The sum $\sum_k z_k q_k$ will be equal to $z_j q_j$, where j denotes the (unique) variety actually bought by a consumer in a particular price-income situation. The total quantity bought of the commodity (in physical units) will be called q; it is of course equal to q_j. For the numbers z_k we can conveniently take the prices p_k^0 in some initial situation; expenditure on the commodity in that situation is consequently

$$v = \sum_k z_k q_k = z_j q_j = z_j q = p_j^0 q. \qquad (2.12)$$

It is then possible to develop a theory, as in the paper by Houthakker (1952c), which is based on the analysis of certain kinds of price movements as described by the equation

$$p_j = \xi + \omega z_j, \qquad (2.13)$$

where ξ, the 'quantity price', does not depend on the quality bought, and ω is the 'quality price' which indicates the price differential between various grades. It will be noted that in the initial situation $\xi = 0$ and $\omega = 1$. In the case of family budgets we are not interested in price changes and we may therefore take for the initial situation the one under consideration. For the rth family we obtain then

$$v_r = z_{jr} q_r = p_{jr} q_r. \tag{2.14}$$

With the aid of this definition we can then study the relation between qualities and income.

It is of course not strictly true that the quality variable z_j is continuous within a certain range, but the approximation involved appears to be well justified by its analytical convenience. The identification of z_{jr} with p_{jr}, however, calls for some qualification, since, as already mentioned, prices for physically identical articles may vary according to location. What this means is that if two families report the same value for p_j they may nevertheless buy different qualities. More precisely it may be that if we identify z_j with the prices p_{js} that hold for the sth family, then for another family ξ may not equal zero and ω may not equal one. Thus, for example, if the different qualities of coal were defined by the price levels ruling in Newcastle it is unlikely that the same definition would be given by the London prices unless perhaps the values of ξ and ω were adjusted. In fact we are most likely to find differences in ξ rather than ω because regional price differences are limited by freight charges which will depend primarily on physical quantity. Ideally in comparing the qualities bought by families in different places an adjustment in ξ should therefore be applied. Other sources of price differences for physically identical items are considered in § 8.12.

The conclusion to be drawn from this section is that while the grouping together of commodities and their varieties inevitably introduces a degree of arbitrariness into the analysis, this can be considerably diminished by the explicit postulation of a quality variable which makes the whole analysis more realistic.

2.5. INTERDEPENDENCE OF PREFERENCES

The basic postulate of family-budget analysis, as remarked at the beginning of this chapter, is in its simplest form that the effects of income changes on consumption may be forecast by examining the consumption patterns of households with differing incomes at the same time. The validity of this has recently been questioned by a number of writers† who suggest that as a result of the interdependence of preferences different responses may be expected according to whether the income of the given household alone changes (other incomes remaining

---

† See Duesenberry (1949), Brady and Friedman (1947).

unchanged), or the income of all households change. In the extreme case of complete interdependence it is argued that if all incomes were to rise in the same proportion this would leave consumption unaffected; it is the relative income level that determines the level of consumption in this case and not its absolute level.

It has been shown by Tobin (1951), on the basis of an examination of records for families kept over several years, that as far as concerns total consumption expenditure the classical postulate, that the absolute income level is the determinant of consumption, gives a better explanation of the data examined by him than does the extreme alternative that only relative income levels matter.

It is clear, however, that the truth must lie somewhere between the two extreme positions of no interdependence and complete interdependence. For most commodities in staple demand the postulate of no interdependence probably gives an adequate description of consumers' behaviour; on the other hand, there can be few commodities for which either of the extreme postulates is fulfilled. For ties, nylon stockings and television sets or, let us say, ostentatious commodities in general, there will be some degree of interdependence which must be taken into account if the results of demand studies are to be properly interpreted.

The model of interdependence given here as an approach to this problem is based on that of H. G. Johnson (1952), which in turn is formally allied to the work of Goodwin (1949). It is here given in its simplest form and the reader requiring further developments should consult these works.

2.51. A MODEL OF INTERDEPENDENCE

It is here assumed that the consumption of a particular commodity by the rth individual, v_r, depends on his income, m_r, and on the level of consumption of all other consumers, $v_1, ..., v_R$ (the notation is here slightly changed from that of earlier sections to simplify the subscripts). The consumption by the rth individual of the commodity considered is thus given by the function

$$v_r = f_r(m_r; v_1, ..., v_R) \quad (r = 1, ..., R), \qquad (2.15)$$

where the right-hand side does not include v_r. For small changes in the variables there results on differentiating (2.15)

$$dv_r = \frac{\partial f_r}{\partial m_r} dm_r + \frac{\partial f_r}{\partial v_1} dv_1 + ... + \frac{\partial f_r}{\partial v_s} dv_s + ... + \frac{\partial f_r}{\partial v_R} dv_R, \qquad (2.16)$$

where $\partial f_r / \partial m_r$ is the marginal propensity of the rth individual to consume the particular commodity, and $\partial f_r / \partial v_s$ is the change in r's consumption resulting from an autonomous unit change in the consumption of s. For subsequent use we define, t_r, the *interdependence coefficient of r* as

D

the change in r's consumption resulting from equal unit changes in the consumption of all other individuals, that is

$$t_r = \sum_{s \neq r} \frac{\partial f_r}{\partial v_s}. \tag{2.17}$$

It is convenient to write the equations (2.16) in the matrix form

$$\mathbf{v} = \mathbf{f} + \mathbf{F}\mathbf{v}, \tag{2.18}$$

where $\mathbf{v}$ is the column vector of length R the elements of which are dv_r, $\mathbf{f}$ is a vector of the same length with elements equal to $(\partial f_r / \partial m_r)\, dm_r$, and $\mathbf{F}$ is a square hollow matrix of order R the (r, s)th element of which is $\partial f_r / \partial v_s$. This equation shows how the changes in the consumption of the various individuals in the society are implictly related; it may be solved to express the changes in consumption in terms of autonomous changes in income, thus

$$\mathbf{v} = (\mathbf{I} - \mathbf{F})^{-1}\mathbf{f}. \tag{2.19}$$

This shows that the effect of a change in a consumer's income on his own consumption, taking into account all the reactions through other consumers, depends both on his marginal propensity to consume and on the interdependence structure of the whole society.

2.52. SOME SPECIAL CASES

To derive any simple results in this complicated situation it is necessary to make some simplifying assumptions about $\mathbf{F}$.

(a) If it is supposed that the consumption of a consumer depends only on those above him in the income scale, $\mathbf{F}$ will be an upper triangular matrix (given that the consumers are arranged in descending order of income). The inverse of $(\mathbf{I} - \mathbf{F})$ will then also be an upper triangular matrix with units as the diagonal elements. It follows that the effect of a rise in a single consumer's income will have the same effect on his consumption as if there were no interdependence.

(b) The same argument holds for the case where consumption depends only on that of consumers lower in the income scale. The reason for these simple results is that while a change in the consumption of a particular individual affects the consumption of others in the society, it only affects precisely those who do not affect him. There is therefore no 'feed-back' and the interdependence is of a special sort.

(c) The most interesting case to consider is that in which the interdependence coefficients of all individuals is the same, that is,

$$t_1 = t_2 = \ldots = t_R = t, \tag{2.20}$$

say, and all the non-diagonal elements of the matrix $\mathbf{F}$ are equal to $t/(R-1)$. This corresponds to the assumption otherwise made of, say, equal income elasticities for all individuals. The inverse of $(\mathbf{I} - \mathbf{F})$ will then have all the diagonal elements equal to

$$D = \frac{1}{1 + t/(R-1)} \cdot \frac{1 - t(R-2)/(R-1)}{1-t}, \tag{2.21}$$

and all the non-diagonal elements equal to

$$N = \frac{1}{(R-1)[1+t/(R-1)]} \cdot \frac{t}{1-t}.$$

(2.22)

If t is small and R large, the non-diagonal elements will be of negligible size, while the diagonal elements are approximately equal to $(1+2t/R)$. Thus the effect of interdependence is to increase the response in a consumer's purchases consequent upon a rise in his own income by a proportionate amount of $2t/R$, which, in general, is negligible.

So far we have only considered the effects of a rise in the income of a single consumer. The more interesting effects of interdependence are, however, to be observed when there is an increase in the income of all consumers. If all the marginal propensities to consume are equal, the effect of an equal rise in all incomes on aggregate consumption will be

$$[D+(R-1)\,N]\frac{\partial f}{\partial m}\,dm = \frac{1}{1-t}\frac{\partial f}{\partial m}\,dm.$$

(2.23)

The effect of interdependence on aggregate consumption is thus measured by the 'multiplier' $1/(1-t)$; if interdependence is positive the effects of income changes are increased, and if it is negative the effects are damped.

(d) If consumers' preferences are interdependent only within certain groups of consumers, and there is no interdependence between the groups, the argument of the above paragraph may easily be extended. For the interdependence matrix may then be partitioned such that those sub-matrices lying about the diagonal are similar to **F** and the remainder are composed only of zeros. The sub-matrices may then be inverted separately, to give results similar to those of the last paragraph.

(e) If the elements of **F** differ then it is not possible to make any general statement about the effects of variations in individual incomes. We can, however, assure ourselves that the interdependence multiplier lies between certain limits, and that the argument of the previous paragraphs is therefore not wholly irrelevant.

We assume that all the elements of the interdependence matrix, to be denoted by f_{ij}, are positive,[†] and that the degree of interdependence of each individual, t_r, is less than unity. Let the smallest and largest value of t_r be t and T respectively. Denoting by **i** the $R \times 1$ unit vector, the aggregate change in consumption is

$$\mathbf{i'v} = \mathbf{i'(I-F)^{-1}f}$$
$$= \mathbf{i'(I+F+F^2+...)\,f}$$
$$= (\mathbf{i'+i'F+i'F^2+...})\,\mathbf{f}.$$

(2.24)

Since the sum of elements in any row of **F** less than T, it follows that

---

† The subsequent argument holds even if some of the elements are negative, provided that we refer to $|f_{ij}|$ instead of to f_{ij}, etc.

the sum of the elements in any row of $\mathbf{F}^n$ is less than T^n; for consider $n = 2$, the (i, j)th element of $\mathbf{F}^2$ is $\sum_k f_{ik} f_{kj}$. The row sum of these elements is

$$\sum_j \sum_k f_{ik} f_{kj} = \sum_k f_{ik} \sum_j f_{kj}$$

$$\leqslant T \sum_j f_{kj}$$

$$\leqslant T^2, \tag{2.25}$$

and the result for the nth power may be demonstrated by induction.

Hence each element in the vector $\mathbf{i}'(\mathbf{I} - \mathbf{F})^{-1}$ will be less than

$$1 + T + T^2 + \ldots = \frac{1}{1 - T}, \tag{2.26}$$

and the aggregate change in consumption is given by

$$\mathbf{i}'\mathbf{v} \leqslant \frac{1}{1 - T} \mathbf{i}'\mathbf{f}. \tag{2.27}$$

Similarly, it may be shown that

$$\mathbf{i}'\mathbf{v} \geqslant \frac{1}{1 - t} \mathbf{i}'\mathbf{f}. \tag{2.28}$$

Now $\mathbf{i}'\mathbf{f}$ is the change in aggregate consumption in the absence of interdependence. It is therefore seen that, under the simplified conditions assumed, the effects of interdependence are to vary this quantity by a multiplier the value of which is between $1/(1 - t)$ and $1/(1 - T)$. It may be noted that (2.23) is a special case of this when $T = t$.

It may be possible with the help of the above argument to attempt an empirical analysis of the demand for ostentatious goods. But the object in giving this comparatively extensive treatment to a subject which is of little practical importance at the present stage of the analysis of family budgets has been not to contribute towards that problem but, rather, to provide an insight into an assumption which lies so close to the basis of family-budget analysis. As has been seen in the above discussion the concept of an income elasticity still retains its central importance, but it requires modification by an 'interdependence multiplier' the value of which depends on the attitude of society as a whole towards that commodity.

2.53. THE INCOME EFFECTS OF INTERDEPENDENCE

The argument given in the above sections is, however, not rigorous since no account has been taken of the constraint that, whatever be the effect of the interdependence of preferences on particular expenditures, in no case may the total of expenditures exceed the income of the consumer. Thus, on summing (2.16) over all commodities for the rth consumer, there results

$$\Sigma\, dv_r = dm_r \Sigma \frac{\partial f_r}{\partial m_r} + dv_1 \Sigma \frac{\partial f_r}{\partial v_1} + \ldots + dv_s \Sigma \frac{\partial f_r}{\partial v_s} + \ldots + dv_R \Sigma \frac{\partial f_r}{\partial v_R}, \quad (2.29)$$

where Σ denotes summation over commodities, and this equation must hold identically for all values of the variables. Since $dm_r = \Sigma\, dv_r$ it follows at once that

$$\Sigma \frac{\partial f_r}{\partial m_r} = 1 \qquad\qquad (2.30)$$

that is, as is well known, the marginal propensities to consume sum to unity for any consumer; and

$$\Sigma \frac{\partial f_r}{\partial v_s} = 0 \qquad\qquad (2.31)$$

that is, if there is an autonomous change in the sth consumer's expenditure on a particular commodity this can only effect the rth consumer's expenditures on the various commodities in such a way as to leave his total expenditure unchanged. It will be seen that the change in expenditure on the particular commodity by the sth consumer thus necessarily affects all the expenditures of the rth consumer and for this reason the simple formulation given in (2.15) is inadequate from a more rigorous point of view.

If the expenditures on all the n commodities by the R consumers were explicitly introduced into (2.15) there would result nR conditions of the type (2.31) which would provide constraints on the interdependence coefficients. These constraints may be said to arise from the income effects of interdependence, by analogy with the usual theory of the effects of price changes on the consumer's budget. A particular consequence of these constraints is that if some of the coefficients are positive, then others must be negative. It is quite possible that the positive effects are concentrated in a few commodities while the negative effects are dispersed over a great many other commodities where they may hardly be discernible in practice. This is especially likely to be the case when the commodity has only a small weight in the budget so that its income effects are generally negligible.

It follows that the applicability of the kind of simplified analysis suggested in § 2.52 requires the qualification that it should be applied only to those objects of conspicuous consumption which do not absorb a large part of the household's total expenditure.

2.54. IMPLICATIONS FOR EMPIRICAL ANALYSIS

The above argument has been concerned with the analytic problem of the difference between the reaction to a change in the incomes of all consumers and that of a single consumer only. The next question to be considered is how this should affect the interpretation of empirical estimates of income elasticities. If these estimates are based on aggregative time-series and it is assumed that there are equal (or equi-proportionate) changes in the income of all consumers throughout the period of observation, then the value will incorporate whatever effects of interdependence there are present as measured by the interdependence multiplier. In the case of family-budget data, however, while there is information on the incomes of many consumers, for no single consumer is there available the information on all the other consumers who affect his consumption. The analysis only distinguishes the income of the consumer as the determining variable, the effects of the other consumers being subsumed under an error term. If this term can be assumed to be random, then the income elasticity derived from family budgets may provide a fairly good estimate of what would happen if the income of a single consumer alone were to change. But if the effects of interdependence are significant this estimate requires correction by an interdependence multiplier before being used in aggregative forecasts.

CHAPTER 3

THE COLLECTION OF INFORMATION ON CONSUMERS' EXPENDITURE BY HOUSEHOLD SURVEYS

3.1. INTRODUCTION

The preceding chapter has set out the theoretical framework which has influenced the approach and concepts underlying the investigations to be presented in later chapters. If that were the only approach to the subject and as a result there were only a single direct question or set of questions which could be answered by a survey of consumers' expenditures, then the planning of such a survey would be a straightforward matter. But there are of course many possible approaches to the subject and many objects which a survey fulfils; its planning will therefore involve the fine art of balancing conflicting criteria.

Little that is generally applicable can be said here on the optimum methods of carrying out a survey of consumers' expenditures—the more so since the experience of the writers has centred on the interpretation of data rather than on their collection. The task of this chapter is therefore to set out as concisely as possible the methods adopted in collecting the information of the two surveys, the results of which are presented in Part III, together with a general background of the principles which govern the organization of surveys. The reader may thus appraise the value of the methods adopted for himself and judge the reliability, efficacy and appropriateness of the data in their subsequent applications.

Only the major features of the surveys will be described here; for further practical details reference should be made to the original accounts given by the Ministry of Labour (1949) and by Massey (1942), on which the description given here is largely based.

This chapter and that following will accordingly be concerned with the practical matters arising in household surveys. This chapter will be largely devoted to a description of the two pre-war budget inquiries and the next section describes the objects of the surveys, the selection of the households and the period of observation covered. The third section will discuss the extent to which the two samples may be judged to represent the habits of the population of Britain as a whole; and the final section will set out the criteria that have influenced the presentation of the data in Part III.

The limitations of the data are not discussed in this chapter except *en passant*, the whole matter being reserved for the succeeding chapter.†

† The reader who wishes to explore further some of the problems raised in these two chapters should consult Yates (1949) and, for a concise discussion of the problems encountered in family budget surveys, Utting and Cole (1953).

3.2. THE MAJOR FEATURES OF SURVEYS OF HOUSEHOLD EXPENDITURES

3.21. THE IMPORTANCE OF A REPRESENTATIVE SAMPLE

In attempting to obtain information on consumption patterns and standards of living two kinds of survey can be envisaged as relevant. The first kind—an analytic survey—would obtain information on consumption units with given characteristics, such as households consisting only of old-age pensioners, and compare their consumption patterns with those of other households, say, households consisting of a husband and wife and two children. A survey directed to this particular end would differ in organization from a survey of the second kind, which attempts to obtain as reliable estimates as possible of a number of characteristics of the population. These characteristics which are to be regarded as variables taking a number of values—for example, the consumption of butter—vary between different sections of the population. If a good estimate is to be obtained of the average value it is important that every substantial section of the population be represented in the sample. Such a survey may be termed 'picturesque', since its object is to obtain a picture of the situation.

While an analytic survey may be primarily directed towards the discovery of causal relationships and a picturesque survey towards the evaluation of a number of parameters describing the population, the difference between them is in reality not as great as may appear at first thought. For the object of obtaining a reliable estimate of a parameter as in the second type of survey is—almost inevitably—to relate it to another parameter by what may be interpreted as a cause and effect process. The number of such relationships existing in the population which are of interest is very large, and it is only possible to investigate those which are quantitatively of greater importance. If partial relationships based on this kind of survey are to give useful insights into the nature of the population it is necessary that the sample of observations should be representative of the population in all possible respects.

While the two kinds of survey may logically have the same object it will generally be the case that an analytic survey will lead to a much greater understanding of a particular problem than will a picturesque survey. Picturesque surveys are carried out because information is expensive to obtain and it is required over a wide field.

3.22. THE OBJECT OF THE SURVEYS AND THE SELECTION OF THE SAMPLES

In surveys of consumers' expenditure the household is regarded as the basic sampling unit.† While some expenditures are made by individuals for their own purposes without regard to the household it

---

† It is possible to to regard the individual as the basic sampling unit and this may be desirable in certain contexts; cf. Gray and Corlett (1950, p. 21).

seems to be the case that the majority of expenditures are carried out by members of the household on its behalf; often, indeed, it will be difficult to allocate expenditures as being on behalf of a particular person. Once the precise definition of the household has been settled it will be found that there are certain consumers who will have to be left out of the survey if it is to be conducted economically; thus, for example, persons living in hotels were excluded from our two surveys. Again, there will inevitably arise a number of borderline cases which require a decision on whether they are to be included in the survey or not. Thus lodgers who dine with the household were regarded as part of the household, but such lodgers and such households were excluded from the surveys on account of the difficulty of obtaining reliable information about them. Lodgers who obtained their own meals were regarded as separate households and were included in the surveys.

The overriding object of the survey conducted by the Ministry of Labour was to obtain information for a revision of the cost-of-living index. This, in effect, requires reliable estimates only of the proportions of total expenditure devoted to the various items. Since the cost-of-living index was conceived as applying to the working class only, this meant that the survey could be restricted to that section of the population, and this survey is accordingly here termed the working-class survey.

The registers of persons insured against unemployment provided the frame from which the sample was drawn. This covered all manual workers (whatever their income) and non-manual workers with incomes not exceeding £250 per year. Certain classes of workers who were not insured for some historical reason, for example, employees in the permanent service of railway companies, were included in the survey by special arrangements. Households in which the principal wage-earner had been unemployed for a considerable period of time were excluded from the inquiry.

The second survey is that conducted by the Civil Service Statistical and Research Bureau and was intended to complement the working-class inquiry in that it covered a section of the population omitted entirely from that inquiry—non-manual workers with incomes exceeding £250 per annum. The frame in this case was the lists of members of three groups of professional organizations: civil servants, local government officials and teachers. This inquiry is here termed the middle-class inquiry, but consideration of whether its results can in fact be considered to reflect the behaviour of the British middle classes is deferred to Chapter 11.

From these lists names were selected at regular intervals, the interval being chosen so as to yield a sample of the required size. As there is no reason to expect any cyclicity in the occurrence of the names this should yield a sample which does not differ from one based on tables of random numbers.

3.23. METHODS OF COLLECTING THE INFORMATION AND THE PERIOD OF THE INQUIRY

Once the households have been selected the information on expenditures may be obtained by a number of approaches. These are: (1) by postal contact which may merely notify the householder when an interviewer will call, or may ask the householder to complete and return an enclosed questionnaire; (2) by personal interview which involves the householder in answering oral questions put by the interviewer; or (3) the interviewer may leave a questionnaire to be completed over a period of time, the interviewer calling back to collect the completed form and to help the householder on any points of difficulty. The effective choice in this country is between the interview method and the personally collected questionnaire method; postal methods are little used.

The appropriateness of the above methods depends on the length of the period of 'observation' and that, in turn, depends on the frequency with which the purchases on a particular commodity are undertaken. For frequent expenditures, such as foodstuffs, it may be that reliable estimates are best obtained from records of a week's expenditure collected by means of a questionnaire. For infrequent expenditures it should be noted that the observations on a given household in successive weeks are not independent; if a household has bought a refrigerator this week it is unlikely to buy another next week. A convenient method for obtaining information on such items is, perhaps, to ask for the date at which an expenditure was last incurred and obtain an estimate of the average expenditure per week by finding the average period of replacement for the item. In practice, some combination of all the above methods may be adopted, taking into account the importance attached to the various items of information the survey is to provide.

In our inquiries the questionnaire method was used. The items were detailed under about 150 heads, about a third of which were food items. It may be noted, however, that in the questionnaire method it is not necessary to make a precise list of all the items; the householder may be left to describe the items bought in detail and the office staff may later classify them under a suitable number of heads.

Useful information on the quantities of foodstuffs bought as distinct from expenditure on the items is more difficult to obtain, since many items are bought in terms of arbitrary units, as a box of cheese or a lettuce. From a nutritional point of view information on quantities is more important than information on expenditures, and it may be worth going to considerable trouble to ensure the accuracy of the quantity information. The investigator may even leave a spring balance with the housewife.†

In our inquiries quantity information was requested for most of the food items and a few non-food items. Little emphasis was, however, laid

---

† Cf. *The Urban Working-Class Household Diet, 1940–1949* (Ministry of Food, 1951, p. 97).

on obtaining complete information, and in the case of the middle-class inquiry what information had been collected was to a large extent discarded in summarizing.† For the working-class inquiry the information has been published as averages for a number of commodities, but we have been able to give in Part III a more complete classification of the data.

The inquiries were each conducted in two parts as far as concerns the length of time they cover. In the major inquiries the households were asked to record a week's expenditure in each of the four quarters of the year. Additional inquiries were made of a proportion of these households who were asked to keep records of their expenditure on clothing for a whole year, since, while clothing forms a considerable portion of the households' total expenditure, it was held that the infrequency of the expenditure makes it desirable to base estimates on a longer period.‡

The weeks chosen for the working-class inquiry were those beginning on 17 October 1937, 23 January, 24 April and 17 July 1938. The middle-class inquiry began some six months after the beginning of the working-class inquiry, and the results are therefore not quite comparable. The dates of the middle-class inquiry are the weeks beginning 24 April, 3 July, 9 October 1938 and 15 January 1939. The annual clothing inquiry in each case covered the 52 weeks beginning with the first week of the main inquiry.

3.24. THE RESPONSE TO THE INQUIRIES

The response to the inquiries are set out in Table 1, in which are distinguished (a) the number of households selected by the sampling procedure, which are given to the nearest thousand; (b) the number of households who supplied adequate information for all four weeks of the major inquiry; and (c) the number of households who participated in the subsidiary clothing inquiry, which are given to the nearest hundred.

TABLE 1. THE RESPONSE TO THE BRITISH INQUIRIES OF 1937-9

	Number selected at random	Number supplying budgets for all four weeks	Number in clothing inquiry
Working class	22,000	10,800	2,700
Middle class	6,000	1,400	700
Total	28,000	12,200	3,400

† We are indebted to Mr T. C. B. Watson for providing us with some information on average prices and quantities which he had summarized from the middle-class inquiry; we were, however, unable to make much use of it in the calculations presented in Chapter 8 on account of the differences in the dates of the two inquiries.

‡ In the middle-class inquiry annual estimates were also obtained for expenditure on education.

As far as the major inquiries are concerned records for approximately a half of the possible number of households were used; though for the middle-class inquiry the proportion is only a quarter. It should be added that there were a number of households who supplied information for some of the four weeks and might have been used if less stringent criteria were adopted. The above proportions accordingly somewhat under-estimate the response rate.

To what extent the records of those supplying budget information may be regarded as representative of all working-class and middle-class households is a matter of judgement on which there can be no firm opinion. The facts have been set out above, and there can be little doubt that all concerned in the inquiries were anxious to obtain representative results. There must, however, remain a desire to have some investigations into the nature of the types of households who do not co-operate in these inquiries.†

3.3. THE PROPORTION OF THE HOUSEHOLDS OF BRITAIN REPRESENTED BY THE INQUIRIES

If the results of the two inquiries are to be applied to the population of Britain as a whole some estimate must be made of the numbers of households in the population of which each of the inquiries can be regarded as representative and, again, some estimate must be made of the proportion of the population which cannot reasonably be regarded as being represented in these inquiries. In particular, if the results of the two inquiries are to be combined to yield better estimates for the country as a whole they should be weighted in proportion to the numbers of households which they represent. Accordingly, this section discusses the basis from which estimates of such weights may be obtained; the argument throughout ignores any bias which may result from differential rates of response of different sections of the population.

In order to derive estimates for this purpose census figures of national totals have to be used and, as there is little information available on the number of households, the argument will be in terms of the numbers of persons in the population, for which there are reliable estimates.‡

The working-class inquiry was based on the number of persons in-sured against unemployment which, as given in the *Annual Abstract of Statistics*, was 15·3 millions in 1937. From this must be subtracted the number of unemployed who were not covered by the survey, and there must be added the number of those who were included in the survey (such as railway employees) but who were not insured. These adjust-

---

† Some information may be obtained by comparing the results of questionnaire inquiries with interview inquiries in which there is a higher response rate; see Gray and Corlett (1950, p. 32).

‡ The computations given here follow those of Ross (1948, p. 157). Reference should be made to Barna (1945, Appendix F, p. 272), and to Chapman (1953, pp. 17 et seq.) for other relevant estimates of national totals. Since approximate estimates are sufficient for purposes of weighting little attention is here paid to the finer definitional details of the figures quoted.

ments change the figure by a small amount to 14·6 millions. An estimate of the corresponding number of households in the population may be obtained by using the figure of 1·75 wage-earners per household given by the sample. Since this last estimate may, however, include other wage-earners, such as housewives and daughters in domestic work who are not included in those insured against unemployment, an adjustment should be made at any rate for the largest section of these, that is, for those in non-resident domestic service. Chapman† gives the number in private domestic service in 1938 as 1·7 millions. This figure should be increased since it is given as the number of full-time equivalent working persons and many were only in part-time employment, and it should be reduced for domestic servants forming part of the household of the employer; in the absence of information it is left unadjusted.

The total number of households so calculated is 9·3 millions and, making use of the estimate of 3·77 persons per household given by the sample, the number of persons represented in the working-class inquiry is found to be 35 millions.

For the middle-class inquiry it is rather more difficult to make an estimate. If the inquiry is held to represent only the civil servants, local government officials and teachers from whose associations the sample was drawn, the figure of 190,000 members‡ in receipt of incomes exceeding £250 per annum may be used as a minimum for the number of earners.

While the households represented by these form one section of the middle classes it seems unrealistic to regard them as representative of the whole of the middle classes, which include merchants, sole traders and the like whose patterns of life and patterns of expenditure must differ in many ways from the salaried professionals covered by this survey. Since there can only be a negligible number of households in this survey whose heads have an income exceeding £1000 per annum, a maximum to the numbers represented may be obtained from the Inland Revenue figure of 2·2 million incomes between £250 and £1000 per annum in 1938. Some of these will have been earned by manual workers covered by the working-class inquiry and some will be profit-earners. On the other hand, on account of supplementary earnings some of the households will have an income in excess of £1000 per annum. Perhaps 1·5 millions may be taken as the number of salary-earners who can, at the most, be regarded as represented in the middle-class survey.

Performing the same calculations as for the working-class inquiry above the number of persons in the population covered by the middle-class inquiry may be judged to be 4 millions.

Knowing the total number of persons in the population, the number not represented by either inquiry can be found by difference. The numbers on the basis of the above assumptions are set out in the first column of Table 2 and the proportions in the final column. From this

† Op. cit. p. 216.   ‡ Given by Massey (1942, p. 189).

it is seen that unless extreme assumptions are made as to the representativeness of the middle-class inquiry it should receive a comparatively low weight when used in combination with the other inquiry in order to obtain national averages.

TABLE 2. ESTIMATED NUMBER OF PERSONS REPRESENTED
IN THE BRITISH INQUIRIES OF 1937–9

	Number of persons (millions)	Percentage
Working-class inquiry	35·1	74
Middle-class inquiry	4·0	8
Not represented	8·4	18
Total population	47·5	100

The weights allocated will depend on the judgement made as to the behaviour of households not represented in either inquiry, and it may therefore be useful to remind the reader interested in such calculations of these categories. They are: unemployed workers; old-age pensioners living on their own; non-manual employees of private persons or firms with an income exceeding £250 per annum; professionals working on their own account; directors; farmers; shopkeepers, sole traders and employers generally; and others whose entire income is derived from unearned sources.

In the absence of information on the expenditure patterns of these categories their weight will have to be apportioned between the two surveys. The estimated proportions given by Stone et al. (1954),† based on an estimate of the distribution of families by income groups in Great Britain in 1937, show 21 % of the households as middle class and the remainder as industrial and agricultural working class. On converting to numbers of persons for comparison with the figures in Table 2 these estimates are equivalent to 19 % for the middle-class survey and 81 % for the working-class survey.

It is not to be expected that the omitted categories of households will affect the reliability of the estimates of all commodities equally, and an estimate better than that to be obtained by simply weighting the two inquiries as above can, no doubt, often be made (for example, on the basis of regression analysis) to meet a particular need. It is, however, as well to keep the above estimates of the representativeness of the data not too far back in one's mind.

3.4. THE PRESENTATION OF THE DATA IN PART III

The principal results of the two inquiries have already been published by the Ministry of Labour (1940–41 and 1949) and by Massey (1942) in the form of tables of average expenditures on the various items. In

† See Stone et al. (1954, p. 168).

the present study of family budgets the interest has inevitably been to obtain records which are as complete and reliable as possible, even if this involved some sacrifice in the representativeness of the sample. In this way it was hoped to facilitate new lines of research both immediately and from a more long-term point of view. The data which are presented in Part III accordingly fulfil a dual role in that they are intended as a support for the investigations in Part II of this book and, in addition, are intended to make material available to the research student in sufficient detail to allow of further investigations. The latter object has guided us in the questions that have arisen in presenting the data, and we have on the whole given the data to more rather than less significant figures than is warranted by their nature.

The data from the working-class inquiry given in Part III relate to those households who co-operated in the annual clothing inquiry and whose main earners were engaged in industrial, commercial and clerical occupations. Households whose main earners were engaged in agriculture and households in rural areas were omitted.† There were thus available some 2200 budgets.

To obtain comparable figures for the middle-class inquiry which were of sufficient accuracy it was necessary to use all the available data both for the four-weekly inquiry and for the annual clothing inquiry; the information given in Part III therefore relates, at the most, to about 1,400 households. Reference to Table 1 will make clear what portion of the available data is here tabulated.

The main features of the present tabulations may be summarized under three heads.

First, the average expenditures on the various commodities are given in a two-way classification—by total expenditure and by the number of persons in the household. This makes possible the investigation of the effects of household size on consumption; confusion on this matter in the past has, in no small part, been due to the lack of a suitable quantity of data so classified.

Secondly, the aim has been to present the two inquiries in a comparable form so as to allow the investigation of social-class factors in consumption. The absence of any income information in the working-class inquiry forced us to use total expenditure in both inquiries as the classifying variable. The main tables in Part III are in two halves, working class and middle class, and the items are defined on a comparable basis. Certain extra items which are only available for one of the inquiries are given at the end in § X. The average total expenditure of the middle-class households is naturally above that of the working-class households, but it has been possible to arrange for three of the total expenditure groups to coincide and two further groups to overlap in part.

The third feature of the present tabulations is the presentation of quantity information for the working-class inquiry from which average

† The organization of this section of the inquiry differed slightly from that for the industrial, etc., households; for details see the publications by the Ministry of Labour.

prices have been computed. This information has made possible the analysis of quality variations given in Chapter 8.

The data in Part III give the average expenditures in ninety-five household groups. For the working-class sample the data are classified by eight income ranges and seven household sizes; two of the cells are empty, thus giving fifty-four groups. For the smaller middle-class inquiry seven income ranges have been used and six household sizes; one cell is empty giving forty-one groups.

There are many further points of detail that could be mentioned in addition to these principal features. While the above account is adequate for the reader concerned only with the results of the analyses presented in subsequent chapters, the student who proposes to use the data in Part III for further calculations should read the 'Guide to the Tables' given at their head.

CHAPTER 4

THE LIMITATIONS OF THE DATA

4.1. ENDS AND MEANS

The limitations of family-budget data, as of any other means, are relative to the ends for which they are required. In this chapter an attempt will be made to set out some of the relevant limitations and the possible sources of bias that may arise in obtaining the information.

The difficulties to be overcome in the case of picturesque surveys will naturally be more serious than in the case of analytic surveys, and the limitations correspondingly greater, since the sample must be representative of the population in a large variety of characteristics. But in a particular analysis it may not matter that the sample is not altogether satisfactory; for example, even if the highest and the lowest income groups are not represented in the sample it may still be possible to carry out a satisfactory analysis of the variation of consumption with respect to the income level of the household on the basis of the income groups that are in the sample.

4.11. EXPENDITURE, CONSUMPTION AND INTAKE

The discussion has so far implicitly assumed that the definition of household expenditure is a straightforward matter. That this is not always so may be seen by comparing it with the allied concept of consumption defined so as to allow of stock variations. Thus the consumption of potatoes by a particular household during a period may be found by adding the stocks of potatoes at the beginning of the period to the quantity of potatoes bought during the period, and subtracting the stocks at the end of the period. Consumption so defined must be distinguished from intake which, for potatoes, would be the quantity eaten by each of the members of the household in the period whether obtained from their own purchases or from other sources, after allowing for wastage in their preparation.†

It does not generally matter from an economic point of view whether consumption is considered or expenditure. For, provided the households are not such as to make a virtue of accumulating potatoes, the amount of potatoes bought will tend to equal the amount of potatoes consumed as the period of the inquiry is lengthened. If, however, goods are customarily bought on credit, or on monthly account, it is necessary

---

† A further distinction is occasionally drawn between intake proper, which is the amount of food actually absorbed in the process of digestion, and the input of food which is the 'intake' defined in the text.

E

to decide whether the information to be collected in a survey should refer to the receipt of goods by the consumer or to his payment of money to the shopkeeper.

From the nutritional point of view, intake is clearly the most appropriate concept. It differs from consumption in allowing for wastage in the preparation of the food, and further, whereas consumption figures may refer to the total for the household, figures of intake should refer to individual members of the household.

4.12. THE ECONOMICS OF INFORMATION

The above considerations do not represent ultimate limitations on the value of family budget data in particular applications. The limitations only arise in so far as data collected, say, on consumption are used as approximations to data, say, on intake. With sufficient trouble and sufficient expense there is no reason why satisfactory data on intake should not be collected. But the expense of collection (considering expense in its widest sense) is, in fact, the crux of the matter. Expense limits the size of the sample, the frequency with which an inquiry is held and the pains taken to ensure the representativeness of the sample.†

The applicability of pre-war data to a post-war situation may also be thought a limitation, but as already indicated in the first chapter, this is not entirely so, since as rationing and controls are relaxed consumption patterns tend to the pre-war form. An inquiry relating to 1938 may therefore be of greater interest today than one relating to, say, 1950.

Since the size of the sample is limited by expense, sampling variability may limit the accuracy of a particular estimate obtained from the inquiry. In planning the inquiry the accuracy with which a particular estimate is required will be weighed against the expense of collecting the information in determining the sample size. Sampling variability is thus more or less under control; what requires much more thought are the various sources of bias that may affect the data. The following three sections therefore discuss the possible sources of bias at three stages: (*a*) in selecting the households, (*b*) in recording the information, and (*c*) in interpreting the information. In the final section the main results of our inquiries are compared with other estimates to assess their general reliability.

4.2. BIAS IN SELECTION AND RESPONSE

Since the survey method relies on the voluntary co-operation of households biases may arise if some types of households are more likely to co-operate than others. On the one hand, there are likely to be too many expansive and 'extroverted' households in the sample who are only too happy to tell the suffering investigator of the way the money is

† In connexion with these topics, cf. the distinction between economic design and statistical design made by Stone (1951*b*, p. 10).

spent and at the same time all the intimate details of their family life.†
These households no doubt have certain characteristic (abnormal)
patterns of expenditure, too many television aerials for example, possibly
too much expenditure on social activities in general, and they possibly
tend to dissave. On the other hand, there are likely to be too many
households in the sample which are of a cautious nature, who already
record every penny leaving the coffers and for whom little extra trouble
is involved in filling out what, for them, is in the nature of a duplicate
expenditure schedule. In general there is also a 'literacy bias', for if
the household is good at reading, writing and arithmetic there will be
less difficulty in obtaining its co-operation.

Apart from the possibility of these general biases there are particular
motives which affect the degree of a household's co-operation. These
again work in opposite directions. Rich households, if they can be
persuaded to co-operate at all, are likely to understate their frivolous
expenditure (this includes the working man's expenditure on beer as
much as the director's expenditure on mink coats). Poor households—
especially in a cost-of-living inquiry—are, on the other hand, tempted
to overstate their expenditure on what they may judge society to judge
as necessities. Poverty is here a relative concept, and this motive may
be equally at work in the middle-class inquiry covering the 'underpaid'
professions.

The only way of keeping, at any rate, a partial check on biases of this
nature is by recording a certain amount of 'control information' which
may be compared with known population values. For example, the
number of households co-operating in each geographical region may be
compared with the numbers in the population to check whether any
regional bias has arisen.‡

Of course, a faulty frame may lead to biases which can later be
corrected. In the working-class inquiry, for example, households. in
which both husband and wife were in insured employment had a twofold chance of inclusion in the sample, since it was drawn from the
registers of insured workers. Any bias which may arise on this account
can easily be corrected by giving returns from such households only
half their weight in constructing averages. This was the method adopted
in tabulating the results of the main working-class inquiry, but it may
well be thought that this was an over-refinement.

The use of 'control information' may be illustrated from our inquiries
by comparing the proportions in the various age and sex groups with
the proportions in the population; for the latter the estimate for 1939 by
the Registrar General is used, and the figures are set out in Table 3.

It will be seen that the proportions correspond quite well, the only
noticeable difference being an excess of children of and below school
age. This may result from an over-representation of households with

† Some investigators consider this to provide a fruitful link between psychology and
economics.
‡ Cf. Ministry of Labour (1949, p. 10).

children, since housewives with children are more likely to be at home when the interviewer calls. This brings out the importance of repeating calls at households if no one is at home;† an immediate substitution of another address will lead to a sample more heavily biased with children. In view of the importance of children in determining consumption patterns it is worth paying attention to this point.

TABLE 3. AGE AND SEX COMPOSITION OF THE
SAMPLES AND THE POPULATION[1]

Age-sex category	Average number of persons per household		Proportions in samples		Proportions in population
	Working class	Middle class	Working class	Middle class	
Males, over 18	1·21	1·00	32	31	35
Females, over 18	1·25	1·26	33	39	39
Males, 14–17	0·17	0·11	4	4	3
Females, 14–17	0·17	0·12	4	4	3
Children, 5–13	0·67	0·52	18	16	13
Children under 5	0·31	0·25	8	8	7
Total	3·77	3·26	100	100	100

[1] In this and subsequent tables it may be found that there is a discrepancy between the total figure and the sum of the components: this is the effect of rounding-off figures to a given number of places.

A comparison of income and total expenditure may be of interest in casting light on the general nature of the households and the order of magnitude of the biases that may arise. It is well known that family-budget inquiries generally show an excess of expenditure over income due to biases in recording, combined with the low level of savings by households in all but the top income groups. The figures below should therefore only be taken as an indication of the order of magnitude of the errors that may arise. To obtain estimates of savings in households it is now generally agreed that specially designed surveys are necessary, based on accounts of assets held and the like.‡

In Table 4 are summarized the results of a tabulation of single-earner households in the middle-class survey. The households have been grouped by the earned income of the head of the household and the table gives the average income in the eight groups, the income-tax paid, and the total expenditure. It will be seen that the averages show a slight but uniform excess of expenditure over income less tax. Only in the highest income group is there a balance.

There is thus no single predominating factor leading to a bias in one direction or another; there are, rather, a number of factors at work

† A method of weighting the information inversely with the amount of time spent at home by the informant has been suggested by Politz and Simmons (1949); this may be used in order to avoid bias resulting from the under-representation of households who spend a large proportion of their time away from home.

‡ See Lydall (1951).

which may lead to the participation of certain kinds of households and consequent biases in the results. As far as total expenditure is concerned there seems to be a small degree of over-statement,† but from the internal evidence of our surveys it is difficult to arrive at any conclusion as to the magnitude of the bias involved in the estimate of any particular item. The technique of interviewing orally a subsample of the households who refuse to co-operate in a questionnaire inquiry may in the future give some insight into this problem.

TABLE 4. INCOME AND EXPENDITURE IN THE MIDDLE-CLASS SURVEY: SINGLE-EARNER HOUSEHOLDS GROUPED BY INCOME (£'S PER ANNUM)

Income group	Number of households	Average income before tax	Income tax	Total expenditure
250–300	219	278	3	319
300–350	278	322	3	382
350–400	231	370	5	433
400–450	120	415	6	454
450–500	50	471	8	525
500–600	103	545	21	587
600–700	40	640	33	684
Over 700	54	877	78	810

4.3. BIAS IN RECORDING

Apart from the biases that may result from a faulty selection of households included in the sample, there are biases that may occur in the process of obtaining and recording the information. These arise in a number of ways and different methods are appropriate for minimizing their effect.

4.31. SURVEY SUGGESTION

First, there is the possibility of bias due to what may be termed *survey suggestion*; as a result of the very process of keeping accounts the housewife may begin to feel that, on some criterion, she is spending too much‡ on certain items. This may happen if accounts are required over, say, a fortnight, when the expenditure in the second week will be influenced by the accounts of the first week. It may also arise if the housewife feels that in the week of the inquiry she ought to provide the interviewer with what to her seems a representative week's expenditure, with the result that exceptional expenditures on, say, furniture are postponed till the inquiry is completed.

† In this middle-class inquiry, which refers essentially to government employees, the reported income figures are probably substantially correct; but it is worth nothing that in surveys of other kinds of households in which income figures have been requested it has been found that these tend to be understated.

‡ Or, indeed, too little.

If this is thought to be a serious source of bias the method of an oral interview covering a short period in the past—asking what was bought yesterday—would seem to have advantages over the questionnaire method. With interviewers there is, of course, the danger that the way in which the question is put, and the mannerisms of the interviewer may affect the informants' reply. But interviewer bias of this kind can be eliminated fairly simply by comparing the results reported by different interviewers.†

4.32. END-PERIOD EFFECT

A second kind of bias arises from the tendency to include expenditure incurred just before the beginning of the inquiry; this may be termed the *end-period effect*. It is probable that this effect is of greater importance in the case of exceptional expenditures which would otherwise have a zero entry; thus on meeting the item 'clothing' in the questionnaire the enthusiastic housewife puts down the cardigan she bought last week-end (only so as not to disappoint the investigator), though there has been no expenditure on the item in the period strictly covered by the inquiry.

The annual inquiry on clothing provides estimates that are of interest in this connexion. Three estimates may be obtained of the average expenditure on clothing items: (*a*) that based on all households participating in the four-weekly inquiry; (*b*) that based on the annual expenditure of those households participating in the subsidiary annual inquiry; and (*c*) that based on the expenditure in the four weeks of the main inquiry by households also participating in the subsidiary annual inquiry. These estimates are not independent since estimates (*a*) and (*b*) both include the information in estimate (*c*). Three independent estimates can, however, be obtained as follows: (1) using the information from those households participating in the four-weekly inquiry but not participating in the annual inquiry; (2) using the information from the forty-eight weeks of the annual inquiry not coinciding with the four weeks of the inquiry; and (3) using the information on expenditure in the four weeks of the main inquiry by those households participating in the annual inquiry. Estimate (3) is, of course, the same as estimate (*c*).

TABLE 5. ALTERNATIVE ESTIMATES OF EXPENDITURE ON CLOTHING (WEEKLY AVERAGES PER HOUSEHOLD)

	Main inquiry 4 weeks (1)	Subsidiary inquiry	
		48 weeks (2)	4 weeks (3)
	s. *d.*	*s.* *d.*	*s.* *d.*
Working class	9 7	8 1	8 7
Middle class	25 6	15 1	20 4

† See Hansen, Hurwitz, Marks and Mauldin (1951).

The results are set out for the two inquiries in Table 5, from which the existence of the end-period effects may be judged. Comparing columns 1 and 2 in the table it is seen that the estimates given by the four-weekly inquiry are considerably higher than those of the annual, in the working-class inquiry by about 20%, and in the middle-class inquiry by about 70%. On the other hand, a comparison of columns 2 and 3 shows that those households who participated in the annual clothing inquiry recorded a higher expenditure on clothing in the four weeks of the main inquiry than they recorded in the rest of the year. This may of course be ascribed to an abnormality of the weeks chosen for the main inquiry, but it seems more likely that the low estimates in column 2 are due to a lack of care in recording all expenditures in the rest of the year.

The systematic nature of the end-period effects may be examined in Table 6, which gives the expenditure on clothing under six subheadings estimated from the annual and four-weekly data. The estimates are not independent, but the main effect of a proportional overestimate in all items is apparent.

TABLE 6. EXPENDITURE ON CLOTHING IN THE FOUR-WEEKLY AND ANNUAL INQUIRIES (WEEKLY AVERAGES PER HOUSEHOLD)

	Working class				Middle class			
	Four-weekly		Annual		Four-weekly		Annual	
	s.	d.	s.	d.	s.	d.	s.	d.
Men's clothing	2	10	2	4	6	5	4	1
Women's clothing	2	6	2	7	9	1	6	4
Children's clothing		11	1	0	2	10	2	1
Clothing repairs		2		2		6		4
Boots and shoes	1	11	1	6	2	10	1	11
Boot and shoe repairs	1	0		7	1	2		9
Total	9	4	8	2	22	10	15	6

4.33. LYING

The third sources of bias may be termed *specific non-disclosure* or, more simply, *lying*. Whenever there is a motive for not disclosing a particular item of expenditure the household has a strong incentive not to participate at all in the inquiries, and for this reason this source of bias has already been mentioned in § 4.2. The fear of arousing the suspicion of the taxation authorities may be an important motive in preventing the co-operation of some households, but other factors will influence the degree of lying about specific expenditures.

The most well-known instance of this bias is the expenditure on drink and tobacco for which reliable estimates of national consumption can be obtained (for example, from the excise authorities). The national estimates given by Stone (1954) are quoted in Table 7 after adjustment to a per person basis, for comparison with the results of our inquiries.

It is apparent that the survey method as applied in these inquiries cannot yield reliable estimates for these items.

TABLE 7. EXPENDITURE ON DRINK AND TOBACCO: A COMPARISON WITH NATIONAL ESTIMATES (PER PERSON PER WEEK)

	Working-class inquiry	Middle-class inquiry	National estimate
	s. d.	s. d.	s. d.
Alcoholic drink and table waters	3	7	2 6
Tobacco and tobacco products	9	1 0	1 5

4.34. IGNORANCE

In part the motive for understatement of this kind may be wilful lying consequent on a sense of shame associated with lustful expenditures; or it may be that the drinking husband merely wants to hide from his nagging wife the amount that he has available for drink after giving her the housekeeping money. But it must be admitted that in part, at any rate, there is a fourth reason for making an understatement of frequent and small items of expenditures; the difficulty of remembering the amount spent when the schedule is completed in the evening. This bias is thus due to *ignorance* or, possibly, subconscious lying.

4.4. BIAS IN INTERPRETATION

A final source of bias may arise from a faulty interpretation of the data even if they were correctly recorded from a properly chosen sample. The number of such biases is, of course, not enumerable *a priori*, and it is one of the main objects of an investigation of family-budget data to reveal hitherto unsuspected sources of bias. Some examples may, however, serve as an indication of the kind of difficulty involved.

A first example arises in using family-budget data to estimate national consumption for the whole year. The assumption has then to be made that the weeks of the inquiry are representative of the rest of the year. If this is not so the inquiry may provide good estimates of national expenditure in the particular weeks of the inquiry, but bad estimates for the remainder of the year.

Secondly, there is a danger of bias if, as indicated in the first section of this chapter, estimates of expenditure are interpreted as estimates of intake.

A final example would be that of a commodity whose consumption depended only on household size and not on income. If the data were then grouped by income, consumption would vary directly or inversely with income according to whether the correlation between income and household size was direct or inverse.

4.5. A Comparison with the Results of other Inquiries

No doubt after this depressing list of sources of error it may be as well to reassure the reader that, on the whole, there is no reason to expect the magnitude of the biases to be large. Confirmatory evidence on the reliability of the results can be based on either internal checks of consistency, or checks with data based on other inquiries.

Internal checks must to a large extent consist in the rejection of data that seem to the investigator to be unplausible, say, a price paid for tea which is ten times the average market price.

Occasionally a more precise check is possible. Thus in the middle-class inquiry there were returns on the income-tax paid in the year which, knowing the composition of the household, could be used to provide a check on the income of the household. This check was applied in the case of single-earner households for which the total earned income was known, in order to obtain by difference an estimate of possible additional sources of unearned incomes. The results indicated that in this sample the amount of unearned income was negligible.

For an external check it is possible to rely on another household survey of expenditures carried out in 1936–7 by Crawford and Broadley. This survey was confined to foodstuffs. More interesting, however, is the check which can be applied by comparing our results with those of Stone's (1954) estimates of national expenditure† which are generally based on sources of supply. The alternative estimates are given in Table 8, using Stone's grouping of the commodities.

The first two columns of the table refer to our inquiries. The third column of the table is based on the returns of agricultural workers in the Ministry of Labour's inquiry.‡ The fourth column is a weighted average of the previous three, the weights (21, 73 and 6) being in proportion to the numbers of households in the populations§ and is Stone's assessment of the evidence provided by the budget inquiries. The fifth column gives the estimates of Crawford and Broadley for 1936–7.

The sixth column is intended to show how regression analysis can be used to improve estimates that may be otherwise biased. If the main reason for the different estimates in columns 1–3 is the different levels of income then an adjustment can be made to any one of them to bring them to the average income of the population. The method used was to adjust the estimates in column 2, which refers to the larger portion of the population, by the elasticities derived in Chapter 7 below so as to take into account the difference between the average total expenditure of £69 per person per annum found in these budgets, and that of £91 given by the National Income estimates for 1938.

---

† The data are from Stone (1954, pp. 167–9).
‡ See Ministry of Labour (1949, pp. 25–42), or Ministry of Labour (1940).
§ See § 3.3 above for a discussion of the weights.

TABLE 8. A COMPARISON OF ESTIMATES OF EXPENDITURE ON FOODSTUFFS (PENCE PER PERSON PER WEEK)

Commodity group	Family-budget data						Stone's time-series
	Middle class	In-dustrial working class	Agri-cultural working class	Average of all classes	Crawford and Broadley	In-dustrial working class adjusted for income	
	(1)	(2)	(3)	(4)	(5)	(6)	(7)
Bread and cereals	18·7	17·1	17·7	17·5	15·3	18·5	18·1
Meat, poultry and eggs	39·9	31·9	25·9	33·1	33·3	36·0	40·9
Fish	5·8	3·3	1·9	3·7	5·2	3·9	3·7
Dairy products	30·1	21·1	16·8	22·5	19·9	23·5	20·1
Margarine and other fats	2·3	3·0	3·6	2·9	2·2	3·1	2·2
Vegetables	9·8	7·9	3·0	8·0	8·0	8·9	9·0
Fruit and nuts	13·3	5·7	3·8	7·0	7·1	6·8	7·6
Sugar	3·6	3·3	4·1	3·4	2·6	3·6	2·4
Tea, coffee and cocoa	6·4	5·9	5·6	6·0	6·9	6·5	5·6
Other foods	11·1	6·0	4·5	6·9	5·9	7·2	7·6

Finally, in column 7 are given Stone's estimates of consumer's expenditure. It will be seen that there is good agreement between the last four columns, especially if it is remembered that the time-series estimates may also be subject to error. Only two comments are made here: (a) the high estimate for fish given by Crawford and Broadley is due to the inclusion of fried fish which in the other columns is included in 'other foods';† (b) the high estimate for margarine and other fats given by our budget inquiries may be due to the exclusion of certain groups in the population for which these commodities are inferior.

The above comparisons have been confined to comparatively broad groups, and it is no doubt the case that with particular items of expenditure the possible biases surveyed in the earlier sections of this chapter will be more serious. Care is therefore necessary in using a figure from these inquiries for a particular purpose, and consideration should always be given to the nature of the biases that may arise in the process of obtaining the estimate.

† There are a number of other minor variations in the definitions of the commodity groups for this survey but these do not substantially affect the comparisons; see Stone (1954, p. 167) for the details.

CHAPTER 5

THE ESTIMATION OF STATISTICAL RELATIONSHIPS

5.1. PRINCIPLES AND THEIR APPLICATION

5.11. INTRODUCTION

A comparison of the facts of consumers' behaviour with a theory purporting to describe them can only be made on the basis of some statistical model held either implicitly or explicitly. The existence of an implicit model is to be inferred whenever a smooth curve is fitted by eye to a scatter of points on a diagram and a judgement is made about the satisfactoriness of the fit; an explicitly held model, on the other hand, may be used for precise tests of significance and to obtain numerical estimates of confidence limits. Implicit and explicit models, and graphical and numerical methods, should be regarded as complementary and not as competitive tools, each having a proper place in the process of research.

It is convenient to distinguish three stages between the original formulation of a theory of consumption, as in Chapter 2, and the final derivation of relationships which characterize the behaviour of consumers in the population investigated. First, it will generally be necessary to refine the original theory on the basis of a broad inspection of the available facts. This will involve a decision as to the number and the importance of extraneous (say, social) factors at work which may prevent the straightforward investigation of a theory about economic factors. It will also be necessary to consider whether the measurable variables coincide sufficiently with those specified by the theory; is it, for example, necessary to adjust the measure of money income received for income in kind, or can this complication be ignored? Further, it may be necessary to restrict the range of observations investigated to ensure stability of the parameters.

The second stage will generally involve a graphical inspection of the data, as when the effect of income on the consumption of a particular commodity is being investigated. An examination of the characteristics—the size, age and sex composition, and the like—of households corresponding to outlying points may then lead to a further refinement of the theory and suggest the form of the relationship at work. In complicated situations, when there are more than three or four important factors at work, graphical examination will be difficult; it may then be postponed till a preliminary regression analysis has been attempted on the basis of which 'partial' scatter diagrams can be drawn.

The third stage in the derivation of a relationship may take the form of a regression analysis and will involve the postulation of a functional form, the estimation of its parameters by an appropriate technique, and the assessment of their reliability on the basis of a statistical model. The main concern of this chapter is with this third stage; the first two stages, the refinement and development of a theory prior to its testing, form the hard core of research, and what general comment is possible on these is best postponed to later chapters.

The virtues of adopting a statistical model and numerical estimation procedures in scientific research require no emphasis here depending, as they do, on the desirability of having objective standards. But it must be kept in mind that classical statistical procedures depend on certain special assumptions which summarize the general features of most problems but may not fit the facts of a particular application exactly. The more precise object of this chapter is therefore to present some of the statistical problems encountered in family-budget analysis and to indicate at which points the classical procedures require extension.

The order of discussion will be as follows. In the remainder of this section the main assumptions of the least-squares regression model are set out so as to provide a framework for the subsequent developments. The second section will take up the problem of the non-linearity of the regression equation and the choice of determining variables, and the third section will consider the heteroscedasticity of the error term. The fourth section will be concerned with problems arising out of the grouping of observations; and the final section will indicate some further lines of enquiry.

5.12. THE LEAST-SQUARES MODEL

The assumptions and results of regression analysis by the method of least squares have recently been elegantly presented by Stone† and his approach and notation will be followed here. In brief, the method supposes that there are n observations of a dependent variable y which are determined by a linear combination of k determining variables, X_i, and an additive error term, ϵ; so that the n observations are supposed to arise from a process

$$\mathbf{y} = \mathbf{X}\boldsymbol{\beta} + \boldsymbol{\epsilon}, \tag{5.1}$$

where $\boldsymbol{\beta}$ is a column vector‡ of k parameters,§ $\mathbf{y}$ and $\boldsymbol{\epsilon}$ are column vectors of order n, and $\mathbf{X}$ is a matrix of order $n \times k$. It is assumed, first, that the expected value of the error term is zero for each observation;

---

† The reader should refer to Stone (1954, pp. 280 et seq.).

‡ While a matrix notation is used wherever this simplifies the mathematical exposition, it is hoped that the accompanying literary exposition will make the problem clear to those who are not so familiar with it.

§ One of these parameters represents the constant term in the equation and arises in the present notation from a dummy determining variable which is unity for all observations. By means of this device the treatment is more concise mathematically; it is also to be recommended for computational purposes whenever there are facilities for the efficient inversion of matrices.

secondly, that the error terms in different observations are independent, and their variances are the same for all observations and equal to σ^2; thirdly, that the determining variables are either fixed in repeated samples or, alternatively, are random variables the joint distribution of which is independent of the error term, so that ϵ expresses the variability of $\mathbf{y}$ for given $\mathbf{X}$; fourthly, it is assumed that there are at least as many (independent) observations as there are parameters to be estimated, and that there is no exact linear relationship between the determining variables.

On the basis of these assumptions it can be shown that the regression coefficients $\mathbf{b}$ given by

$$\mathbf{b} = (\mathbf{X'X})^{-1}\mathbf{X'y} \tag{5.2}$$

are unbiased estimates of β and have a smaller variance than any other linear estimate, the variance matrix of $\mathbf{b}$ being given by

$$\mathscr{E}\{(\mathbf{b}-\boldsymbol{\beta})(\mathbf{b}-\boldsymbol{\beta})'\} = \sigma^2(\mathbf{X'X})^{-1}. \tag{5.3}$$

The first problem to be taken up is that of the basic supposition that the relationship whose parameters are to be estimated is a linear function of the type (5.1).

5.2. NON-LINEARITY OF THE BASIC RELATIONSHIP

5.21. REASONS FOR ADOPTING A NON-LINEAR FORM

When a relationship is expected to exist between a number of variables the simplest assumption that can be made about its form is that it is linear. Provided that the range of variation in all the variables is small this assumption is generally adequate and leads to the well-known and straightforward solution of the resulting normal equations. The linear form may become inappropriate for two reasons. First, if the range of variation in the variables is large, different estimates may be obtained for the regression coefficients according to the range of variation investigated. While the application of the least-squares linear regression technique will still lead to a minimization of the sum of the squares of the residuals, they will not be minimized uniformly, and over some ranges the fit will be much better than over others. The adoption of an appropriate non-linear form thus has the purpose of minimizing deviations *uniformly* over the whole range investigated and is therefore a refinement on the general least-squares criterion.

A second reason for adopting a non-linear form is that it may be suggested by some underlying theory. In this case even if the range of variation is small it may be desirable to estimate the parameters of the non-linear form instead of deriving a round-about approximation to it by means of a linear or polynomial form. It may be thought that in economics as compared, say, with physics this reason will very rarely be operative, since economic theory, at the most, suggests the variables to be taken into account in explaining a given situation but not the form in which they enter. In Chapter 9 below there is presented a problem in which a non-linear formulation is required if its essence is not to be obscured, and there can be little doubt that this kind of problem is encountered more frequently than is usually hinted at.

Corresponding to these two reasons for adopting non-linear formulations there are two kinds of problems that arise in treating them. First, since the normal equations are no longer linear there will be difficulty in solving them to obtain estimates of the parameters. This, however, does not imply a rejection of the principle of least squares; all that is required is the discovery of some convenient method of solving the equations that arise in a particular application. In the problem of Chapter 9 it will be seen that an iterative method was adopted; such a procedure generally involves computing the residual sum of squares for different values of the parameters and choosing those values which minimize it.

The second problem that arises is the need for some method of measuring the degree of linearity of the fit, or, in consonance with the argument above, the degree of *uniformity* of the goodness of fit.

5.22. THE METHOD OF TRANSFORMING THE VARIABLES

With these considerations in mind it is next necessary to examine a method for avoiding at any rate the first of these problems, namely, the method of transforming the variables. This method is frequently used in analysing econometric relations between a number of variables, when their logarithms are treated as the fundamental variables instead of their absolute values. The parameters $\boldsymbol{\beta}$ then become Marshall's elasticities,

$$\beta_k = \frac{x_k}{y}\frac{dy}{dx_k} = \frac{d(\log y)}{d(\log x_k)}, \tag{5.4}$$

the estimation of which may, in any case, be the object of the investigation.

Suppose the relationship to be investigated is of the form

$$y = \phi(\mathbf{x}'\boldsymbol{\beta}) + \epsilon, \tag{5.5}$$

that is, the dependent variable is determined by some function ϕ, such as the logarithm or the inverse, of a linear combination of the determining variables, and an additive error term. This is, of course, not the general case of a non-linear relationship, but it is a type which frequently occurs in practice. One method of treating (5.5) would be to obtain an approximation to ϕ by a Taylor series expansion and fit the first few terms by polynomial regression; this method may also be used in treating the general non-linear form. But polynomial regression, besides being laborious in application, is subject to the difficulty of having to decide which terms to include in the analysis. It may be that a term in x^2 will remove an insignificant portion of the variance, but this does not always exclude the possibility that a term in x^3 will be significant.† Polynomial regression is therefore to be avoided where possible. A more satisfactory treatment depends on the possibility of finding a function ϕ^{-1} which is the inverse of ϕ, that is,

$$\phi^{-1}\phi = 1. \tag{5.6}$$

For example, if ϕ were the logarithm, ϕ^{-1} would be the anti-logarithm.

Applying ϕ^{-1} to both sides of (5.5) gives

$$\phi^{-1}(y) = \phi^{-1}\{\phi(\mathbf{x}'\boldsymbol{\beta}) + \epsilon\}, \tag{5.7}$$

which, on writing ψ for ϕ^{-1} and expanding in a Taylor series, simplifies to

$$\psi(y) = \mathbf{x}'\boldsymbol{\beta} + \psi'\epsilon + \tfrac{1}{2}\psi''\epsilon^2 + \dots. \tag{5.8}$$

In this equation $\psi(y)$ is a linear function of $\mathbf{x}$, the parameters of which can be estimated in the usual way except for the fact that the error term has been transformed at the same time so that its distribution is no longer the same as in the original formulation (5.5).

Suppose, for example, that the error term in (5.5) is normally distributed with zero mean and a variance of σ^2, and that the first two derivatives of ψ are large, but that the others may be neglected. The mean value of the error term in (5.8) will then be given approximately by

$$\mathscr{E}\{\psi(y) - \mathbf{x}'\boldsymbol{\beta}\} = \mathscr{E}\{\psi'\epsilon + \tfrac{1}{2}\psi''\epsilon^2\}$$
$$= \tfrac{1}{2}\sigma^2\psi'', \tag{5.9}$$

so that if the constant term in (5.8) is estimated by the usual methods the estimate will be biased. Further, the variance of the residual of (5.8) is given by

$$\mathscr{E}\{\psi(y) - \mathbf{x}'\boldsymbol{\beta}\}^2 = \mathscr{E}\{\psi'\epsilon + \tfrac{1}{2}\psi''\epsilon^2\}^2$$
$$= \sigma^2\psi'^2 + \tfrac{3}{4}\sigma^4\psi''^2, \tag{5.10}$$

where use has been made of the result that the third moment of the normal distribution is zero and its fourth moment is $3\sigma^4$. Since the value of the derivative of ψ will depend on the values of $\mathbf{x}$ the variance will now no longer be the same for each observation, and the method of least squares may therefore require amendment as in the next section.

When transformation of the variables is in practice desirable in order to achieve simpler methods of estimation little consideration will, rightly, be given to the precise implications of the transformation for the distribution of the error term as considered in the last paragraph, since so very little is generally known of its original distribution. The algebra has, however, been worth developing on account of two applications. The first arises from the fact that if the variance of the residual was originally not constant, then it may become approximately constant after transformation. Suppose, for example, that it is approximately proportional to the square of the expected value of y or,

† For a related difficulty see Kendall (1951, p. 20).

equivalently, that the basic model has a multiplicative error term so that

$$y = \phi(x) + \epsilon\phi(x) = \{\phi(x)\}\{1 + \epsilon\}. \tag{5.11}$$

Taking logarithms of both sides will then make the error term additive and of approximately constant variance.

5.221. TAKING THE LOGARITHM OF ZERO

The second application is also concerned with the taking of logarithms. If a constant elasticity form of equation is posited with additive error term,

$$y = Ax^\beta + \epsilon, \tag{5.12}$$

the appropriate transformation in order to estimate β is, as is well known, to take logarithms of both sides. In some applications, as in our work where y would represent the expenditure on a particular commodity by a household and x its income, values of y may be encountered which are very small or even zero. The application of the method of (5.8) gives

$$\log y = \log Ax^\beta(1 + \epsilon/Ax^\beta)$$
$$= \log A + \log\beta\ x + [(\epsilon/Ax\beta) - \tfrac{1}{2}(\epsilon/Ax\beta)^2 + \tfrac{1}{3}(\ \ )^3], \tag{5.13}$$

and if expenditure by a particular household is zero, so that $\epsilon = -Ax^\beta$, the series on the right of (5.13) will diverge to minus infinity. Even if there were no zero value of y, the existence of a number of small values may lead to substantially different estimates for β according to whether the residuals of (5.13) are minimized or those of (5.12).

Assuming that an iterative method of estimating β in (5.12) is to be avoided the most appropriate procedure can, in such a case, only be decided by considering the nature of the facts investigated. In our example a zero expenditure on a particular commodity by a particular household may result from a number of causes. It may be that the household never buys the commodity; for example, a vegetarian household will not buy any meat; or it may be that it has forgotten to enter the item in its return, that is, there is an error of observation; or, and this is especially likely in non-food items, while the commodity is generally consumed by the household it so happened that in the particular week of observation it did not buy any.

If the first possibility is ignored on the argument that households which *never* buy the commodity should in any case be treated separately, it is possible to argue that, regarded as an error of observation, the zero should be replaced by some small positive quantity as if it had occurred through rounding-off an item the true value of which was less than half the least significant recorded figure. The average value of such items will then be a quarter of a unit (if any value between zero and a half is equally likely), and before carrying out the regression analysis each zero may be replaced by a quarter. In order not to disturb the average value of the variable, items recorded as a unit may be reduced by an appropriate amount. While this method certainly avoids the problem of having to correlate a variable one of the values of which is minus infinity, it follows from the argument above that this procedure will generally lead to estimates which have a substantial bias† and is therefore not satisfactory.

An alternative procedure is based on the last reason for the occurrence of zeros: that households buy the commodity only infrequently. It is known that as the period of the inquiry is lengthened the number of zero returns diminishes, and this suggests that a method based on averaging zero returns with the values of the purchases of households that are in similar circumstances is not unduly at fault. This was the method adopted here in the calculation of constant elasticity expressions and follows from our method of grouping the data; instead of correlating the values of expenditures by individual households, the values for households having the same total expenditure and the same household size were averaged, and these were treated as the fundamental variables. In the few cases where this still left a zero value, the observation was ignored, though this may lead to a slight upward bias in the general 'height' of the curve.

5.23. A MEASURE OF NON-LINEARITY

The discussion has so far been concerned with the treatment of a non-linear form when it has been specified on some *a priori* basis. The second problem mentioned in § 5.21—that of measuring the degree of linearity of fit—arises when the form of the relation has to be determined from the data themselves. This requires that a choice be made among a number of transformations of the variables which seem plausible *a priori*.

Two classical methods for investigating non-linearity are well known, there is the method using the correlation ratio, which is based on sub-dividing the total range, investigating the variability of the data in each portion, and comparing it with an estimate of the variability about the linear regression. If the scatter of points is in fact linear the two estimates should not differ significantly. The difficulty in this method is the basic arbitrariness of the extent of subdivision of the range which affects the stability of the measure. The other method is that based on testing the significance of polynomial terms, the difficulties of which have already been stated.

The method of testing for non-linearity proposed here is based on a much more general notion of what is meant by non-linearity. In effect every systematic deviation from randomness in the residuals is taken to be an indication that the form adopted does not 'explain' all the variation in the data and accordingly requires modification. The nature of the criterion is best explained by reference to Fig. 3 *a*, in which

---

† In some experimental calculations it was found that the value of the regression coefficient was significantly sensitive to the precise values which were substituted for the zeros.

a straight line has been drawn through a number of points which result from a relationship which is in fact curved. Non-linearity will be seen to consist in the occurrence of adjacent deviations which tend to be of the same sign. Accordingly, the degree of serial correlation between residuals when arranged by the magnitude of the determining variable

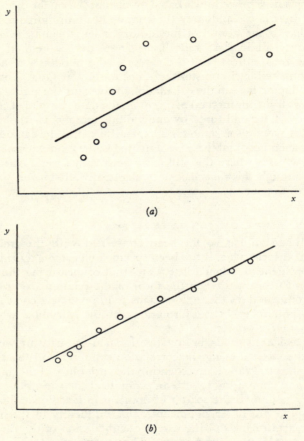

Fig. 3. Non-linear regressions.

may be taken as the measure of non-linearity. According to this measure, it may be noted, it does not matter how small in magnitude is the degree of non-linearity; so long as the deviations are systematically related they will be shown up by this criterion (cf. Fig. 3*b*).

5.24. DURBIN AND WATSON'S *d* AS A TEST OF NON-LINEARITY

The next problem is how to test this criterion for statistical significance. Two tests will be mentioned. For the more exact of these we are fortunate in being able to draw at once on work done in another branch of econometrics, that of regression analysis based on time-series. There, the existence of serial correlation between the errors in successive observations may indicate a lack of independence between the observations and the seriousness of the problem has been recognized since the days of Yule.† Durbin and Watson (1950, 1951) have provided a rigorous treatment of the topic based on the statistic

$$d = \sum_{t=1}^{n} (u_t - u_{t-1})^2 \bigg/ \sum_{t=1}^{n} u_t^2, \tag{5.14}$$

where u_t is the value of the tth residual. This statistic is related to the first-order serial correlation coefficient, r_1, as may be seen on expanding (5.14) thus,

$$d = \sum_{t=2}^{n} u_t^2 \bigg/ \sum_{t=1}^{n} u_t^2 - \sum_{t=2}^{n} u_t u_{t-1} \bigg/ \sum_{t=1}^{n} u_t^2 + \sum_{t=2}^{n} u_{t-1}^2 \bigg/ \sum_{t=1}^{n} u_t^2. \tag{5.15}$$

The first and last term tend to unity and the middle term to r_1, so that the approximate relation between r_1 and d is given by

$$r_1 \sim 2 - d. \tag{5.16}$$

Thus by arranging the observations in order of magnitude of the determining variable, calculating the ratio of the sum of squares of differences between successive residuals to the sum of squares of all residuals, and consulting the table of bounds given by Durbin and Watson (1951, pp. 173–5) a rigorous decision can be taken as to the significance of the degree of non-linearity.

5.25. APPROXIMATE TESTS FOR NON-LINEARITY

The not inconsiderable labour of calculation involved in evaluating the residuals makes it desirable to find some simpler criterion which can be more easily applied. A non-parametric test based on the theory of runs of random events would seem to be applicable and have the advantages both of being valid under more general conditions and of being simple to calculate. Many such test statistics can be constructed according to length of run considered, corresponding to the order of the serial correlation coefficient in the parametric case. The basis of such tests is that only the sign of the residual is considered and not its magnitude, so that a residual can be only positive or negative.

One such test would then be as follows. Let there be N observations. Count the number of adjacent residuals which are of the same sign; let this value be R (for Run). Next count the number of adjacent residuals which are of opposite sign; let this number be C (for Cross). Since adjacent residuals must be either of the same or opposite sign, it will, of course, be true that

$$R + C = N - 1. \tag{5.17}$$

An indicator of first-order serial correlation is then given by

$$(R - C)/(N - 1). \tag{5.18}$$

† For a general account of the problem in connexion with time series, see Stone (1954, chapter XIX, § 4, pp. 287–91).

The reason for this can be seen by supposing that all the residuals have the values ± 1, so that the sum of cross-products of the residuals is $R - C$, and the sum of squares is $N - 1$, after adjusting for the number of observations.

Another test[†] is based on the definition of a run as a sequence *of any length* of adjacent residuals of the same sign. Let the number of runs so defined be D, so that in the series

$$- + + - + - - - +$$

D is six. Let P be the number of positive deviations in the series and Q the number of negative deviations, then provided P and Q are greater than about ten, D is approximately normally distributed about a mean of

$$\mathscr{E}(D) = 1 + 2PQ/N, \tag{5.19}$$

and a variance of

$$\sigma^2 = 2PQ(2PQ - N)/N^2(N - 1). \tag{5.20}$$

If the number of observations is large, and p and q represent the proportions of positive and negative residuals, (5.19) and (5.20) reduce approximately to $2pqN$ and $(2pq)^2N$ respectively.

On the basis of these quantities a test of non-linearity can be made very rapidly. In particular, the test quantity

$$\lambda = \frac{\xi(D) - D}{\sigma} \tag{5.21}$$

is used in Chapter 7 below.

These tests suffer from the drawback that it has been the object of the work of Durbin and Watson to overcome, namely, no allowance is made, as there is in their limits for the distribution of d, for the non-randomness introduced into the residuals by the fitting of a regression line. It would clearly be desirable to have some similarly easily calculable measure which allows for this difficulty. In the meantime, its importance may be minimized by using the measures only in comparisons of the results of a number of experiments so that only broad inferences are drawn—whether one form of curve is *generally* more linear than another—and by the admittedly inelegant device of omitting from consideration points that lie unduly close to the line.

The approximate test (5.21) or the more exact test (5.14) may be used as sensitive criteria for distinguishing between the linearity of fit of alternative transformations of the variables. From the point of view of statistical tests of significance the variable x^3, say, is of course regarded as quite different from the variable x, and once the transformations have been chosen, the classical tests of significance based on (5.3) should be carried out.

While the discussion above has been in terms of the bivariate case, it may be noted that the extension to the multivariate case is straight-

[†] The account which follows is based on Mood (1950, pp. 391–4).

forward, requiring only that the residuals be arranged according to the order of magnitude of each of the determining variables in turn.

In general it is to be expected that some degree of positive serial correlation will be found in all regression analyses of experimental data, and by fitting alternative forms it will only be possible to reduce this to some sufficiently small level. What that level should be will depend on the theoretical framework in which the data are examined and the use to which the results are to be put. In particular if, as often happens in econometrics, an estimate is required of the slope of a curve at some distance away from the mean of the observations it may be wise to be on the strict side in applying the criterion.

It remains to consider the possibility of negative serial correlation in the residuals. This would indicate that on the whole the observations lay at two levels so that the residuals changed sign more frequently than in a random series. This could occur if the observations fell into classes with different means, or in general, if a variate has been omitted from the analyses. Negative serial correlation should thus be a warning to the investigator to search further.

5.3. THE DISTRIBUTION OF THE ERROR TERM†

5.31. THE VARIANCE OF THE ERROR TERM

The next problem to be considered is that of the distribution of the error term in (5.1). The second assumption of the method of least squares‡ requires that its variance be the same for all observations; but in considering the nature of the determinants of a household's expenditure on a particular item it seems likely that the variability will be greater, the greater is the average level of expenditure on the item. In order to investigate this, the variance (about the group mean) of expenditure on tea—there seems no reason to question its typicalness—in the working-class sample was calculated for each of the fifty-four basic groups according to which the material has been tabulated. On the assumption that the averages of each of the groups is 'explained' by the behaviour equation, these variances provide estimates of the variance of ϵ.

The results are shown in Fig. 4, in which the variance of each group has been plotted against the square of its mean expenditure. The observations lie on a strikingly straight line passing through the origin and suggest that an appropriate hypothesis for the variance of the residual is that it is proportional to the square of the expected value of the dependent variable. This result is in conformity with the investigations of Brady (1938) and Friedman (1937), which may be consulted for further diagrams of a similar nature.

† For a more extensive treatment of the matters discussed in this and the next section, see the paper by Prais and Aitchison (1954).
‡ See p. 47 above.

The existence of heteroscedasticity—as the inconstancy of the variance is termed—does not affect the unbiased property of least-squares estimates. This depends only on the assumption that the distribution of the error term is independent of the determining variables, as may be seen by substituting from (5.1) into (5.2) to give, on taking expected values,

$$\mathscr{E}\{\mathbf{b}\} = \mathscr{E}\{(\mathbf{X}'\mathbf{X})^{-1}\mathbf{X}'[\mathbf{X}\boldsymbol{\beta} + \boldsymbol{\epsilon}]\}$$
$$= \mathscr{E}\{\boldsymbol{\beta}\} + \mathscr{E}\{(\mathbf{X}'\mathbf{X})^{-1}\mathbf{X}'\boldsymbol{\epsilon}\}$$
$$= \boldsymbol{\beta}, \tag{5.22}$$

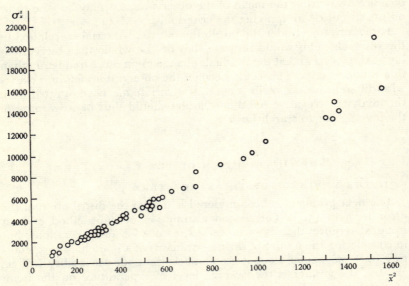

Fig. 4. Variance of expenditure on tea and square of mean expenditure: British working-class households, 1938.

since the second term on the right-hand side vanishes as it is a linear combination of terms each of which has an expected value of zero. Heteroscedasticity only implies that the estimates given by (5.2) will not be of minimum variance, that is, they are inefficient.

5.32. AN EFFICIENT TREATMENT OF HETEROSCEDASTICITY

The correct method of combining observations of unequal variances is to weight each of the observations inversely by its variance so that the less reliable is the information (as measured by the magnitude of its associated variance), the less it contributes to the estimate. To take the general case where the variance matrix of the residuals is $\sigma^2\boldsymbol{\Omega}$, the sum of squares to be minimized, as noted by Aitken† (1935), is

$$\boldsymbol{\epsilon}'\boldsymbol{\Omega}^{-1}\boldsymbol{\epsilon}, \tag{5.23}$$

† See Stone (1954, p. 288) for an application to serial correlation and a general discussion.

and the resulting minimum variance estimator of β is

$$\mathbf{b} = (\mathbf{X}'\boldsymbol{\Omega}^{-1}\mathbf{X})^{-1}\mathbf{X}'\boldsymbol{\Omega}^{-1}\mathbf{y}, \tag{5.24}$$

and its variance is given by the relatively simple expression

$$V\{\mathbf{b}\} = \sigma^2(\mathbf{X}'\boldsymbol{\Omega}^{-1}\mathbf{X}). \tag{5.25}$$

In our case $\boldsymbol{\Omega}$ is a diagonal matrix the elements of which are the squares of the expected values of $\mathbf{y}$; the difficulty in applying this method here is, of course, that these values cannot be estimated until the equation has been fitted.

If efficient estimates are thought important it is nevertheless possible to apply this method without too much difficulty by iteration. The procedure would be to obtain a first estimate of β using, say, the estimator (5.2). On the basis of these estimates a first trial value of $\boldsymbol{\Omega}$ could be calculated, say $\boldsymbol{\Omega}^{(1)}$, and used to obtain a new estimate of β from (5.24). This would then lead to $\boldsymbol{\Omega}^{(2)}$, and so on. This is the method which in effect is used in probit analysis and, as recently shown by Finney (1951) in that context, it would only rarely be necessary to go beyond the estimation of $\boldsymbol{\Omega}^{(1)}$.

An alternative would be to begin the iteration using as weights the observed values of y after adjusting the zeros and any patently extreme observations. This may be a little inelegant, but should lead to even better convergence.

5.33. THEIL'S CORRECTIONS TO THE VARIANCES OF THE CLASSICAL ESTIMATORS

Instead of adapting the classical procedures to the present special case as above, it is possible to approach the problem in three other ways. The first is to attempt to minimize squares directly† on the basis of a model with a multiplicative error term as in (5.11). It will be found, however, that the resulting normal equations are non-linear and not soluble except by an iterative procedure, which would then involve a return to the method just discussed. The same result would follow if the method of maximum likelihood were applied.

The second alternative, suggested by Theil, is to continue to use the inefficient classical estimator (5.2) since it is simple to apply and is unbiased, but to compute its variance correctly taking into account the heteroscedasticity. The variance matrix of the estimator may be derived as follows from (5.22):

$$\mathscr{E}\{(\mathbf{b}-\beta)(\mathbf{b}-\beta)'\} = \mathscr{E}\{(\mathbf{X}'\mathbf{X})^{-1}\mathbf{X}'\boldsymbol{\epsilon}\boldsymbol{\epsilon}'\mathbf{X}(\mathbf{X}'\mathbf{X})^{-1}\}$$
$$= \sigma^2(\mathbf{X}'\mathbf{X})^{-1}(\mathbf{X}'\boldsymbol{\Omega}\mathbf{X})(\mathbf{X}'\mathbf{X})^{-1}. \tag{5.26}$$

The variance matrix $\boldsymbol{\Omega}$ is unknown, but for the purposes of estimating the 'weighted' variance matrix $(\mathbf{X}'\boldsymbol{\Omega}\mathbf{X})$ for (5.26) it may be replaced by the estimate $\boldsymbol{\Omega}^{(1)}$ defined in the last section.

† The treatment which follows relies considerably on the work of Theil (1952a).

Since the variances in the classical case are given by $\sigma^2(\mathbf{X'X})^{-1}$, the factor $(\mathbf{X'\Omega X})(\mathbf{X'X})^{-1}$ can be regarded as a correction for heteroscedasticity. Computationally the best method of calculating (5.26) would appear to be to calculate each of the moment matrices separately and then multiply them out; but it is apparent that an alternative would be to evaluate the correction factor directly in terms of the fourth moments of the determining variables. Where there is only one determining variable Theil has shown† that this may be expressed as

$$\frac{2B^{(1)}Rc + (B^{(2)} - 1)R^2c^2}{1 + R^2c^2},\tag{5.26a}$$

where R is the correlation coefficient, c is the coefficient of variation of the dependent variable, and $B^{(1)}$ and $B^{(2)}$ are Pearson's moment ratios of the third and fourth order for the determining variable, equal respectively to $\Sigma x^3/(\Sigma x^2)^{\frac{3}{2}}$ and $\Sigma x^4/(\Sigma x^2)^2$, where x is measured from its mean value.

To illustrate the size of the ratio (5.26a) its values have been computed for the semi-logarithmic curve considered in Chapter 7 below, using the data for the working-class inquiry. The results are given in Table 9 in the form of the percentage underestimate of the true standard error given by the classical estimator. The coefficient of variation for typical commodities is about 0·5, and it will be seen that the degree of underestimate is then small. In some numerical examples for Dutch data Theil found an underestimate of about one-quarter.

TABLE 9. THEIL'S CORRECTIONS FOR HETEROSCEDASTICITY BASED ON THE WORKING-CLASS INQUIRY

R / c	0·2	0·4	0·6	0·8
0·2	0	0	0	1
0·5	0	2	6	11
1·0	2	11	22	32
1·5	6	22	36	47

For the calculations to be presented below the classical estimators have accordingly been used, but Theil's correction has not been taken into account since it is unlikely to affect the significance of any of the results presented.

The final method of treating heteroscedasticity which it is occasionally worth considering is that of transforming the variables. This has already been considered in § 5.22 above and requires no further comment here except to note that heteroscedasticity *by itself* is not sufficient justification for adopting a particular transformation. Where both the assumption (5.22) and a transformation to logarithms are appropriate it is accordingly not necessary to apply the corrections of Theil.

† Op. cit. p. 144.

5.4. GROUPING THE OBSERVATIONS

5.41. THREE METHODS OF GROUPING

The problems so far discussed have been problems of principle in which an explicit extension of the theoretical framework is the only possible treatment; the problems which arise on account of grouping, on the other hand, can always be avoided by a sufficient amount of extra work. Grouping is thus a device for saving computational labour and is unobjectionable, and, indeed, desirable, provided care is taken to avoid methods which lead to biased estimates.

Three kinds of grouping may be distinguished here in order to clarify the issues involved. First, the observations may be grouped in such a way that the answer is (arithmetically) the same as that to be obtained from the original observations. This may arise, for example, when the sum of cross-products is required between expenditure on an item and household size. An efficient method of calculating this sum would be to group the observations by the size of household, which is a discrete variable taking on only a limited number of values, find the average expenditure in each of these groups, and then compute the required sum by weighting these averages by the number of persons in each group.

A second kind of grouping occurs when the observations of a variable of $y = f(x)$ is tabulated for certain intervals of x, and the average value of y is centred at the mid-point of the interval. In this case it may under certain conditions be desirable to use Sheppard's corrections for grouping.†

A third type of grouping occurs when the average values of y are associated with the average values of x that are actually observed in the sample instead of with their central values as in the second method. This is the kind of grouping that was adopted in the present work and will be the concern of the remainder of this section.

This method of grouping consists of replacing the values of a number of observations by their average. To treat this method in a concise manner it is necessary to establish a 'grouping matrix' which transforms the original observations into the grouped observations.

5.42. THE GROUPING MATRIX

Suppose the observations are grouped in threes; then the first three observations are transformed thus:

$$\begin{pmatrix} \overline{y}_1 \\ \overline{y}_2 \\ \overline{y}_3 \end{pmatrix} = \begin{pmatrix} \frac{1}{3} & \frac{1}{3} & \frac{1}{3} \\ \frac{1}{3} & \frac{1}{3} & \frac{1}{3} \\ \frac{1}{3} & \frac{1}{3} & \frac{1}{3} \end{pmatrix} \begin{pmatrix} y_1 \\ y_2 \\ y_3 \end{pmatrix}, \tag{5.27}$$

† For a further discussion of these two kinds of grouping, the reader should consult the paper by Dwyer (1942).

where $\mathbf{y}$ represents the original observations, and $\bar{\mathbf{y}}$ the grouped observations which are, of course, all the same in this case. If the matrix of (5.27) is denoted by $\mathbf{G}_3$, the transformation of the whole set of observations may be written as

$$\bar{\mathbf{y}} = \mathbf{Gy}, \tag{5.28}$$

where

$$\mathbf{G} = \begin{pmatrix} \mathbf{G}_3 & & & \mathbf{0} \\ & \mathbf{G}_3 & \ddots & \\ \mathbf{0} & & & \mathbf{G}_3 \end{pmatrix}, \tag{5.29}$$

and the sub-matrices $\mathbf{G}_3$ are repeated down the leading diagonal the required number of times and there are zeros elsewhere. In general, $\mathbf{G}_n$ is a matrix each of whose elements is equal to $1/n$, and the matrix $\mathbf{G}$ will have the sub-matrices $\mathbf{G}_n$ repeated down the leading diagonal; different values of n may occur in the same matrix $\mathbf{G}$.

$\mathbf{G}$ is then symmetric and idempotent, that is,

$$\mathbf{G} = \mathbf{G}' = \mathbf{GG}, \tag{5.30}$$

as may be easily seen on inspecting the matrix of (5.27).

The vector of the average values of the dependent variable is thus given by (5.28), and in the same way the matrix of determining variables $\mathbf{X}$ is replaced by $\bar{\mathbf{X}}$, where

$$\bar{\mathbf{X}} = \mathbf{GX}, \tag{5.31}$$

and the matrix of the transformation is the same as in (5.28).

If these grouped values are then substituted into the classical estimator (5.2), there results on using (5.30)

$$\bar{\mathbf{b}} = (\bar{\mathbf{X}}'\bar{\mathbf{X}})^{-1}\bar{\mathbf{X}}'\bar{\mathbf{y}}$$

$$= (\mathbf{X}'\mathbf{GX})^{-1}\mathbf{X}'\mathbf{Gy}. \tag{5.32}$$

This estimator is unbiased as may be seen on substituting for $\mathbf{y}$ to give

$$\bar{\mathbf{b}} = (\mathbf{X}'\mathbf{GX})^{-1}\mathbf{X}'\mathbf{G}(\mathbf{X}\boldsymbol{\beta} + \boldsymbol{\epsilon})$$

$$= \boldsymbol{\beta} + (\mathbf{X}'\mathbf{GX})^{-1}\mathbf{X}'\mathbf{G}\boldsymbol{\epsilon}, \tag{5.33}$$

and on taking expected values the last term vanishes as before. The variance matrix of $\bar{\mathbf{b}}$ is given by

$$\mathscr{E}\{(\bar{\mathbf{b}} - \boldsymbol{\beta})(\bar{\mathbf{b}} - \boldsymbol{\beta})'\} = \mathscr{E}\{(\mathbf{X}'\mathbf{GX})^{-1}\mathbf{X}'\mathbf{G}\boldsymbol{\epsilon}\boldsymbol{\epsilon}'\mathbf{GX}(\mathbf{X}'\mathbf{GX})^{-1}\}$$

$$= \sigma^2(\mathbf{X}'\mathbf{GX})^{-1}$$

$$= \sigma^2(\bar{\mathbf{X}}'\bar{\mathbf{X}})^{-1}. \tag{5.34}$$

That is, the variance matrix may be computed by the classical formula (5.3) using the grouped values instead of the original values.

The above treatment has implicitly assumed that in computing the requisite cross-products for (5.32) and (5.34) the grouped average values have been weighted by the number of observations in the group, so that the matrices $\bar{\mathbf{y}}$ and $\bar{\mathbf{X}}$ are of the same order as $\mathbf{y}$ and $\mathbf{X}$. The correctness of this procedure might have been inferred from the treatment in the previous section on taking into account the well-known result that the variance of an average is inversely proportional to the number of observations; the variance matrix Ω of (5.23) can thus be derived from $\mathbf{G}$.

5.43. THE EFFICIENCY OF GROUPED ESTIMATORS

The efficiency of a method of grouping is to be measured by the ratio of the variances of the estimates as obtained from the grouped data with those that might have been obtained from the original data, that is, by the ratio of the elements of $(\mathbf{X'GX})^{-1}$ to the corresponding elements of $(\mathbf{X'X})^{-1}$. Maximum efficiency will be obtained in the trivial case when $\mathbf{G=I}$, or when the variables take on the same values for a number of observations so that $\mathbf{X=GX}$ and grouping has no effect. In the general case grouping will lead to an underestimate of the diagonal elements of $\mathbf{X'X}$ (as may be shown by using the familiar Schwartzian inequality), but the other elements may be either increased or decreased. Any method of grouping the data will, however, give an unbiased estimate provided always that the same grouping is used for the dependent and determining variables.

From the point of view of testing for significance, the number of degrees of freedom is reduced by grouping (since the rank of $\mathbf{G}$ is equal to the number of groups), and this has to be taken into account in computing standard errors; an estimate of the residual variance is obtained by dividing the residual weighted sum of squares by the number of degrees of freedom, which is equal to the number of grouped observations less the number of fitted parameters.

It should be noted that the correlation coefficient obtained from grouped observations is not a satisfactory estimator of the correlation coefficient in the population; for while a satisfactory estimate can be obtained of the residual variance, it is not possible to obtain an estimate of the original variance on the basis of the grouped data (except in the trivial case when the grouping is done randomly). Correlation coefficients based on grouped data can thus only be used for comparative purposes.

Where the loss of efficiency because of grouping is great, but it is impossible to use the original data, it may occasionally be worth using a compromise estimator based on the original data for the determining variables, but on grouped data for the dependent variable: that is, the estimator would be

$$\mathbf{b}_1 = (\mathbf{X'X})^{-1}\mathbf{X'Gy}. \tag{5.35}$$

Such a situation might arise if the values $\mathbf{X}$ were available on punched-cards but $\mathbf{y}$ were a function of a number of variables too complicated to work out for each of the original observations.

This estimate is, however, biased, the expected value of $\mathbf{b}_1$ being given by

$$\mathscr{E}\{\mathbf{b}_1\} = (\mathbf{X'X})^{-1}\mathbf{X'GX}\beta = \mathbf{K}\beta, \tag{5.36}$$

say, where $\mathbf{K}$ may be termed the bias matrix. The variance of $\mathbf{b_1}$ is then given by

$$V\{\mathbf{b_1}\} = \sigma^2 \mathbf{K}(\mathbf{X'X})^{-1}, \tag{5.37}$$

but unless $\mathbf{K}$ is close to the unit matrix it is not worth proceeding with the calculation.

5.5. SOME FURTHER PROBLEMS

In the last three sections comparatively detailed attention has been given to a number of problems that arise in the analysis of family budgets. It will be clear that it has not always been possible to give a completely satisfactory treatment of all the issues raised, and even when an efficient treatment is possible mathematically it is not always the case that it is worth undertaking computationally. The motive has been to clarify the issues as far as possible so as to allow a proper appraisal of the results to be presented in later chapters.

In this section, at the risk of raising undue doubts in the reader's mind, some further problems are briefly mentioned, though for these, as far as the authors know, there are no satisfactory treatments as yet available. Consider, first, the possibility which results from the interdependence of consumers' preferences (see § 2.5 above) that the error terms of households in adjacent income groups are not independent. This may not be a serious problem in the applications made here, but if it were desired to obtain some measure of the interdependence of preferences further thought would have to be given to this problem.

A more serious question is that in the discussions above no attention has been given to the problem of errors of measurement in the variables. An error in the dependent variable, of course, does not matter, since it is merged with the error in the equation, but errors in the determining variables may lead to an overstatement of their variances and hence may bias the regression coefficients downwards. If an estimate were available of the proportion of the variance ascribable to errors of measurement it would, under certain circumstances, be possible to correct for this bias as suggested by Wold,[†] but in its absence it does not appear that anything useful can be done. By making sure that there is a sufficient range of variation present in the determining variables the importance of this problem can be minimized.

Finally, it is necessary to mention the kind of consideration which naturally occurs to anyone familiar with the 'simultaneous equations approach' to econometrics. The difficulties which arise are twofold. First, consider the relationships between each item of expenditure (including savings) and income. These will not be independent since all the items must sum to income, and any one relationship could be derived as a residual. In order to make full and correct use of all the information available, theory suggests that this dependence be taken into account.

---

† Wold (1944, p. 115). But see Durbin (1954) who suggests that there are economic contexts in which errors in variables do not bias the regression coefficients.

Secondly, since in practice income figures are often not available or, if available, are not reliable, it may be necessary to use total expenditure as an approximation to it. In this case in addition to the first objection there is the further difficulty that the errors in the dependent and determining variables are not independent, and biased estimates may result. So long as the item of expenditure is a small proportion of the budget it is not to be expected that serious biases will result, provided, of course, that a correction is made for the elasticity of total expenditure with respect to income.

CHAPTER 6

COMPUTATIONAL METHODS

6.1. HANDLING BULK DATA

Analysing family-budget data differs from other econometric work in the amount of computation that is necessary before a result can finally be derived. The magnitude of the computations does not, it is true, differ from that customary in many branches of the natural sciences, such as crystallography or astronomy, and in a monograph on these subjects it would not normally be necessary to devote much space to a discussion of computational methods, since, in their very nature, useful points that can be made are highly specialized—referring to a short-cut method suitable in a particular application—and accordingly of little use in other applications. In economics, however, computational problems have only recently become of any magnitude and there is little experience generally available in this field. In the next decade computational methods will, no doubt, receive more attention with the growing interest in input-output studies and linear programming apart from that in the analysis of household surveys. It is hoped that the brief discussion given in this chapter may serve as a useful record of our experience.†

6.11. THE EXTENT OF INSTITUTIONAL ASSISTANCE

The main general problems encountered in handling bulk data are, first, the cost and organization of the personnel engaged on the work, and secondly, the organization of the time-table within which the work is to be completed. The analysis of family-budget data, if it is to be at all extensive, is beyond the resources and capacity of an individual worker both on account of the range of problems encountered and the number of operations to be performed; the help of an institution with suitable computational facilities is therefore essential.

In preparing the results of the present publication at the Department of Applied Economics in Cambridge there were on the average about two persons engaged in full-time computation for a period of three years—all this aside from the assistance derived from punched-card equipment and the electronic computer‡ to be described below. A certain minimum of computational assistance is necessary at the institution

---

† Some of the problems raised in this chapter are well discussed by Yates (1949, pp. 109–27) to which the readers should refer, especially for a more detailed description of punched-card machines.

‡ The convention followed in this chapter is to describe the machine as a comput*er* and the person operating it as a comput*or*.

at which the work is carried out, but we have no firm opinion on whether that minimum should be exceeded by carrying out punched-card operations at the institution rather than by outside contractors. The difficulty of the latter course is that time is spent in forwarding instructions, transporting punched-cards, and in correcting mistakes. On the other hand, if punched-card operations are carried out at the institution too much of the detailed work of organizing the operations tends to fall on those whose time is better spent in directing the general lines of the inquiry.

An advantage of working in an institution in which other projects are also in progress arises from the possibility of calling on extra computors when required for short periods. Thus, while an average of two computors were engaged on the work it was at times possible to call on up to six when results were required rapidly so as not to delay subsequent analysis on automatic equipment.

6.12. PLANNING THE TIME-TABLE OF RESEARCH

The second general problem to be faced in handling bulk data is the necessity of planning the programme and the time-table of research with considerable precision. In scientific research it is generally desirable to proceed step by step, continually evaluating intermediate results and planning the next stage on their basis. The length of time required to prepare bulk data for analysis makes it desirable that as many as possible of the second steps in an analysis are contemplated when the first step is taken.

An example—in which the required forethought was not exercised in the present analysis—may bring out the nature of the difficulty. In beginning the present analysis it was thought that it would be sufficient, for all analyses likely to be undertaken, to group all the observations by household size and the value of total expenditure and to work in terms of the grouped data only. In particular, it was thought that the information on household composition—the number of children, etc.— in these groups would be adequate for any subsequent analysis. When, however, an analysis was undertaken of the effect of household composition on consumption it was found that there was an artificially high correlation between types of persons as calculated from the data so grouped. The reason is that the average of a number of households of the same size will contain more types of person than there are in individual households of that size.† It was accordingly necessary to go to considerable trouble to obtain the correlations from the original (ungrouped) data involving two thousand observations instead of the fifty grouped observations. More forethought would have indicated the desirability of grouping the observations by household types so as to avoid the biased correlations between types of persons, even though the other analyses were not carried out in these terms.

The organization of the personnel and the time-table are the main

† This problem is discussed in further detail in § 9.44 below, p. 139.

problems that require consideration in carrying out an analysis of this type. The precise course adopted will be influenced by the extent of the available institutional facilities and in particular by the mechanical and automatic computing devices to which the investigator has access. The devices at present available and their potentialities are discussed in the next section of this chapter. This is followed, in the third section, by a discussion of their relative appropriateness at the various stages of the computations and, in the final section, some attention is given to the vexing problem of checking the results.

6.2. MECHANICAL AND AUTOMATIC AIDS TO COMPUTATION

When the amount of data involved in a computation is small it does not matter in which form the data are recorded and stored, as it is a comparatively small operation to transfer from one type, say written records, to another, say punched-cards. But if bulk data are involved this is not so, and the mechanical devices used as aids in the computation have to be considered with the associated forms of record.

6.21. THE DESK MACHINE

An electric desk machine is probably the minimum requirement for the efficient handling of econometric computations. Modern machines generally multiply and divide automatically and allow for the storage of one or two numbers. It is possible, for example, to store a multiplier in the machine which can then be applied to a number of multiplicands in turn without intermediate resetting. Again, sums of cross-products of two series of numbers can be accumulated without requiring the writing down of any intermediate results; and with a little ingenuity it is possible, though not necessarily economical, to obtain the sums of the multipliers and multiplicands at the same time, as is generally required in correlation problems.

Written records are the basis of calculations carried out on desk machines, and the facility of intermediate storage both saves the labour of writing down and decreases the number of errors which arise in transferring numbers from paper to machine and back again. Desk machines are useful once the data have been summarized, but in the process of summarizing they are very much inferior to any machine in which the data are recorded in a 'mechanized' form.

6.22. PUNCHED-CARD EQUIPMENT

Punched-cards have now become the classical form of storage for bulk data. The machines available for handling these cards can still, however, perform only a limited set of elementary operations, though these are by no means unimportant on that count. Sorting and adding machines are available that work efficiently, but multiplication is a slow process better avoided whenever possible, and division can only be undertaken by indirect methods.

6.23. ELECTRONIC COMPUTATION

The recent development of electronic computing devices would seem to be of the greatest importance for the computations encountered in econometric work. We were fortunate in having access to an electronic computer, and this proved to be of great service in the calculations presented in later chapters.

The machine on which our experience is based is that of the University Mathematical Laboratory in Cambridge known as the EDSAC, a name formed of the initial letters of Electronic Delay Storage Automatic Calculator. This is a high-speed general-purpose machine capable of performing all mathematical operations that can be put in numerical form. Its input is on paper teleprinter tape, and output either on similar tape or on a typewriter.

Punched-tape may therefore be considered as a form of storage alternative to punched-cards. Since it is continuous it is not so well adapted for sorting operations as are discrete cards, but this is no doubt only a temporary limitation. The development of magnetic tape storage with auxiliary facilities for the rapid transfer of information may well make electronic computers superior to punched-card machines also in this respect.†

The development of electronic equipment is so rapid that there is a danger that some of the details and even the general principles discussed in these paragraphs may become outdated before they reach the reader. The advances in computing techniques made possible by these devices are, however, so great that it seems worth setting down some of the applications that have been made in Cambridge and the economies thereby achieved. For a more extensive discussion, with references to the literature, the paper by Brown, Houthakker and Prais (1953) may be consulted.

The advantages of electronic computation arises from three features. First, there is the large store, or 'memory', for holding data and intermediate results. It has already been seen that the efficiency of modern desk machines lies in the possibility of storing numbers which are either used several times in a calculation, or only required at an intermediate stage of the calculation. The EDSAC has a store which can hold about five hundred numbers of approximately ten decimal digits in length or twice as many if the numbers are only half as long. More involved computations can therefore be handled efficiently.

Part of this storage space will be occupied by the *programme* controlling the sequence of the machine's operations. The programme is a sequence of coded *orders* to the machine, also fed into the machine by teleprinter tape, and contains in precise detail the sequence of instructions to be followed in carrying out the computations. The orders are of the form, 'add the number in storage location 50 to the contents of the accumu-

† The value in the meantime of a device for transferring information from punched-cards to tape may be noted.

lator', and this is punched on to tape by means of a special 'typewriter' in the code form, A50. There are many types of orders, but only one requires special mention here. This type is for the transfer of control to different sequences of orders according to the outcome of an intermediate calculation. For example, in evaluating a function by means of an infinite series it is desirable to stop computing extra terms after their magnitude falls below a given level of significance, say 10^{-10}. One of the orders for the transfer of control tests whether the value in the accumulator is $\geqslant 0$, when control is transferred to another part of the programme or, if it is < 0, control proceeds serially. To decide when to stop summing the series and move to the next stage in the computations it is therefore only necessary to compute an extra term in the series, subtract 10^{-10}, and then test the result by means of this order. There are six other orders for the transfer of control under specified circumstances.

In this way parts of a programme may be repeated either a specified or an unspecified number of times. It is the orders for the conditional transfer of control which make for the 'automatic' operation of the machine, and these may therefore be regarded as the second feature of an electronic computer.

The third feature of an electronic computer is the short time required for each operation which is of the order of a thousandth of a second. Some examples will be given in the next section of the time taken for completing some typical computations.

In assessing the relative suitability of these various devices as aids in a large-scale computation it is important to keep in mind the degree of skill required for handling the devices and the extent to which it is possible to call on the aid of other persons in the course of the inquiry. In the case of an electronic computer the main problem to be solved is that of *programming*, and the feasibility of a whole research project may depend on whether it is possible to devise economically a programme suitable for the machine at hand. Accordingly, a large part of the work of programming must fall on those directing the main lines of the inquiry.

In the case of punched-card machines the corresponding work is that of preparing the plug-board and setting the switches which control the machine. The technical knowledge required for this and for the general operation of a punched-card machine is widely dispersed, and most of the methods useful in statistical problems are well established. By contrast, the research worker must expect to invest a good deal of time, sometimes many weeks, in programming a new problem for an electronic computer. Accordingly, even if electronic methods are clearly the best if a programme exists, they may be eschewed if such a programme is likely to be used no more than once. In general, if the amount of time which can be spared for programming is limited, it will pay to invest it in the construction of programmes of the most general validity, even though this may require that in most applications of the programmes it will be necessary to carry out a considerable amount of subsidiary calculation on desk machines.

6.3. THE FOUR STAGES OF A COMPUTATION

The choice among the various types of machine has to be considered in relation to the processes which are carried out in a typical investigation of family-budget data. For the purposes of this discussion four stages may be distinguished in the process of a computation: (1) preparing the original and office records of the data; (2) classifying and sorting; (3) summarizing; and (4) estimating numerical relationships.

6.31. PREPARING THE RECORDS

A considerable amount of paper work is inevitably involved at the first stage. The field worker can obtain data on a wide variety of subjects, some of which will be precise figures written down on paper either by himself or the informant, while some may only be in the form of a general impression, say that the informant was lying in his replies to particular questions. Not all of these data will require subsequent analysis, and accordingly they will not all be transferred to 'mechanized' records such as punched-cards.

It may be convenient in particular inquiries to prepare written intermediate or office records from the field records, selecting the portion of the data subsequently to be transferred to punched-cards and arranged in a convenient order for this purpose. At the same time checks can be applied to the data to ensure that no misreadings occur; for example, it should be ascertained that the total expenditure is equal to the sum of expenditures on the individual items, and sub-totals should be prepared for use in the subsequent checking of the punched-cards.

But in well-organized inquiries, such as a continuous inquiry carried out for governmental purposes rather than research, it is more economical to design the forms so that office checks can be carried out on them, and also so that cards can be punched directly from them. Intermediate records were prepared in our inquiries both because the items of expenditure had to be classified in a uniform manner (it was left to the informant to describe the precise nature of his food purchase on the form) and on account of reasons of confidentiality.

6.32. CLASSIFYING AND SORTING THE DATA

Even after the process of selecting the material to be recorded has been completed, it will still generally be the case that little progress can be made till the data have been classified and sorted. For example, it may be desirable in a particular analysis to concentrate only on households of two adults and   or two children. The problem, by no means trivial, is then encountered of selecting the records of these households from the mass of information facing the investigator. The use of a punched-card sorting machine† is here very efficient; it is

† The tabulator also contain *distributors*, usually relay devices, by means of which separate sub-totals can be obtained for groups of households, defined by characteristics recorded on the cards, without previously sorting the cards.

doubtful whether any considerable economies can be achieved by the use of electronic equipment in view of the little time spent in 'computation' compared with that spent in reading the information.

6.33. SUMMARIZING

In addition to sorting the data by a number of criteria it may be desirable to summarize them and examine the average values in each group. In the present investigation the averages (as given in Part III) were required in terms of a grouping by total expenditure and household size. The punched-card tabulator was used for this, as all that is required after sorting the data is their addition and the printing of sub-totals. The subsequent division of the totals by the number of households was done on desk machines. It would seem that electronic devices have a greater part to play in this operation, since the transformation of the data, for example, from ounces to pounds and from annual totals to weekly averages, which is often required at this stage, can be easily carried out at the same time. Further, the machine can print out the results in page format immediately suitable for photographic reproduction and subsequent printing.†

Our inquiries were substantially at too advanced a stage when electronic computing facilities became available to make use of them at this stage of the computations, but, in view of the considerable costs of this stage, an investigation of these possibilities deserves attention.

6.34. THE ESTIMATION OF NUMERICAL RELATIONSHIPS

The final stage of a computation is the estimation of numerical relationships which in our investigations has generally taken the form of a regression analysis. At this stage the electronic computer is of the greatest value, and a number of programmes have been developed for the Cambridge computer which have substantially reduced the labour of the computations encountered in econometric work. A description of the operation of these programmes may serve to indicate the possibilities in this field.

The first problem to be solved was that of finding a suitable method for computing the moment matrix of a number of variables. The principal problem that arises here is that of the difficulty of storing all the numerical information in the machine at one time as this may exceed the capacity of the memory. A convenient solution is to arrange operations so that the numerical information is only read into the machine when required for computing and not before. The computation of a moment matrix is equivalent to multiplying the matrix of observations by its transpose, and for this it is necessary to take into the store only one row of the matrix at a time, then (*a*) form the cross-products

---

† Of course, if the necessary calculations can be conveniently carried out on punched-card machines it is also possible to print out the results in a suitable format.

of the elements,† (*b*) add them to the previous partial sums of corresponding cross-products, and finally (*c*) proceed to the next row of observations. The size of the memory then sets no limit to the number of observations that can be taken into account, but the number of variables may not exceed twenty-five with the present size of the EDSAC memory.

There is a slightly more complicated programme which gives weights to the observations as is required if they are derived from grouped data. In the case of weighted regressions the gain in time in electronic computation is particularly impressive because most desk machines are not well suited to the accumulation of triple products. It takes about seven minutes on the EDSAC to compute all the fifty-five weighted sums of squares and cross-products of ten variables with forty observations, in addition to about four hours for punching and checking the number tape and verifying the results by a sum check. A computor with an electric desk machine would probably need about eighty hours for this calculation, so that over seventy hours of labour are replaced by seven minutes of machine time.

The next step in regression analysis is the inversion of the moment matrix and requires a much more complicated programme; such a programme applies, of course, to all symmetric positive-definite matrices. Among the various methods of inverting matrices one had to be chosen which could be split into successive stages so as to save storage space, and which avoided divisions as much as possible so as to save time. We selected the so-called Choleski method which involves converting the original matrix into the product of a triangular matrix and its transpose, inverting the lower triangular matrix and multiplying the inverse triangular by its transpose to give the inverse of the original matrix. The three phases can be programmed separately and do not require the storing of any intermediate results; at each stage only $\frac{1}{2}k(k+1)$ numbers (*k* being the order of the matrix) have to be in the memory. The only non-linear operation is the taking of *k* inverse square roots, which is done by an iterative process. The routine works at a very satisfactory speed; for instance, it takes less than five minutes to invert a matrix of order ten and as much again to reinvert the result as a check. Only one-half of this time is spent in actual computation; the remainder is used for reading the programme and the original matrix, and for printing the inverse. At present the EDSAC can deal with matrices up to the eighteenth order with this programme.

In the case of matrices or orders less than thirteen it is not necessary to split up the programme to save storage space, and reading time can be saved by leaving it in the memory in its entirety. This makes it possible to invert several matrices in succession without interruptions for programme input. In this way twenty matrices of order five could be inverted and reinverted in thirty minutes, that is, forty-five seconds for each inversion.

† If there are *k* variables only $\frac{1}{2}k(k+1)$ cross-products need be formed as the moment matrix is symmetric.

By combining these routines most of the computations in regression analysis can be performed automatically. For particular problems it is on occasion worth taking a further step. Thus a number of programmes have been developed which derive the parameters of different types of Engel curves (with their correlation coefficients and standard errors) directly from the basic data. The development of these programmes was worth while since the main burden of the work is to find the regressions of about 150 variables, the expenditures on various commodities, on a few 'fixed' variables—household size, income, and the like.

The value of electronic computation for statistical research is shown even more clearly in the case of calculations that would not be attempted without its aid. Least-squares regression analysis has customarily been confined to formulae where the parameters (possibly after some transformation) enter linearly, so that the normal equations are linear and can be solved by classical methods. Although this approach is satisfactory in many investigations it has proved too restrictive for some problems, particularly that of estimating unit-consumer scales which forms the subject of Chapter 9 below. The special methods adopted for this problem will be described there.

The above discussion should make clear that it is only rarely the case that a particular computational device can be said to be obsolete. The variety of problems encountered in handling a computation involving bulk data is so wide that the investigator must continually set himself the problem: has full use been made of all the available equipment?

6.4. CHECKING THE RESULTS

The process of checking, while generally tedious, must be regarded as an integral part of a calculation and should be planned as such from the beginning. The degree of accuracy required in a calculation varies at its different stages, and depends to some extent on the purpose of the calculation. In fact, just as economic problems are encountered in planning a survey, the increase in size and cost of sample having to be weighed against the increased accuracy of the resulting information, so in checking the subsequent computations it is necessary to weigh the costs of checking against the seriousness of the errors likely to be committed, and the costs of correcting an error against the proportional degree of improvement in the results. In an exploratory investigation it may be that an error in the third significant figure will have no sensible effect on the result, and it is not worth going to any trouble in correcting it despite the possible penalties that may be incurred at a later stage. If, however, the calculation is to be used in 'political' applications, as in the case of the cost-of-living index, it may be desirable to insist on accuracy to the final digit.

Errors in a result may arise from the human failings of computors or from the mechanical and random defects of computers. Different methods of checking are appropriate according to the computing device employed.

In the use of desk machines errors due to the human element are relatively frequent and every computation requires checking. Checking methods are well developed for the kind of calculations performed on these machines which are, in any case, elementary. The only points that require mention are that some form of cross-check is always preferable to a mere repetition of the calculation, and that it is better that the check figure be prepared by another computor.

In the more automatic punched-card and electronic machines errors due to human failings are less frequent, but the problem of checking is no less serious on this count. In the punching, sorting and tabulating of punched-cards it is important to provide a flow of check totals parallel with the main flow of the work.

The punched-card tabulating machines appear to be moderately sensitive to changes in the operations performed. In typical problems encountered in the commercial field the same operations are performed week after week, and a fault in a part of the machine not actually used in the calculation will not affect its accuracy. In research work, however, different kinds of tabulations are constantly required, so that the machine has to be at a generally higher state of efficiency. Errors often arise from a small fault such as the momentary failure of a relay in the machine which does not affect its general working, but occasionally causes it to print a wrong total.

In this respect it differs from the electronic computer where a minute fault in one part of the machine generally affects its total workability, so that the existence of faulty working is soon detected. In part, this superiority of electronic equipment is a reflexion of the more complicated calculations which it performs; an insignificant error at one stage is usually transformed into a gross and noticeable error by the time the result is printed out.

For punched-card machines the most thorough checking is therefore to be recommended, using cross-checks whenever possible and repeating the more complicated calculations in a different way. Two examples may be given. The use of an extra field on a card with the sub-totals of the items of expenditure on that card is well worth while for cross-checking purposes, despite the expense in extra cards that may be necessary and the extra punching. Again, in forming sums of cross-products on a rolling-total tabulator it is essential to check that $\Sigma AB = \Sigma BA$. In this kind of calculation errors may occur in more than a tenth of the totals printed out.

The main problem in electronic computation is making sure that the programme is right. The skill required in programming is different from the skill in checking developed for punched-card equipment, and considerable experience is necessary in achieving a balanced approach. An exposition of some of the problems encountered is given in Chapter 5 of the book by Wilkes, Wheeler and Gill (1951).

The standards of checking adopted in presenting the tables in Part III have in some ways been on the low side on account of the institutional limitations within which the work has been carried out. In general, it was felt that errors which affect only the fourth significant figure were not worth tracing, since the accuracy of the original data will generally be far less than this. Errors in the third significant figure have occasionally been tolerated. In computations on the EDSAC, problems were encountered about when and how to round-off, and the number of significant figures to be retained in a calculation.† These were found to be of surprisingly large importance in the calculations of the regression coefficients given in Chapter 7. In these the third significant figure is generally not reliable. The criterion adopted in calculations in which there is a sampling error associated with the estimate was that it was not worth correcting an estimate where the error was only a fraction of the standard error.

The limitations mentioned in the last paragraph are of course not essential in electronic computation and are primarily due to the desire to explore the new possibilities with the minimum of delay. Virtually any number of significant figures can be retained in a suitably programmed computation; the programme for inverting matrices, for example, works to about seven significant figures.

The computational problems encountered in analysing family-budget data are thus seen to be of a magnitude requiring institutional assistance and considerable planning on the part of the investigator. The use of modern computing devices is essential for an efficient handling of these problems, and though their magnitude is greater than that usually encountered in the social sciences they are not atypical of those customary in the natural sciences. With the development of research institutions of comparable magnitude and efficiency computational problems may cease to require so much thought and energy on the part of research workers engaged on particular projects.

† After the present calculations were completed this type of problem was considerably eased by the introduction of a new order in the EDSAC order code. This transfers controls when the accumulator overflows and thus allows an easy check to be maintained on the number of significant figures.

PART II

THE ANALYSES

PROLEGOMENA

Before proceeding to the detailed analyses of the next four chapters it is appropriate to comment on the logic which underlies the order of the investigations.

It will already be clear from the considerations presented in Part I that there are a number of factors which may be expected to have a significant influence on the pattern of expenditure. In attempting to separate the precise effect of each of these factors two simple procedures are in general possible. First, the effect of any one factor may be examined by holding the levels of all other factors constant. This means, in practice, that in examining, say, the effect of differences in income, only those households would be selected for examination which had the same number of persons and the same household composition; further, it might be necessary to consider only households belonging to a particular social class and the main earner of which was in a particular occupational group. This method of *isolating* the effects of the particular factor to be investigated is the one customarily adopted in the natural sciences and must be adopted to a greater or less extent in all sciences. In the study of family budgets it is possible to adopt this method to some extent, but in general it leads to such a considerable decrease in the number of available observations as to make it impracticable in the applications given in the following chapters.

The second simple method for distinguishing the separate effects of a number of factors is that adopted when each of the factors act in a manner that can be reduced to a linear effect. In this case the method of multiple regression analysis can be used. The assumption of a linear form is, however, only appropriate where the range of variation of the factors is comparatively small or where interest is only centred on obtaining approximations valid for small changes in the factors. One of the virtues of family-budget data is that there is a sufficient range of variation in the data to allow for the more precise investigation of the form of the relationships, and it is therefore inappropriate to proceed by merely listing the variables and relying on linear regression analysis.

The above two methods are of course constantly used in the work presented subsequently, and the above remarks must not be interpreted as casting doubt on their efficacy in the appropriate contexts. By themselves, however, they do not provide a sufficient basis for the analysis. The further principle adopted here is that it is possible to make a precise study of the effects of a particular factor even if only approximate corrections are made for the effects of other factors, these approximate corrections being based on the two simpler methods of analysis. A principle of this type must underlie any approach to the analysis of a non-linear problem involving a number of variables.

It naturally follows from this approach that in the early stages of the argument it will be necessary to make assumptions of an approximate nature which at a later stage should be given a more precise investigation. Further, the final testing of the sensitivity of the original results to the changes in the assumptions indicated by the subsequent investigations must be regarded as an important part of the argument. It must be admitted, however, that on account of the complicated form of the relationship finally derived it has not proved possible to do this in the desired detail; but it is thought that the results presented are sufficient to justify the reliability of the main conclusions.

An implication of this approach is that it makes particularly clear the extent to which the present research work is indebted to that of previous work. Without the results of Allen and Bowley presented in their *Family Expenditure* it would have been impossible to formulate the more precise relationships investigated here. In the same way if the investigations were to be repeated there can be little doubt that by making initial corrections for other factors on the basis of the present results it would be possible to obtain improved estimates for the effects of any particular factor.

The plan of the next four chapters is therefore as follows. In Chapter 7 the effects of income variations on quantities are investigated on the basis of a preliminary correction for household size. The effects of varying household composition are at this stage by-passed by examining only averages of a number of households. This is supplemented in Chapter 8 by an investigation of the effects of income variations on the quality of the commodities bought, again with a simplifying assumption as to the effects of household size. In Chapter 9 the effects of household composition are investigated by means of unit-consumer scales based on the behaviour equations thus far established. Finally, in Chapter 10, the more precise effects of household size are investigated so as to take into account the possibility of economies of scale in consumption. At the same time the implications are set out of the effects of this development on the estimates obtained in the earlier chapters.

CHAPTER 7

THE ENGEL CURVE

7.1. DEFINITION

The basic result to be derived from an econometric analysis of family budgets is the relationship showing how expenditure on (or the consumption of) a particular commodity varies with the income level of the household. This relationship is generally termed the Engel curve after Ernst Engel, who began his systematic investigations of this subject over a century ago. Before proceeding to a more precise discussion it may be useful to set out, as an illustration of the kind of result which is the interest of this chapter, some of the results which Engel derived from his early studies of family budgets as presented in his paper of 1857. These are: (1) that food represents the largest item of expenditure in the family budget; (2) that the proportion of expenditure devoted to food decreases as the standard of living of the household increases; and (3) that the proportion of expenditure on rent and clothing is approximately constant and that on 'luxury' items increases with a rise in the standard of living. In his later study of 1895 Engel realized that the first and third of these propositions are an inadequate representation of the facts; the second proposition has been repeatedly confirmed in later investigations and has become known as Engel's Law.

In so far as expenditure on a commodity depends on other factors besides income, this relationship is to be regarded as a partial relationship drawn on the assumption that the other factors are held constant; in particular, at this stage it is to be supposed that each household size is to be described by a separate curve.

In this chapter a number of investigations are presented which attempt to carry the analysis of the Engel curve somewhat further in two directions. The first is an attempt to integrate the effects of household size variations with those of income variations and thus lay the foundations for the analysis in Chapters 9 and 10; the second is an attempt to take into account explicitly the curvature of the relationship. The remainder of this section discusses the definition of the Engel curve, and in the following two sections are set out the formulations chosen for investigation and the reasons for the choice. The fourth section is devoted to a first formulation of the effects of household size. The results for food and non-food items are given respectively in the fifth and sixth sections, and the seventh section gives some calculations on related topics. The argument is summarized in the eighth section, and in the final section the results of the analyses are given for the British budgets.

7.11. THE DEPENDENT VARIABLE

It is next necessary to consider more precisely the definition of the two variables entering into the relationship. For the dependent variable expenditure may be used or quantity. If the commodity considered is indeed obtainable only in a unique variety, so that it is always bought at the same price, there will be no need for a choice, since both will give the same result except for a proportionality factor equal to the price. But if a number of varieties are on the market, as in practice is always the case, it will be necessary, as pointed out in Chapter 2, to distinguish the effects of income variations on the three variables: quantity, expenditure and average price paid. Only two of the three analyses need be carried out, since the behaviour of the remaining variable may be derived from the identity $v_i = p_i q_i$.

In practice the choice of the analyses will be guided by the availability and reliability of the data. There is, however, an argument which suggests that the correct decision is to analyse the dependence of expenditure and average price paid on income, and to derive the implied relationship for quantity as their ratio. The argument depends on the fact that the average price paid rises rather smoothly with income (as will be seen explicitly in the following chapter), and the implication that expenditure, being the product of quantity and average price, will rise more smoothly than quantity bought. In regression analysis it is always advisable to choose variables so that the relationship is as smooth as possible, and this principle allows a choice to be made here. It may be noted that this principle suggests that the use of the proportion of expenditure on the commodity as the dependent variable is inadvisable, since for some commodities this has a distinct maximum with respect to income.

An advantage of using expenditure as the dependent variable is that no difficulty is encountered in forming composite commodities such as 'dairy produce' in which, if quantity were the basic concept, there would be the difficulty of adding a number of eggs to pints of milk.

7.12. THE DETERMINING VARIABLE

For the definition of the determining variable, income,† the relevant considerations are rather more complex. If the income stream accruing to the consumer and his needs were steady over time it could be argued that the conditions of the static theory of consumers' demand, as considered in Chapter 2, were substantially satisfied and that the income received (net of statutory deductions) was the appropriate measure. This supposition is, however, patently unrealistic; both the income of a household and its needs change over time, and the income received in a particular period may be a very poor indicator of its standard of

† The determining variable will henceforth be referred to as income wherever this makes it simpler to convey the sense of the sentence; no confusion should arise on this count.

life. The true determinants of the expenditure pattern of a household in a dynamic situation are a complicated function of past, present and expected incomes, and though this function can analytically be formulated in a precise way it is of little help here. The success of an empirical analysis must depend on the choice of some simple, readily obtainable, measure which substantially represents the facts.

The use of total expenditure as the determining variable in the Engel curve can be justified on the assumption that while total expenditure may depend in a complicated way on income expectations and the like, the distribution of expenditures among the various commodities depends only on the level of total expenditure.†

The objections to this assumption can most conveniently be discussed by considering the nature of the demand for durable goods. If the survey is conducted for only a short period, a week, say, households buying expensive durables will, if total expenditure is used as the measure of 'income', be placed in too high an 'income group'; that is, their expenditures on other items will be more like those of households with a lower total expenditure. It may be argued, however, that the bias due to exceptional expenditures on a particular item in the period of observation is to some extent reduced by the tendency for households to offset such expenditures by lower expenditures elsewhere.

A second objection is that while expenditures on staple items may be satisfactorily correlated with total expenditure in the period of observation, in the case of durables and, in particular, postponable expenditures, changes in income level may be of substantial importance in determining the date of purchase. When the information is available it may therefore be desirable to introduce some measure of past or expected incomes.

In most sample surveys of household expenditures the limitations of the material effectively limit the choice to that between the two measures, income received and total expenditure in the period of observation; on the basis of the above discussion the latter seems preferable *a priori*, at any rate for those items that are not household durables. Of the two surveys examined here only in the middle-class inquiry was there the alternative of using income as the determining variable, and some calculations comparing the alternative results are set out in §7.71.

For the working-class inquiry only figures of total expenditure were available. Values of the households' expenditures on clothing for a whole year were available in addition to the four-weekly total, and so it was possible to obtain another estimate of total expenditure for the four-weekly period of observation by replacing the four-weekly expenditure on clothing by the appropriate proportion of the annual value. On account of the tendency to offset exceptional expenditures in other directions mentioned above this adjustment was not carried out.

† See Vickrey (1947) for a discussion of some of the points made here.

7.2. Criteria for an Algebraic Formulation
of the Engel Curve

Having defined the Engel curve and outlined the considerations which in practice influence the precise way in which the variables are to be measured, it is a straightforward matter to plot on a graph the observations given by a particular survey and thus obtain an impression of the relationship at work. Progress in the analysis of family budgets must, however, depend on the formulation of this relationship in algebraic terms, taking into account the statistical element so that deviations from the assumed relationship can be investigated and the formulation, in consequence, refined. Both economic and statistical considerations influence the choice of the algebraic formulation to be adopted.

7.21. ECONOMIC CONSIDERATIONS

While the abstract considerations of Chapter 2 do not give very much guidance for the algebraic formulation of the Engel curve, there are two simple properties which it may be thought desirable to incorporate into the formulation. These are: (*a*) that there is an initial income below which a commodity is not purchased, and (*b*) that there is a satiety level, that is, a maximum to the quantity of the commodity consumed which is not exceeded however high income may rise. Whilst it is clear that not all commodities will have Engel curves with these properties (the reader may at this point find it convenient to refer again to the discussion in §2.41), yet for the staple commodities, especially when considered in small groups, the properties seem plausible, and it is therefore worth developing some of their implications.

First, the simplest type of curve which has these properties is the hyperbola

$$v_i = \alpha - \beta/v_0, \qquad (7.1)$$

where v_i is expenditure on the particular commodity, v_0 is total expenditure or income, and α and β are parameters. This curve has an initial income of β/α and an asymptote equal to α. The elasticity of the curve diminishes continually as income rises, and there is one income level at which the elasticity is unity. This point may be determined by drawing a line from the origin tangent to the curve, since at the point of tangency $dv_i/dv_0 = v_i/v_0$, that is, $v_0\,dv_i/v_i\,dv_0 = 1$. This point may be termed the luxury point, since to its left the income elasticity of demand for the good is greater than unity and the good is technically a luxury; to its right the good is, correspondingly, a necessity.

Secondly, the notion of a satiety level will only be applicable to items of expenditure for which there is no great shift to higher qualities as income rises. For most commodities such shifts take place sooner or later (sugar seems to be the only substantial exception we have found), with the result that, if expenditure on the commodity is measured on the vertical axis rather than its quantity, the satiety level will have an upward slope. It is not to be expected, however, that this will offset the general tendency of a diminishing income elasticity.

In addition to these two properties which arise on general grounds there is a third point which it may be thought should be considered in an algebraic specification of the Engel curve. This is the constraint imposed on the parameters of the curves so that the sum of all expenditures is equal to income at all income levels. More explicitly if the Engel curve for the ith commodity is given by

$$v_i = f_i(v_0), \qquad (7.2)$$

it may be argued that the f_i should be chosen so that

$$v_0 = \Sigma v_i = \Sigma f_i(v_0) \qquad (7.3)$$

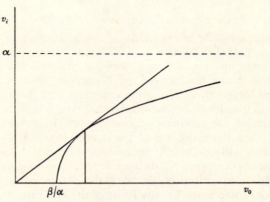

Fig. 5. A hyperbolic Engel curve.

identically. For example, if the f_i are ascending polynomials for all commodities, that is

$$v_i = f_i(v_0) = a_i + b_i v_0 + c_i v_0^2 + \dots, \qquad (7.4)$$

it is apparent that the constraint (7.3) is fulfilled if

$$\Sigma b_i = 1 \qquad (7.5)$$

and $$\Sigma a_i = \Sigma c_i = \dots = 0. \qquad (7.6)$$

Since, however, the curves are only defined in the positive quadrant it is apparent that there will be additional restrictions on the coefficients besides (7.5) and (7.6). In particular, the constant terms a_i cannot be negative if at low values of v_0 the equations are not to give negative values of the dependent variable, and in conjunction with (7.6) this implies that the a_i must all be zero.

An immediate consequence of this 'adding-up' criterion is that the Engel curves for all commodities cannot have asymptotic values; for then there would be some income level at which the whole of income

6-2

would not be spent. In other words, this criterion leads to the conclusion that if there are some commodities which have a satiety level, there must be others which do not.

It is, however, easy to overestimate the importance of the adding-up criterion. In building aggregative models of the economy as a whole it is clear that if it is ignored there is danger of introducing spurious behaviour properties. But in examining the detailed form of the Engel curve for a particular commodity it may be unwise to restrain the formulation by imposing the same algebraic form on the curves for all items of expenditure; a better representation of consumers' behaviour may be obtained by postulating different forms of Engel curves for different types of commodities. It will be seen below that this was found to be the case in the present investigations.

7.22. STATISTICAL CONSIDERATIONS

Though in fact little use is made of the adding-up criterion in the investigations below there is a neat theorem concerned with the estimation by least squares of Engel curves that fulfil this criterion. In essence this theorem was proved by Nicholson[†] but is here given a more general formulation. The theorem states that if the same form of Engel curve is fitted to all commodities and the form is such as to allow the fulfilment of the adding-up criterion (or, in general, any linear constraint), then the estimates of the curves obtained by the method of least squares will also satisfy the adding-up criterion (or, in general, the same linear constraint). This may be shown as follows. In order to fulfil the adding-up criterion, ignoring the complication of non-negativity, it is only necessary for the form of the equation to be a sum of terms which may be chosen arbitrarily except that one of the terms must be linear in income; that is, in addition to the polynomial terms as in (7.4) there may be included any other terms at will (the logarithm of income, household size and the like).[‡]

Let there be k such determining variables and let the values of these variables for a given household be denoted by the vector $\mathbf{x}$ of order $k \times 1$, the first element of the vector for convenience being income. Let $\mathbf{y}$ denote the vector of order $(n+1) \times 1$, the first n elements of which are the expenditures on the n commodities and the last element is income. The constraint that the sum of expenditures is equal to income may then be represented by the equation

$$\mathbf{y}'\mathbf{\theta} = 0, \tag{7.7}$$

where $\mathbf{\theta}$ is the (column) vector $[1, 1, ..., 1, -1]$.

[†] See Nicholson (1949, pp. 388–9).

[‡] In an earlier paper by Prais (1953), setting out some of the preliminary results of this chapter, it was said that only polynomial terms would satisfy the 'adding-up' criterion. This error was subsequently pointed out by a number of people and is noted by Worswick and Champernowne (1954). In that note there is also given a proof of the associated theorem in least squares using the conventional summation notation to which the reader who is unfamiliar with the matrix notation adopted here may find it convenient to refer.

The equation relating any element of **y** to the variables **x** is given for a particular household by

$$y = \beta'\mathbf{x} + \epsilon, \tag{7.8}$$

where β is a vector of k parameters and ϵ is a random element. By a natural extension of (7.8) the equations for all the variables **y** can be written in a matrix notation as

$$\mathbf{y} = \mathbf{B}'\mathbf{x} + \epsilon, \tag{7.9}$$

where **B** is a matrix of parameters and is of order $k \times (n+1)$. The last column of **B** will, of course, be null except for a unit in the first place, since it is the trivial equation for income. The least-squares estimates of the elements of **B** are given, in the usual way, by

$$\mathbf{B} = (\mathbf{X}'\mathbf{X})^{-1}\mathbf{X}'\mathbf{Y}, \tag{7.10}$$

where **X** and **Y** are the matrices of the observed values of the determining and the dependent variables. They are of order $\omega \times k$ and $\omega \times (n+1)$ respectively, where ω is the number of observations.

Let **y*** be the forecast values corresponding to any arbitrary value **x*** of the determining variables, that is,

$$\mathbf{y}^* = \mathbf{B}'\mathbf{x}^*. \tag{7.11}$$

It is then required to show that the 'forecast' values satisfy the same constraint as did the original observations. This now follows at once on using (7.10) and (7.7), for

$$\begin{aligned}
\mathbf{y}^{*\prime}\theta &= \mathbf{x}^{*\prime}\mathbf{B}\theta \\
&= \mathbf{x}^{*\prime}(\mathbf{X}'\mathbf{X})^{-1}\mathbf{X}'\mathbf{Y}\theta \\
&= 0.
\end{aligned} \tag{7.12}$$

Thus it is seen that if for some purpose it is required to obtain a set of equations which are consistent, in the sense that forecast values from the equations will satisfy exactly the same constraint as the original observations, this may be achieved by taking least-squares estimates based on the same set of determining variables. However, even if the fitted curves are such that they cannot satisfy the adding-up criterion exactly, they cannot fail to satisfy it approximately† if the basic data to which they are fitted add up and if the goodness of fit is at all close. This provides some justification for the neglect of this criterion in the work reported here.

Before leaving this topic it may be noted that the above theorem is of general application, since the 'consistency' vector θ may be of any given parameters. The theorem can therefore be applied, for example, to estimates of elements in a set of accounts which have to balance.

In specifying the algebraic form of the Engel curve it is important to consider the ease of numerical estimation of its parameters. There are

---

† What deviations there are will normally occur only in the very extremes of the range of observation and in extrapolations beyond that range.

occasions when a non-linear formulation is unavoidable if the features of the phenomenon are not to be observed, as in the problem to be considered in Chapter 9. But in general it is desirable to specify a form of equation which is linear or which can be reduced to the linear form by appropriate transformations of the variables.† For this reason the general hyperbolic forms proposed by Tornquist (1941), which are of the type

$$v_i = \alpha v_0^\delta \frac{v_0 - \beta}{v_0 - \gamma}, \qquad (7.13)$$

with $\delta = 0$ or 1, and α, β, γ as parameters, are not examined. If δ is zero and either β or γ is zero the form becomes linear and suitable for treatment by the ordinary least-squares methods. For, if $\beta = 0$ the form may be written as

$$v_0/v_i = v_0/\alpha - \gamma/\alpha, \qquad (7.14)$$

and if $\gamma = 0$ the form is

$$v_i = \alpha - \beta/v_0. \qquad (7.15)$$

The latter form is examined below; similar simplifications hold when $\delta = 1$.

It might be thought that the problem of specifying the form of the equation to be used as the basis of the regression analysis is trivial, since a polynomial of sufficiently high degree can assume any required shape. The flexibility of a polynomial is, however, only an advantage if the degree of scatter of the observations is small enough to allow a precise determination of the parameters of the polynomial. The data provided by family budgets do not seem to have sufficient regularity to make this possible, and it is therefore necessary to choose a form of expression with few parameters which substantially represents the required form. The object of the following sections of this chapter is to examine the Engel curves for those commodities which have a regular behaviour and which will allow of a choice between such alternative forms; the form chosen will then be applied in estimating the Engel curves of the other and less regular items.

In choosing a simple algebraic form it has been argued that the transformations of the variables used should be such as to yield residuals which are of approximately constant variance (or homoscedastic).‡ The view adopted here is that it is more natural to investigate the form of the function independently of this criterion and then, if necessary, make the appropriate adjustments to the estimating procedures. For this reason this topic finds its place in the earlier chapter on statistical methods (§5.3).

† With the development of electronic computation techniques the desirability of using only simple linear forms becomes less pressing; thus Brown and Aitchison, in their forthcoming article on the Engel curve, present calculations based on a non-linear form which is estimated by an iterative process.

‡ See, for example, an article on the savings function by Klein and Morgan (1951).

7.3. THE FORMS INVESTIGATED

With the above considerations in mind the following five basic forms were chosen for investigation:

$$\log v_i = \alpha + \beta \log v_0, \qquad (7.16)$$

$$\log v_i = \alpha - \beta/v_0, \qquad (7.17)$$

$$v_i = \alpha + \beta \log v_0, \qquad (7.18)$$

$$v_i = \alpha + \beta v_0, \qquad (7.19)$$

$$v_i = \alpha - \beta/v_0. \qquad (7.20)$$

As will be seen below a number of adjustments were made to these forms in the course of the investigations, but in essence they remain the basis of the investigations and the conclusions derived are, inevitably, limited by the possible existence of more suitable forms with which a comparison has not been made.

The reasons for the choice of these forms are as follows. It was thought desirable to investigate the forms that had been most used in past investigations, and this accounts for (7.16), the double-logarithmic form used extensively by Stone and others, and for (7.19), the linear form used by Allen and Bowley. The hyperbola (7.20) allows the investigation of a saturation level in its simplest form, while (7.17) has a sigmoid shape, passing through the origin and having an asymptote. (7.18) has a form which for the relevant portion of the curve is very similar to the hyperbolic but it has no asymptotic value; it has, however, the advantage of always giving a positive initial income; for when $v_i = 0$, the initial income is antilog $(-\alpha/\beta)$, which is positive irrespective of the signs of α and β.

The examination of alternative regression forms can be regarded as testing between alternative hypotheses about the income elasticity or the marginal propensity to consume. From this point of view forms (7.16), (7.17) and (7.18) are equivalent, respectively, to the hypotheses that the income elasticity is constant, that it is inversely proportional to the level of income, and that it is inversely proportional to the level of consumption. The forms (7.19), (7.18) and (7.20) can conveniently be expressed in terms of the marginal propensity to consume, and are equivalent respectively to the hypotheses that the marginal propensity is constant, that it varies inversely with income, and that it varies inversely with the square of income.

A priori it is difficult to express any preference as to which of the above hypotheses is the most reasonable. The linear hypothesis (7.19) implies that the income elasticity for all goods tends to unity as income increases, and this may be thought unreasonable. Again, there is some ground for not favouring the first two forms since they pass through the origin and thus do not give an initial income. Further, they lead to difficulties in the treatment of households that have no expenditure on the commodity, a matter that has been discussed in §5.221 above. These reasons are not, however, sufficient to reject these forms, since (7.16), for example, provides the simplest means of testing the hypothesis that the income elasticity is constant. Of course, if some alternative and equally simple method were found of testing this last hypothesis which did not have these disadvantages it would be possible to reject the form (7.16) on *a priori* grounds.

This again emphasizes the fact that it is only possible to test the reasonableness of a hypothesis against a limited number of specified alternatives.

7.4. VARIATIONS IN HOUSEHOLD SIZE

While the main interest of this chapter is the investigation of the effects of income variations on the level of consumption, it is difficult to proceed with the examination of family-budget data unless some correction is first made for differences in household size.

It might be thought that since household size is, in a sense, a non-economic factor it would be possible to proceed by treating it as a random variable whose effects are superimposed on those of income, and that its effects could be ignored by examining only the averages of a number of households of different sizes. This simple treatment is not suitable for two reasons. First, in most samples of household expenditures that are available there is a positive correlation between house-hold income and household size, so that biased estimates will result if household size is not explicitly treated. Secondly, variations in house-hold size have comparatively large effects on consumption, so that in most samples of household expenditures the magnitude of the variations in consumption due to household-size variations is, for some commodities, greater than that due to income variations. This again suggests that it is important to consider household size explicitly in the formulation of the Engel curve.

7.41. THE HOMOGENEITY HYPOTHESIS

The simplest hypothesis allowing for the effects of variations in house-hold size is given by supposing that *comsumption per person depends only on the level of income per person*. This is adopted as a working hypothesis in this chapter. It corresponds to the assumption of constant returns to scale often made in the theory of production; the existence of economies of scale in consumption would lead to the consequence that, if income per person were the same, larger households would enjoy a higher standard of living in the sense, say, that they will have a larger expenditure per person on luxuries. These considerations are only mentioned in this context to give the reader some appreciation of the significance of the assumption made here. The matter will be taken up again explicitly in Chapter 10, where it will be seen how the formulation of the consumption function may be refined to take into account the possibility of economies, or diseconomies, of scale.

The working assumption that there are no economies of scale will be referred to as the homogeneity hypothesis, since it asserts that the function

$$v_i = f_i(v_0, n), \qquad (7.21)$$

relating consumption to income and household size (represented by n, the number of persons in the household), is homogeneous of degree one. For the multiplication of v_0 and n by an arbitrary factor, λ, leads to an increase in v_i to λv_i, that is

$$f_i(\lambda v_0, \lambda n) = \lambda f_i(v_0, n), \qquad (7.22)$$

as is apparent on rewriting (7.21) in the more direct manner

$$v_i/n = g_i(v_0/n). \qquad (7.23)$$

Household size may at this stage be considered as measured by the number of persons in the household. It is apparent that there are a number of characteristics of the members of the household—age, sex and occupation—which may have an important influence in the consumption of particular commodities and the present formulation is therefore inadequate. The elaboration of the formulation in this direction is the object of Chapter 9 below; in the treatment in the remainder of this chapter this complication does not seem important since, first, only those commodities are considered for which this effect seems intuitively to be of small magnitude (thus differing from the problem of taking into account the general effect of household size); and, secondly, since the analyses are based on averages of a number of households not grouped by age or sex the differential effects of variations in composition are likely to average out between households.

7.42. SOME IMPLICATIONS

The adoption of the homogeneity hypothesis allows a number of simplifications in the theory of the household which are of importance in empirical analysis. The first is that the Engel curves for households of different sizes are likely to cross if examined over their full range. This may be seen by combining the homogeneity hypothesis with the hyperbolic form (7.20) to yield the set of curves

$$v_i/n = \alpha - \beta n/v_0 \qquad (7.24)$$

or

$$v_i = \alpha n - \beta n^2/v_0. \qquad (7.25)$$

From this it can be seen that the initial incomes from the households of various sizes are given by

$$n\beta/\alpha, \qquad (7.26)$$

and the satiety levels by

$$n\alpha. \qquad (7.27)$$

Since these are both proportional to n it follows that the curves must cross as in Fig. 6.

The second point to notice in connexion with household-size variations is that they may be used to discriminate between luxuries and
necessaries. A common definition† of a luxury is that it is a good the
income elasticity of which is greater than unity; correspondingly, for
a necessity it is less than unity. An alternative procedure suggested by
the above considerations is to define a good as a luxury if its consumption
decreases with an increase in household size; that is, it is sacrificed to the
consumption of necessaries the demand for which increases with household size. This alternative definition seems to fit in well with *a priori*
notions of the nature of luxuries and necessaries, but the remarkable
feature of these two sets of definitions is that if the homogenity hypothesis
hold they are equivalent.

This may be shown most simply by applying Euler's theorem on
homogeneous functions to (7.21) to give

$$v_0 \frac{dv_i}{dv_0} + n \frac{dv_i}{dn} = v_i, \tag{7.28}$$

so that

$$1 - \frac{v_0}{v_i}\frac{dv_0}{dv_i} = \frac{n}{v_i}\frac{dv_i}{dn}. \tag{7.29}$$

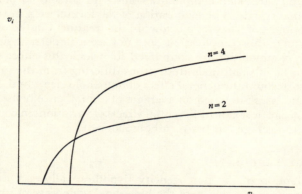

Fig. 6. Hypothetical Engel curves for households of different sizes.

The left-hand side provides the criterion in terms of the income
elasticity and the right-hand side in terms of variations in household size.

The interpretation of these results in graphical terms provides a conclusion which was of considerable help in the preliminary analysis of
the data given in Part III. If a good is a necessity over the whole range
it is to be expected that scatter diagrams will show the Engel curves for
larger households lying systematically above those for smaller households.
For luxuries, on the other hand, the curves for the smaller households
will be higher. In the intermediate case, when the income elasticity
is about unity, it is to be expected that the curves will cross each other
and will show little systematic variation with the size of the household.

† Cf. the discussion in Allen and Bowley (1935, pp. 5 et seq.).

7.43. TWO TYPICAL COMMODITIES

It has already been indicated that the main task of assessing the adequacy of the homogeneity hypothesis is postponed to a later chapter, but before proceeding with the main empirical analysis it is as well to verify that the considerations of the above paragraphs are substantially in accord with the facts. This may be done by examining almost any of the tables in Part III. For more explicit examination there is shown in Fig. 7 the scatter diagram for butter in the working-class households as given by Table D6 of Part III. Only points representing averages

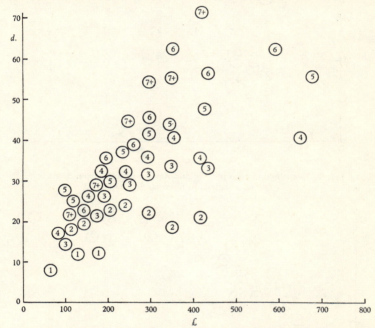

Fig. 7. Household expenditure on butter in British working-class households, 1938.

of over five households are shown. On the vertical axis is measured household expenditure on butter per week, and on the horizontal axis total household expenditure per annum. The size of the household is indicated by the number in the circle.

This commodity is no doubt more regular in appearance than many others; it is chosen here not as a typical commodity, but as a commodity which exhibits certain typical regularities which may be explained on the above theory. The following points should be noted: (*a*) variations in household size have a significant effect on consumption levels; (*b*) the larger households lie systematically above the smaller households; (*c*) at the left of the figure there is some evidence of the curves crossing each other.

Butter was evidently a typical necessary expenditure. As a typical luxury there is shown in Fig. 8 the expenditure by the middle-class sample on midday meals away from home. This diagram is similar to

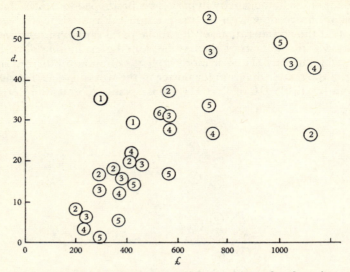

Fig. 8. Household expenditure on mid-day meals away from home in British middle-class households, 1938.

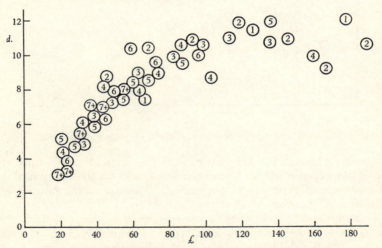

Fig. 9. Expenditure per person on butter and total expenditure per person, in British working-class households, 1938.

the one above. While less regular, it exhibits well the main feature of a luxury expenditure in that the points referring to households of smaller size lie above those for households of larger size.

The justification for the homogeneity hypothesis must be that the Engel curves for households of different sizes can be made to coalesce by dividing both expenditure and income by household size. That this is substantially so can be seen from Figs. 9 and 10 which show the two commodities exhibited above after this transformation.

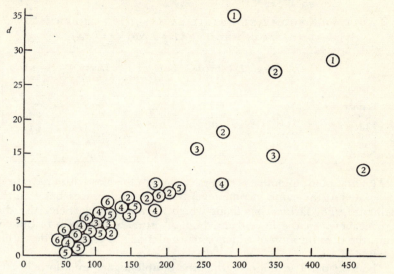

Fig. 10. Expenditure per person on mid-day meals away from home and total expenditure per person, in British middle-class households, 1938.

7.5. Alternative Forms for Foods

In testing the alternative forms of equation listed in §7.3 it is as well to consider commodities the consumers' demand for which is likely to be influenced as little as possible by random elements. To this end the comparisons made in this section are confined to a number of relatively broad food groups the examination of which will suggest a number of conclusions. In the following section the analysis will be extended to non-foods, but since the demand for these is rather less regular it is not to be expected that it will be possible to derive equally firm conclusions.

The six food commodities examined here are: (a) farinaceous foods, (b) dairy products, (c) vegetables, (d) fruit, (e) fish and (f) meat. The exact composition of these grouped commodities is given in the Guide to the Tables, p. 177 below.

7.51. A COMPARISON OF THE ELASTICITIES

The first step is to calculate the regression of expenditure per person, on the various commodities, on total expenditure per person using the transformations of the variables implied by the forms (7.16)–(7.20). The data used are from the working-class sample. The thirty regressions which result are best compared in the present context by considering the income elasticities computed at the mean values of the variables. These are shown in Table 10, in which the figures should be compared a row at a time (the abbreviated names given at the heads of the columns are for ease of reference only and are not conventional).†

TABLE 10. INCOME ELASTICITIES BASED ON ALTERNATIVE REGRESSION FORMS (AT MEAN VALUES)

Form Commodity	Double-log (7.16)	Log-inverse (7.17)	Semi-log (7.18)	Linear (7.19)	Hyperbola (7.20)
Farinaceous	0·36	0·27	0·35	0·30	0·25
Dairy	0·53	0·41	0·48	0·41	0·35
Vegetables	0·62	0·46	0·58	0·50	0·40
Fruit	1·20	0·90	1·03	0·98	0·66
Fish	0·84	0·62	0·76	0·66	0·51
Meat	0·69	0·53	0·62	0·51	0·44

The first point to notice is that even though the elasticities have been calculated at the same income level there are differences between the estimates. For farinaceous foods which have a low elasticity the difference between the lowest and highest estimate is only 0·1; but for fruit, the consumption of which is more elastic, the estimates lie within a range of 0·5.

The next point to notice is that the double-logarithmic form (7.16) consistently gives the highest estimate and the form (7.20) the lowest estimate. The semi-logarithmic form (7.18) gives the second highest estimates.

TABLE 11. INCOME ELASTICITY FOR MEAT AT VARIOUS INCOME LEVELS: ESTIMATES BASED ON ALTERNATIVE REGRESSION FORMS

Income Form	£40	Mean	£100
Double-log (7.16)	0·69	0·69	0·69
Log-inverse (7.17)	0·92	0·53	0·37
Semi-log (7.18)	0·84	0·62	0·48
Linear (7.19)	0·38	0·51	0·60
Hyperbola (7.20)	0·95	0·44	0·24

The differences between the estimates are, of course, greater when calculated at any point away from the mean, since each form makes different assumptions as to the way in which the elasticity varies. To give an impression of the order of magnitude of the differences, the elasticities have been calculated for the meat group of commodities at values of the income variable of £40 and £100 per person per annum (approximately the upper and lower quartiles) for comparison with

† The equations are given in Table 21 at the end of the chapter.

those at the mean value in the sample which is about £60 per person per annum. The results are shown in Table 11 (the value of £100 per annum corresponds approximately to the average income per person in Britain in 1938).

It is clearly desirable to make a choice between the alternative regression forms. The characteristics of these forms have already been discussed in §7.3, and it now remains to be seen whether it is possible to choose between them on grounds of goodness of fit.

7.52. A COMPARISON OF THE GOODNESS OF THE FITS

The large range of variation in the data has received comment on several occasions; the greater part of the data lie in the income per person range of £20 to £200 per annum—a ten-fold range. It is therefore desirable to test goodness of fit both in terms of the closeness and in terms of the linearity of fit.

For the closeness of fit the correlation coefficient is used and the values for the thirty regressions are set out in Table 12.† It will be seen that the values are high and the differences between the coefficients are small. Some conclusions may, however, be hazarded. First, the linear form seems to be inferior except for the case of fruit. This commodity has, however, an elasticity close to unity, so that the constant term in the linear form must be relatively close to zero. For testing the linear form, fruit is therefore an exceptional commodity and little attention should be paid to that result. Secondly, the hyperbola—the simplest form of curve which is acceptable on *a priori* grounds—though generally better than the linear form is inferior to the semi-logarithmic form.

TABLE 12. CORRELATION COEFFICIENTS FOR ALTERNATIVE REGRESSION FORMS

Form / Commodity	Double-log (7.16)	Log-inverse (7.17)	Semi-log (7.18)	Linear (7.19)	Hyperbola (7.20)
Farinaceous	0·82	−0·82	0·82	0·74	−0·80
Dairy	0·94	−0·98	0·92	0·83	−0·90
Vegetables	0·92	−0·93	0·91	0·84	−0·86
Fruit	0·96	−0·98	0·94	0·96	−0·83
Fish	0·94	−0·94	0·92	0·84	−0·84
Meat	0·92	−0·96	0·92	0·81	−0·90

In comparing the correlation coefficients of the last three equations with those of the first two it should be noted that the degree of 'explanation' of the variance of v_i is being compared with that of $\log v_i$. It is possible to make the coefficients more strictly comparable by considering, say, the (weighted) sum of squares of arithmetic residuals in all cases. For example, having fitted the form (7.16), the values of $\log v_i$ should be calculated for the sample using the estimated regression

† The correlation coefficients given in this and subsequent tables are based on grouped data and should be used for comparative purposes only; cf. the remark on p. 61 above.

coefficients, their antilogs taken, and then correlated with the observed v_i. This coefficient would then be comparable with that of (7.18).

The adjustment seems, however, to be of small effect for broad groups of commodities in which there are no low values of v_i, and comparable to fitting strictly the non-linear form

$$v_i = Av_0^b, \qquad (7.30)$$

with additive error term instead of the linear form (7.16) to which it is generally equivalent. In some computations by Theil[†] the effect of 'untransforming' the dependent variable in the way described is to reduce the correlation coefficient by only 0·03. While this may leave a certain latitude in the conclusions the complication does not seem to be of sufficient magnitude to require detailed calculations.

To compare the degrees of linearity of fit the λ coefficient described in §5.25 has been used. Perfect linearity of fit is shown by a value of λ close to zero, significant non-linearity by a value greater than 3. The values of λ for the thirty regressions are given in Table 13. It was not found necessary to omit any of the points in computing the value.

TABLE 13. LINEARITY TEST FOR ALTERNATIVE REGRESSION FORMS

Form / Commodity	Double-log (7.16)	Log-inverse (7.17)	Semi-log (7.18)	Linear (7.19)	Hyperbola (7.20)
Farinaceous	0·3	2·4	0·5	2·0	3·0
Dairy	2·9	0·6	0·1	3·2	2·3
Vegetables	0·2	1·5	−0·4	1·2	1·5
Fruit	2·7	1·9	3·0	2·5	5·7
Fish	−0·8	2·4	2·0	0·3	2·9
Meat	2·9	1·4	0·9	3·2	3·0

Inspection of the table shows that this test is rather more sensitive to the alternative forms than is the correlation coefficient. The hyperbola is unsatisfactory on this test, and the diagrams showed that it has too much curvature and flattens out at too low an income level. The linear form (7.19) may also be judged unsatisfactory on this test except for the fish group. Of the remaining three forms it seems that the semi-log form is the most satisfactory especially if the fruit group—which is not very satisfactory on any of the forms—is left out of account.

These results seem to suggest that so long as the elasticity is less than unity the semi-logarithmic form gives an adequate representation of the commodity.

7.53. A COMPARISON BETWEEN THE TWO SAMPLES

The evidence so far given is not, however, sufficiently strong to require the rejection of the double-logarithmic form, and more particularly it seems unwise to reject the hypothesis that the elasticity is invariant with

† In an as yet unpublished paper on 'The family expenditure of farmers in Holland'.

respect to income level as against the hypothesis that the elasticity declines with the income level or the level of consumption. A comparison was therefore made with the results of the middle-class inquiry in the following manner. Engel curves were computed according to forms (7.16) and (7.18) for the working-class and middle-class inquiries, both separately and combined. Since the average income of the middle-class inquiry is higher than that of the working-class inquiry, it is possible to see whether the elasticity is constant by testing whether the two values of the elasticity could be estimates of the same population value as estimated from the combined samples. The values for the double-logarithmic form are set out in Table 14, the coefficients being here equal to the elasticities.

TABLE 14. REGRESSION COEFFICIENTS FOR SIX FOOD GROUPS, USING DOUBLE-LOG ENGEL CURVES

Commodity	R	Combined samples	Separate samples	
			Working class	Middle class
Farinaceous	0·84	0·34 ± 0·03	0·36	0·33
Dairy	0·92	0·42 ± 0·02	0·53	0·26
Vegetables	0·90	0·53 ± 0·03	0·62	0·40
Fruit	0·95	0·94 ± 0·04	1·20	0·55
Fish	0·92	0·73 ± 0·04	0·84	0·57
Meat	0·89	0·59 ± 0·04	0·69	0·44

A comparison of the last two columns shows at once that the elasticities of demand for the items given in the table are lower in the middle-class households than in the working-class households. One commodity —fruit—is in fact seen to be a luxury for the working-class households and a necessity for the middle-class households.

An approximate test of the significance of the differences as between the elasticities may be made by taking $\sqrt{2}$ times the standard error of the regression coefficient as calculated from the combined samples† and given in the third column of the table. Inspection shows all the differences to be highly significant.

The next step is to repeat the computations using the semi-logarithmic form (7.18). The results, presented in Table 15, stand in contrast to the earlier results. For while there are now still differences between the coefficients in the two samples these are small, and there is no systematic tendency for the results of the one inquiry to be either higher or lower than those of the other. A comparison of differences with their standard errors does not lead to the rejection of the hypothesis that the behaviour of the households in both samples can be described by the same set of Engel curves.

† These have been computed after allowing for a constant difference between the samples representing a social-class factor. The correlation coefficient in the second column refers to this computation.

It is thus seen that if the two samples are regarded as comparable then the differences between the elasticities can be explained by the hypothesis that the income elasticity diminishes with the income level of the household. We are therefore led to prefer an Engel curve of the form (7.18) which expresses this hypothesis algebraically.

TABLE 15. REGRESSION COEFFICIENTS FOR SIX FOOD GROUPS, USING SEMI-LOG ENGEL CURVES

Commodity	R	Combined samples	Separate samples	
			Working class	Middle class
Farinaceous	0·83	15·5±1·2	14·7	16·7
Dairy	0·93	24 ±1·3	27	20
Vegetables	0·90	10·5±0·6	11·1	9·5
Fruit	0·94	15·9±0·9	13·6	19·2
Fish	0·90	8·4±0·5	8·2	8·9
Meat	0·89	36 ±2	37	33

The earlier calculations, however, show that even with this form of curve there is often a degree of residual curvature in the scatter of the points, but it has not been found possible to derive any generalizations which account for the differing behaviour of the various commodities.

7.6. ALTERNATIVE FORMS FOR NON-FOODS

In the last section it has been seen that for foodstuffs a degree of support has been found for the generalization that the income elasticity declines with the income level of the household and is approximately inversely proportional to the value of income per person. This generalization was ultimately based on a comparison of the working-class and middle-class surveys. In this section similar computations are examined for other commodity groups.

Once the domain of food is left it is, however, extremely difficult to find homogeneous groups of commodities. The following six commodity groups were chosen as being more or less homogeneous: (1) net rent and expenditure on house-purchase; (2) expenditure on fuel and lighting; (3) clothing and shoes (including repairs); (4) household durables—ironmongery, brushes, crockery, furniture, etc.; (5) newspapers, books, postage, etc., called, for short, 'literary' activities; and (6) expenditure on tobacco, drink, amusements, etc., which is here called 'vice'.

The comparisons are confined to the double-logarithmic and semi-logarithmic forms in the two samples, and the results of the calculations that have been carried out are given in Tables 16 and 17. These show that what degree of uniformity has been found in the consumption of foodstuffs has not carried over to non-food items. First, the differences between the correlation coefficients on the two forms was generally negligible for foodstuffs, whereas here—especially for clothing, durables and expenditure on literary activities—the differences may be judged as significant (the standard error of a correlation coefficient of 0·9 with 54 observations is 0·03 using the approximate formula $(1 - r^2)/\sqrt{n}$).

TABLE 16. REGRESSION COEFFICIENTS FOR SIX NON-FOOD GROUPS, USING DOUBLE-LOG ENGEL CURVES

Commodity	R	Combined samples	Separate samples	
			Working class	Middle class
Rent	0·91	0·74 ± 0·05	0·90	0·49
Fuel	0·95	0·74 ± 0·03	0·75	0·73
Clothing	0·98	1·05 ± 0·04	0·93	1·24
Durables	0·97	1·75 ± 0·06	1·74	1·77
Literary	0·98	1·12 ± 0·03	1·16	1·05
Vice	0·92	0·95 ± 0·05	1·16	0·61

TABLE 17. REGRESSION COEFFICIENTS FOR SIX NON-FOOD GROUPS, USING SEMI-LOG ENGEL CURVES

Commodity	R	Combined samples	Separate samples	
			Working class	Middle class
Rent	0·87	87 ± 8	82	96
Fuel	0·91	48 ± 3	37	66
Clothing	0·80	145 ± 17	57	282
Durables	0·65	136 ± 20	67	244
Literary	0·84	30 ± 3	15	53
Vice	0·90	43 ± 3	44	42

Secondly, for expenditures on fuel and lighting, household durables and literary activities, the hypothesis of a constant elasticity is appropriate and should be estimated from a double logarithmic Engel curve. In the case of household durables the scatter of the points shows an upward curvature, and a semi-logarithmic Engel curve which flattens out at high incomes does not provide a suitable description of the range of data available in these budgets.

Thirdly, for clothing the calculations show that there are differences in the behaviour of the two samples which cannot be explained by either of the two hypotheses under consideration. The income elasticity for this group of expenditures is higher in the middle-class sample than the working-class sample which contrasts with the results for other commodities. Clothing, however, is an item on which the influence of social class may be expected to be strong. It is therefore advisable to analyse the samples separately, and there seems little point in straining to find a simple 'explanation' of the behaviour of both samples together.

7-2

I

Fourthly, for rent and the items labelled 'vice' there is evidence of saturation effects which lead to a diminishing income elasticity. Semi-logarithmic Engel curves describe the phenomena adequately.

The above calculations are only exploratory. It is evident that the demand for non-food items is more variable than the demand for food items and is governed by more factors. The limitations of a cross-sectional study which neglects dynamic factors, such as income changes, are in consequence particularly marked, But, as will be seen in §7.9, it has been found possible to obtain statistically satisfactory estimates of the elasticities for most of the non-food items even with these simplifications.

7.7. SOME FURTHER DETAILS

The main argument of this chapter is given in the above sections: before summarizing it, consideration is given in this section to two matters allied to the estimation of consumption relationships from family budget data.

7.71. INCOME AND EXPENDITURE

The first matter is one that has been held over from the first section in this chapter and concerns the use of total expenditure instead of income as the independent variable in the consumption relationship.

For the middle-class survey information is available on the income of the head of the household. This is not the sole income of the household, since there is an average of 1·2 wage- or salary-earners in this sample. On the other hand, it can be argued that it is the income of the head of the household which determines its general level of consumption, the income of subsidiary earners being devoted to particular expenses. A comparison of the results using the alternative variables may be of interest, if only as an illustration of the considerations involved.

This comparison is summarily made in Table 18, which gives the correlation and regression coefficients on the double-logarithmic form using first, income per person, and secondly, total expenditure per person, as the determining variable. As far as the correlation coefficient is concerned the twelve commodities fall into two groups. There are some commodities—clothing and household durables—for which the correlation with income is lower than that with total expenditure. This may be explained if the households with a total expenditure different from their income are those households which have incurred exceptional expenditures on these items in the period of the inquiry.

The second group contains the staple items of the expenditure—the six foods and rent—for which the correlation is higher with the income of the household. In part this effect is the converse of that in the first group; the total expenditure for certain households is artificially raised by expenditure incurred in the inquiry period. Further, it can be argued that in the households covered by this survey the income of the head does not fluctuate over time, since he is a salaried official with an assured pension and little chance of losing his job. The conditions therefore approximate to the assumptions of the static theory of choice and income is the appropriate independent variable. For the three remaining items, fuel, literary activities, and vice, the correlation coefficient with income is lower but not significantly so.

TABLE 18. A COMPARISON OF THE USE OF INCOME AND TOTAL EXPENDITURE AS THE DETERMINING VARIABLE IN THE ENGEL CURVE

Commodity group	Correlation coefficient		Regression coefficient	
	Income	Total expenditure	Income	Total expenditure
Farinaceous	0·87	0·82	0·47	0·33
Dairy	0·86	0·84	0·36	0·26
Vegetables	0·86	0·82	0·55	0·40
Fruit	0·90	0·88	0·75	0·55
Fish	0·85	0·82	0·79	0·57
Meat	0·83	0·80	0·60	0·44
Rent	0·92	0·74	0·83	0·49
Fuel	0·91	0·95	0·95	0·73
Clothing	0·76	0·94	1·35	1·24
Durables	0·76	0·95	1·94	1·77
Literary	0·90	0·95	1·36	1·05
Vice	0·74	0·78	0·78	0·61

Turning next to the elasticities it is seen that these are always higher for the regressions on income. In analysing the differences it should be noted that the elasticity of an item with respect to income is the product of its elasticity with respect to total expenditure and the elasticity of total expenditure with respect to income. This may be shown as follows in which Y denotes income:

$$\eta_{iY} = \frac{Y}{v_i}\frac{dv_i}{dY}$$

$$= \frac{v_0}{v_i}\frac{dv_i}{dv_0} \cdot \frac{Y}{v_0}\frac{dv_0}{dY}$$

$$= \eta_{io}\eta_{oY}. \tag{7.31}$$

The regression of total expenditure on the income of the head of the household, η_{oY}, was found to be 1·17 with a correlation coefficient of 0·86. This factor accounts for about half of the differences between two sets of elasticities; the remaining portion may, perhaps, be attributed to the 'error in variables' bias mentioned in §5.5.

The estimated value of 1·17 given in the last paragraph should not be taken as a basis for an estimate of the aggregate marginal propensity to consume, since the income of subsidiary earners has been omitted. To obtain a somewhat better estimate of the marginal propensity to consume a special tabulation was made of the 1095 households (out of the total of 1361) with only one earner so that all the earned income was taken into account. The following regression was obtained:

$$\log v_0 = 0.35 + 0.89(\pm 0.04) \log Y, \qquad (7.32)$$

with a correlation coefficient of 0.94. This suggests that income elasticities may be estimated by diminishing the expenditure elasticities by about one-tenth.

As has been seen in §4.2, the limitations of the data are such that too much reliance should not be put on comparisons of income and total expenditure.

7.72. THE ESTIMATION OF SUBSTITUTION ELASTICITIES

The second matter to be considered in this section is the possibility of estimating substitution elasticities from family-budget data. The temptation to obtain such estimates arises from the observation that households which have, say, an exceptionally large expenditure on butter, will tend to have a low expenditure on its substitute, margarine. The introduction of margarine in the equation explaining butter will therefore lead to a reduction in the unexplained variance.

But consideration will show that no economic significance can be attached to the regression coefficient of margarine in such an equation;† unless data are obtained in which prices vary it is not possible to obtain estimates of elasticities with respect to the own price of the commodity nor with respect to the prices of related commodities. Of course, by comparing the results of family-budget surveys conducted at periods in which prices differed, estimates of substitution elasticities can be obtained, either by the involved method suggested by Wald (1940) or by the more straightforward method recently adopted by Duesenberry and Kistin (1953). Too little work has as yet been completed along these lines to allow an assessment of the value of this method.

7.8. A SUMMARY OF THE ARGUMENT

A wide range of topics has been covered in this chapter, and it is now time to draw the discussion together and assess the results of the calculations that have been presented. The argument may be summarized as follows:

(1) The effects of household size and income on the levels of consumption can to a first approximation be simply described by the hypothesis that consumption per person depends on the level of income per person.

(2) From this relationship it follows that Engel curves for households of different sizes are related according to the nature of the good; a particular corollary is that a good may be defined as a necessity or a luxury according to whether an increase in household size leads to an increase or a decrease in its consumption.

† For some computations and an elaboration of the argument see Prais (1953, p. 98).

(3) The principal problem in fitting Engel curves is to find an algebraic expression which satisfies both certain *a priori* criteria and also certain criteria of a statistical nature.

(4) On *a priori* grounds the curve may be required to have an initial income and in some cases a satiety level.

(5) It is desirable that the parameters of the algebraic expression should represent some behaviouristic constants, should be capable of satisfying statistical tests of significance, and the classical methods of estimating the parameters by least squares be straightforward. Further, expressions involving the logarithm of expenditure lead to difficulties, since the expenditure by a particular household may be zero.

(6) None of the five expressions used in the calculations have been found to be uniformly satisfactory. Certain conclusions have, however, emerged: (*a*) It is always possible to obtain a better estimate than that given by the linear form. (*b*) The double-logarithmic form gives a fairly satisfactory description of the curvature found in most commodities except for the difficulty of treating zero expenditures. (*c*) The semi-logarithmic form gives a satisfactory description of expenditure on most foodstuffs.

(7) For foodstuffs the law of diminishing elasticity seems to hold, the elasticity being approximately inversely proportional to the level of income.

(8) Elasticities with respect to total expenditure may be converted to elasticities with respect to income by multiplying by the elasticity of total expenditure with respect to income. The only evidence available for the present enquiries suggests an estimate of 0·9 for the latter elasticity.

7.9. ENGEL CURVES BASED ON THE BRITISH INQUIRIES

It has been seen that the degree of curvature of the Engel curves varies between commodities. Since it was clearly impracticable to examine each commodity in detail some general form had to be adopted which could be applied to most commodities. On the basis of the above investigations it was decided to analyse all food items on a semi-logarithmic Engel curve and all non-food items on a double logarithmic curve.

As noted by Allen and Bowley, the Engel curve is most suitably described in terms of two parameters, the proportion spent on the commodity and the elasticity of expenditure at the mean income. Denoting the elasticity by η, the proportion of expenditure on the commodity by w, and the marginal propensity to consume by b, the relation between these three magnitudes is

$$\eta = b/w. \qquad (7.33)$$

Table 19 accordingly gives the proportions of expenditure on the various items in two inquiries. They are given as unadjusted averages so as to give a concise impression of the extent to which the results of

TABLE 19. PROPORTIONATE DISTRIBUTION OF EXPENDITURE
IN THE BRITISH INQUIRIES (PER CENT)

No.	Item	Working class	Middle class
C1	Flour	1·0	0·3
C2	Cake mixture	0·2	0·2
C3	Oatmeal	0·1	0·1
C4	Rice	0·1	0·1
C5	Cereals	0·2	0·2
C6	Bread	3·0	3·0
C7	Biscuits	0·4	0·5
C8	Fancy bread, cakes	1·4	0·8
D1	Milk, fresh	3·5	2·7
D2	skimmed	0·0	0·0
D3	condensed	0·3	0·0
D4	dried and preparations	0·2	0·1
D5	Cream	0·1	0·1
D6	Butter	2·8	1·5
D7	Margarine	0·4	0·1
D8	Lard	0·4	0·1
D9	Cheese	0·8	0·3
D10	Eggs	2·1	1·3
D11	Suet	0·3	0·1
E1	Tea	1·9	0·8
E2	Coffee	0·1	0·1
E3	Cocoa	0·2	0·1
E4	Sugar	1·2	0·6
E5	Jam	0·6	0·3
E6	Syrup	0·1	0·1
E7	Sweets	0·3	0·5
F1	Apples	0·4	0·4
F2	Oranges	0·4	0·4
F3	Bananas	0·3	0·2
F4	Other fresh fruit	0·3	0·5
F5	Dried fruit	0·4	0·3
F6	Tinned and bottled fruit	0·3	0·3
G1	Potatoes	1·2	0·5
G2	Green vegetables	0·7	0·4
G3	Root vegetables	0·5	0·4
G4	Onions	0·1	0·1
G5	Dried legumes	0·1	0·0
G6	Tinned and bottled vegetables	0·1	0·1
H1	Fish, fresh	0·6	0·6
H2	shell	0·0	0·0
H3	dried and cured	0·2	0·1
H4	tinned	0·3	0·2
I1	Beef and veal, fresh	2·0	1·3
I2	frozen	0·9	0·3
I3	Mutton, fresh	0·8	0·7
I4	frozen	0·8	0·4
I5	Pork	0·6	0·2
I6	Bacon	2·2	1·0
I7	Sausages	0·7	0·4
I8	Tinned meat	0·2	0·2
I9	Other meat	0·5	0·2
I10	Rabbits and poultry	0·2	0·3
J1	Malt and cod-liver oil	0·0	0·1
J2	Fish and chips	0·4	0·1
J3	Other food	0·4	0·4
J4	Meals at school	0·0	0·1
J5	Other food at school	0·0	0·0
J6	Other meals away from home, dinners	0·6	1·1
J7	Other meals	0·7	0·5

TABLE 19 (cont.)

No.	Item	Working class	Middle class
K1	Drink (alcoholic and soft)	1·0	1·1
K2	Tobacco }		
K3	Cigarettes	3·0	1·9
L1	Rent	9·7	4·4
L2	House-purchase	2·6	7·9
M1	Coal	3·7	2·8
M2	Coke	0·1	0·3
M3	Oil	0·1	0·1
M4	Firewood, candles, etc.	0·7	0·3
M5	Gas, slot meter	1·3	0·2
M6	other meter	0·2	0·6
M7	Gas fittings	0·1	0·2
M8	Electricity, slot meter, current	0·5	0·1
M9	slot fittings	0·0	0·0
M10	other meter, current	0·5	1·1
M11	fittings	0·1	0·2
N1	Men's clothing	2·6	2·4
N2	Women's clothing	2·9	3·7
N3	Children's clothing	1·1	1·2
N4	Clothing repairs	0·2	0·2
N5	Boots and shoes,	1·7	1·1
N6	Boots and shoes, repairs	0·7	0·4
O1	Soap	0·9	0·6
O2	Soda	0·4	0·3
O3	Ironmongery	0·3	0·4
O4	Brushes	0·1	0·3
O5	Crockery	0·2	0·2
O6	Drapery	0·8	1·7
O7	Furniture	1·4	2·5
O8	Carpets	0·8	1·0
O9	Other utensils	0·5	0·5
P1	Education and music lessons	0·4	2·0
P2	Newspapers	1·2	0·9
P3	Books	0·3	0·6
P4	Postages, telephone, telegrams	0·5	1·3
Q1	Cinemas	1·0	0·7
Q2	Theatres	0·4	0·6
Q3	Sports	0·3	0·3
	Travel to and from work:		
R1	by rail: Season	0·3	0·9
R2	Cheap	0·2	0·0
R3	Other	0·1	0·1
R4	by bus, tram, coach, etc.	1·1	0·8
R5	Other travel by rail	0·3	0·5
R6	Other travel by bus, tram, coach, etc.	0·7	0·8
S1	Doctor	1·1	2·8
S2	Medicine	0·6	0·7
S3	Chemists' sundries	0·1	0·4
S4	Hairdresser	0·6	0·6
T1	Laundry	0·6	0·8
T2	Wages for domestic help	0·2	2·1
T3	Payments to hospital funds	0·3	0·4
T4	Trade Union, Friendly Society, etc., subscription	1·7	0·9
T5	Unemployment, N.H. Insurance	2·4	0·5
T6	Payments to pension funds	3·0	6·3
T7	Licences	0·6	0·9
T8	Food for animals	0·2	0·2
T9	Holiday expenditure	0·9	0·3
T10	All other expenditure	3·2	11·6

TABLE 20. ESTIMATES OF TOTAL EXPENDITURE ELASTICITIES BASED ON THE BRITISH INQUIRIES

No.	Item	Working class	Middle class
C1	Flour	0·07 ± 0·05	0·11 ± 0·05
C2	Cake mixture	0·52 ± 0·12	0·30 ± 0·08
C3	Oatmeal	0·14 ± 0·11	0·35 ± 0·14
C4	Rice	0·34 ± 0·03	0·41 ± 0·08
C5	Cereals	0·37 ± 0·12	0·27 ± 0·18
C6	Bread	0·12 ± 0·05	0·21 ± 0·04
C7	Biscuits	0·68 ± 0·06	0·50 ± 0·09
C8	Fancy bread, cakes	0·56 ± 0·04	0·77 ± 0·09
D1	Milk, fresh	0·45 ± 0·03	0·18 ± 0·02
D2	skimmed	− 1·06 ± 0·32	0
D3	condensed	− 0·22 ± 0·33	− 0·08 ± 0·18
D4	dried and preparations	0·60 ± 0·12	0·55 ± 0·30
D5	Cream	0·85 ± 0·14	1·34 ± 0·20
D6	Butter	0·39 ± 0·02	0·35 ± 0·04
D7	Margarine	− 0·25 ± 0·06	0·02 ± 0·06
D8	Lard	0·31 ± 0·06	0·18 ± 0·09
D9	Cheese	0·39 ± 0·05	0·61 ± 0·09
D10	Eggs	0·48 ± 0·03	0·45 ± 0·04
D11	Suet	0·30 ± 0·04	0·29 ± 0·05
E1	Tea	0·37 ± 0·04	0·68 ± 0·08
E2	Coffee	0·74 ± 0·13	1·42 ± 0·20
E3	Cocoa	0·23 ± 0·07	0·25 ± 0·17
E4	Sugar	0·27 ± 0·03	0·37 ± 0·04
E5	Jam	0·31 ± 0·04	0·64 ± 0·12
E6	Syrup	0·46 ± 0·09	0·44 ± 0·13
E7	Sweets	0·79 ± 0·06	0·32 ± 0·06
F1	Apples	0·69 ± 0·05	0·52 ± 0·08
F2	Oranges	0·62 ± 0·06	0·70 ± 0·10
F3	Bananas	0·50 ± 0·06	0·23 ± 0·07
F4	Other fresh fruit	0·86 ± 0·07	1·10 ± 0·15
F5	Dried fruit	0·57 ± 0·04	0·80 ± 0·09
F6	Tinned and bottled fruit	0·69 ± 0·06	0·77 ± 0·08
G1	Potatoes	0·23 ± 0·03	0·20 ± 0·04
G2	Green vegetables	0·64 ± 0·04	0·90 ± 0·11
G3	Root vegetables	0·61 ± 0·03	0·62 ± 0·09
G4	Onions	0·41 ± 0·05	0·57 ± 0·08
G5	Dried legumes	0·19 ± 0·08	0·23 ± 0·23
G6	Tinned and bottled vegetables	0·48 ± 0·06	0·51 ± 0·23
H1	Fish, fresh	0·60 ± 0·05	0·78 ± 0·06
H2	shell	0·62 ± 0·10	1·22 ± 0·46
H3	dried and cured	0·57 ± 0·07	0·55 ± 0·12
H4	tinned	0·70 ± 0·05	0·91 ± 0·22
I1	Beef and veal, fresh	0·45 ± 0·05	0·40 ± 0·07
I2	frozen	0·23 ± 0·05	− 0·18 ± 0·09
I3	Mutton, fresh	0·66 ± 0·06	0·93 ± 0·12
I4	frozen	0·39 ± 0·06	0·12 ± 0·09
I5	Pork	0·53 ± 0·06	0·44 ± 0·15
I6	Bacon	0·51 ± 0·04	0·49 ± 0·08
I7	Sausages	0·41 ± 0·04	0·40 ± 0·07
I8	Tinned meat	0·23 ± 0·05	− 0·18 ± 0·09
I9	Other meat	0·45 ± 0·05	0·38 ± 0·09
I10	Rabbits and poultry	0·75 ± 0·10	1·83 ± 0·20
J1	Malt and cod-liver oil	0·32 ± 0·16	0
J2	Fish and chips	0·28 ± 0·07	− 0·25 ± 0·16
J3	Other food	0·62 ± 0·04	0·77 ± 0·08
J4	Meals at school	0·17 ± 0·50	0
J5	Other food at school	1·09 ± 1·10	− 0·35 ± 0·28
J6	Other meals away from home, dinners	1·08 ± 0·16	2·53 ± 0·45
J7	Other meals	0·91 ± 0·10	2·17 ± 0·25

TABLE 20 (*cont.*)

No.	Item	Working Class	Middle Class
K1	Drink (alcoholic and soft)	1·63 ± 0·13	0·96 ± 0·16
K2	Tobacco	0·76 ± 0·12	0·85 ± 0·16
K3	Cigarettes	0·94 ± 0·07	0·18 ± 0·12
L1	Rent	0·66 ± 0·09	0·57 ± 0·12
L2	House-purchase	1·89 ± 0·13	0·45 ± 0·11
M1	Coal	0·78 ± 0·07	0·86 ± 0·06
M2	Coke	1·35 ± 0·26	0·99 ± 0·20
M3	Oil	0·19 ± 0·18	0·76 ± 0·16
M4	Firewood, candles, etc.	0·66 ± 0·07	0·72 ± 0·09
M5	Gas, slot meter	0·43 ± 0·08	−0·07 ± 0·20
M6	other meter	1·89 ± 0·14	0·67 ± 0·07
M7	Gas fittings	1·93 ± 0·22	0·65 ± 0·13
M8	Electricity, slot meter, current	0·36 ± 0·14	0·14 ± 0·28
M9	fittings	0·63 ± 0·36	0
M10	other meter, current	1·57 ± 0·09	0·51 ± 0·06
M11	fittings	1·60 ± 0·95	0·13 ± 0·11
N1	Men's clothing	0·81 ± 0·04	1·27 ± 0·15
N2	Women's clothing	1·04 ± 0·04	1·35 ± 0·08
N3	Children's clothing	1·45 ± 0·12	1·74 ± 0·18
N4	Clothing repairs	1·43 ± 0·08	1·07 ± 0·12
N5	Boots and shoes	0·52 ± 0·03	0·91 ± 0·12
N6	Boots and shoes, repairs	0·80 ± 0·05	0·61 ± 0·06
O1	Soap	0·69 ± 0·04	0·48 ± 0·05
O2	Soda	0·81 ± 0·05	0·69 ± 0·06
O3	Ironmongery	1·55 ± 0·14	1·34 ± 0·15
O4	Brushes	1·18 ± 0·11	1·27 ± 0·29
O5	Crockery	1·29 ± 0·14	1·19 ± 0·17
O6	Drapery	1·76 ± 0·14	1·55 ± 0·11
O7	Furniture	1·41 ± 0·14	2·53 ± 0·19
O8	Carpets	2·36 ± 0·17	2·10 ± 0·26
O9	Other utensils	2·30 ± 0·17	1·49 ± 0·22
P1	Education and music lessons	1·54 ± 0·39	1·83 ± 0·49
P2	Newspapers	0·87 ± 0·14	0·61 ± 0·11
P3	Books	1·50 ± 0·07	1·10 ± 0·08
P4	Postages, telephone, telegrams	1·50 ± 0·06	0·82 ± 0·08
Q1	Cinemas	1·24 ± 0·06	0·57 ± 0·08
Q2	Theatres	2·02 ± 0·10	1·17 ± 0·09
Q3	Sports	1·59 ± 0·12	0·49 ± 0·10
	Travel to and from work:		
R1	by rail: Season	1·68 ± 0·20	1·67 ± 0·30
R2	Cheap	1·33 ± 0·25	0·34 ± 0·49
R3	Other	1·42 ± 0·26	0·85 ± 0·21
R4	by bus, tram, coach, etc.	1·52 ± 0·12	0·63 ± 0·10
R5	Other travel by rail	1·82 ± 0·16	1·00 ± 0·12
R6	Other travel by bus, tram, coach, etc.	1·63 ± 0·11	0·65 ± 0·09
S1	Doctor	1·62 ± 0·17	1·58 ± 0·18
S2	Medicine	1·35 ± 0·09	0·85 ± 0·07
S3	Chemists' sundries	2·11 ± 0·12	0·63 ± 0·09
S4	Hairdresser	1·54 ± 0·06	1·05 ± 0·09
T1	Laundry	2·01 ± 0·11	1·04 ± 0·07
T2	Wages for domestic help	2·38 ± 0·28	1·38 ± 0·08
T3	Payments to hospital funds	1·08 ± 0·09	1·16 ± 0·15
T4	Trade Union, Friendly Society, etc., subscription	1·05 ± 0·09	0·92 ± 0·14
T5	Unemployment, N.H. Insurance	0·64 ± 0·07	−0·12 ± 0·10
T6	Payments to pension funds	1·24 ± 0·07	1·66 ± 0·09
T7	Licences	1·62 ± 0·17	1·37 ± 0·16
T8	Food for animals	1·60 ± 0·17	1·01 ± 0·18
T9	Holiday expenditure	2·61 ± 0·17	1·10 ± 0·23
T10	All other expenditure	—	—

the two surveys differ. To obtain estimates of the proportions at the income of the population of Britain in 1938 these values should be adjusted by the elasticities given in Table 20. An example of such an application has been given in §4.4.

The elasticities for the various items are given in Table 20. For the non-foods items the calculations have been straightforward with the exception of the clothing items, in which expenditure on children's clothing per child has been treated as the dependent variable, and similarly for women's and men's clothing. The elasticities are given with their standard errors.†

For food items the elasticity varies with income and, in order to allow a comparison between the independent estimates provided by the two samples, the elasticity has always been evaluated at an income of £100 per person per year, which is close to the 1938 average. The confidence limits given in the table are proportional to the standard errors of the regression coefficient.

The figures in the two tables speak for themselves and do not require detailed comment. For a more summary comparison of the inquiries the following percentages of total expenditure may be of interest (the working-class figure is given first): on food, 39 and 23; on housing, both 12; on clothing, both 9; on fuel and light, 6 and 8; on other items, 32 and 49. It will be seen that the elasticities as estimated from the two inquiries are very similar, and only in comparatively few cases do significant differences arise. These will be considered in discussing social-class effects in Chapter 11.

TABLE 21. EQUATIONS USED IN THE CALCULATIONS GIVEN IN TABLES 12 AND 13

Commodity / Form	Double-log (7.16)	Log-inverse (7.17)
Farinaceous	$\log v/n = 0.612 + 0.359 \log v_0/n$	$\log v/n = 1.40 - 8.07 n/v_0$
Dairy	$\log v/n = 0.427 + 0.529 \log v_0/n$	$\log v/n = 1.60 - 12.3 n/v_0$
Vegetables	$\log v/n = -0.196 + 0.617 \log v_0/n$	$\log v/n = 1.16 - 13.8 n/v_0$
Fruit	$\log v/n = -1.45 + 1.20 \log v_0/n$	$\log v/n = 1.19 - 27.0 n/v_0$
Fish	$\log v/n = -0.859 + 0.836 \log v_0/n$	$\log v/n = 0.975 - 18.5 n/v_0$
Meat	$\log v/n = 0.159 + 0.692 \log v_0/n$	$\log v/n = 1.69 - 15.9 n/v_0$

Commodity / Form	Semi-log (7.18)	Linear (7.19)	Hyperbola (7.20)
Farinaceous	$v/n = -8.44 + 15.0 \log v_0/n$	$v/n = 12.9 + 0.080 v_0/n$	$v/n = 24.2 - 319 n/v_0$
Dairy	$v/n = -24.1 + 27.1 \log v_0/n$	$v/n = 14.5 + 0.145 v_0/n$	$v/n = 35.2 - 586 n/v_0$
Vegetables	$v/n = -11.6 + 11.2 \log v_0/n$	$v/n = 4.23 + 0.062 v_0/n$	$v/n = 12.7 - 231 n/v_0$
Fruit	$v/n = -18.8 + 13.7 \log v_0/n$	$v/n = 0.117 + 0.083 v_0/n$	$v/n = 10.7 - 226 n/v_0$
Fish	$v/n = -10.1 + 8.29 \log v_0/n$	$v/n = 1.61 + 0.045 v_0/n$	$v/n = 7.76 - 166 n/v_0$
Meat	$v/n = -40.8 + 37.5 \log v_0/n$	$v/n = 12.9 + 0.196 v_0/n$	$v/n = 41.0 - 801 n/v_0$

† Where the coefficient was found to be less than its standard error, this has been shown as zero.

CHAPTER 8

QUALITY VARIATIONS IN THE CONSUMPTION PATTERN

8.1. THE NATURE OF QUALITY VARIATIONS

8.11. INTRODUCTION

It will now be apparent to the reader, as it has been to most of those who have previously examined family-budget records, that the items recorded in schedules of household expenditures are not uniform homogeneous commodities but represent aggregates of more or less closely related substitutes. This is true even of comparatively precise commodities such as tea, which was the example used by Marshall in discussing the topic which is the subject matter of this chapter:

> The question where the lines of division between different commodities should be drawn must be settled by convenience of the particular discussion. For some purposes it may be best to regard Chinese and Indian teas, or even Souchong and Pekoe teas, as different commodities; and to have a separate demand schedule for each of them. While for other purposes it may be best to group together commodities as distinct as beef and mutton, or even as tea and coffee, and to have a single list to represent the demand for the two combined, but in such a case, of course, some convention must be made as to the number of ounces of tea which are taken as equivalent to a pound of coffee.†

In the analysis of family budgets the degree of aggregation of the commodities is largely determined by the number of items to be included in the schedule of expenditures. Whether the data are collected at an interview or by means of an account book, and however great the number of items originally distinguished by the householder, the analyst must limit the number of items if he is to present a list of manageable dimensions. In the two British inquiries examined here some 150 items of expenditure were distinguished, but that this is by no means the maximum is shown by the Dutch inquiry‡ of 1935–6 where over 500 items of expenditure were distinguished; in the investigations below it will be necessary to refer to this more complete inquiry.

In the remainder of this section the causes of price variations among varieties of ostensibly the same commodity will be considered in some detail. In the following section it will be shown that these variations in the quality of a commodity can be summarized in terms of a 'quality elasticity' which is quite analogous to, and complements, the expenditure elasticity derived in the previous chapter. The third and fourth sections of this chapter are concerned with the formulation and investi-

---

† Marshall, *Principles*, p. 100 n.   ‡ To be referred to as *Huishoudrekeningen*.

gation of a hypothesis describing the systematic variation of the average price paid for a commodity with the income and size of the household. This leads to the formulation of a quality equation which in the fifth section is combined with the results of our investigations of the Engel curve. In the final section the argument is summarized, and measures of the quality elasticities are given for the items in the British budgets.[†]

8.12. CAUSES OF PRICE VARIATIONS

An item of expenditure in a family-budget schedule is to be regarded as the sum of a number of varieties of the commodity each of different quality and sold at a different price. But the different prices which are recorded in family-budget surveys as having been paid for the same commodity arises not only from quality differences but also from a number of other causes which must be considered here if the evidence of price variations in family budgets is to be correctly interpreted.

The first of these causes is the existence of regional variations in the price of a commodity which may affect its component varieties. This will be important for agricultural products as between town and country; for coal as between Newcastle and London; and for water, gas and electricity charges which, before the war, varied considerably according to the municipality. If the commodity can be defined precisely, as, for example, electric current, it will be possible to use family-budget material for the estimation of elasticities with respect to price,[‡] and where similar regional variations are of importance the analysis of this chapter cannot be applied without considerable modification.

The second reason for differences in prices is that there may be discrimination in the prices charged to rich and poor. This mainly occurs in the purchase of services, the classical example being doctor's services. In the majority of commodities for which it is possible to obtain information on prices by means of family-budget surveys there is little scope for the operation of this factor.

The third reason is that there may be differences in the accompanying services purchased together with the commodity. These arise in a number of ways that may not be at all obvious to the consumer: in small local shops extra payment is made for individual attention and the convenience of location; again, payment must be made for the guarantee of quality implied by a trade mark. Discounts for bulk purchases are of the same nature, since the customer (at the margin) gives up the convenience of buying in small quantities. These accompanying services may for the purposes of this chapter be regarded as variations in the quality of the commodity.

[†] It may be noted that at the same time as this approach to quality variations was being formulated in Cambridge two other investigators were proceeding along essentially similar lines in Holland and the United States. The reader may find it of interest to compare these three independent approaches as given by Black (1952), Houthakker and Prais (1952) and Theil (1952*b*). The account in the present chapter has, of course, been influenced by the results of Black and Theil.

[‡] Cf. Houthakker (1951) for the estimation of elasticities from a regional analysis.

A particular kind of price variation, which from the point of view of this chapter is to be treated as a variation in quality, is that of seasonal differences in the prices of, say, strawberries. Richer households may be able to buy strawberries in seasons of scarcity while poorer households will only buy in times of plenty; this will be shown in an annual inquiry into their expenditures by the higher average prices paid for the commodity by the richer households. Though winter strawberries may be the same as summer strawberries as far as concerns their material characteristics, from the point of view of economic analysis they are distinct commodities which are treated as different varieties of the same commodity only as a convenient practical simplification.

The notion of the quality of a commodity is in essence multi-dimensional, and its complete specification may well be a laborious matter in most cases. However, in so far as differences in the quality of a commodity are voluntarily chosen by the consumer in a market supposed to be in equilibrium, these multi-dimensional elements are brought under the measuring rod of money. Provided regional variations are not important the average price paid for the commodity may therefore be taken as an indicator of quality variations, and in an economic analysis it is the average price paid that it will be necessary to explain.

8.13. THE RECORDING OF PRICE INFORMATION

The average prices which are given in Part III are calculated by dividing expenditure on the commodity by the quantity bought. It is only where both these sets of information are collected that it is possible to undertake the kind of analysis presented in this chapter. In general, it may be said that the importance of collecting both quantity and expenditure information has for long been emphasized by those who use the results of family-budget surveys,† but that those who have had the task of organizing these inquiries and presenting their results have been content to provide only one set. Where the interest lay in nutritional considerations the accent has been on quantities; where the main purpose has been to provide weights for a cost-of-living index the accent has been on expenditures.

Cost-of-living index numbers are generally based on the variations in the prices of a number of standard varieties of commodities chosen so that they can be easily defined and are likely to remain unchanged on the market for long periods of time. In fact, these standard varieties will be purchased by only a minority of households; changes in the average prices actually paid by households of a particular income group, though no doubt closely related to the changes in the prices of the standard varieties, may well be different on account of the variations in the average prices paid which, as can be seen from the figures in Part III, are quite substantial for many commodities. The subject

† See for example, Staehle (1934, p. 350).

requires further investigation from this point of view; the interested reader will find some pertinent investigations in the recent work of von Hofsten (1952), where it is shown that quality variations have an economically significant effect on the calculated value of the index number.

A final point that requires mentioning under this head is that the availability of both quantity and expenditure information provides a valuable cross-check on the reliability of the information. By computing the price as a ratio of these two it has on occasion been found possible to throw out extreme observations as being due to errors of recording. It is greatly to be hoped that future budget collections will be so organized that both quantity and expenditure information is made available to the analyst.

8.2. THE MEASUREMENT OF QUALITY VARIATIONS

It follows from the point of view adopted here that the quality, as measured by the average price paid, as well as the quantity of the commodity, will vary with the standard of living of the household, that is, with its income level and household size and composition. The change in expenditure on a commodity in response to a change in any parameter can be decomposed into a change in quantity and a change in quality, thus

$$\delta v_i = p_i \delta q_i + q_i \delta p_i. \tag{8.1}$$

This expression leads naturally to the concept of a quality elasticity with respect to, say, income which has the property that the sum of the quantity and quality elasticities is equal to the expenditure elasticity. This follows from (8.1) on dividing the left-hand side by v_i and the right-hand side by $p_i q_i$ and taking the derivative with respect to income, v_0. Thus

$$\frac{v_0}{v_i}\frac{\partial v_i}{\partial v_0} = \frac{v_0}{q_i}\frac{\partial q_i}{\partial v_0} + \frac{v_0}{p_i}\frac{\partial p_i}{\partial v_0}. \tag{8.2}$$

Similar expressions hold, of course, with respect to variations in household size.

The last term on the right-hand side of (8.2) may be taken as the measure of quality variations. It is termed the quality elasticity to avoid confusion with the conventional price elasticities which refer to changes in the prices of the individual varieties.

A useful way of looking at (8.2) is to note that the quantity elasticity may be derived as the difference between the expenditure elasticity and the quality elasticity. This means that if, when dealing with aggregates of commodities, it is required for some particular purpose to obtain a measure of the change in the physical quantity consumed, it is unnecessary to consider the variations in the physical quantity of each commodity separately, provided that the quality elasticity of the aggregate is measured in addition to the expenditure elasticity. This has two applications: first, in nutritional investigations where the accent is always on quantities consumed rather than on expenditure; and secondly, in demand analyses based on time series. In the latter the income elasticities from family budgets, which are used to correct time-series of consumption for the effects of income variations, should be adjusted for the quality effect, since the time series are generally estimated by weighting a number of quantity series with constant prices.

8.3. The Quality Equation

It is the purpose of this section to establish the nature of the equation describing quality variations, and it is therefore to be regarded as complementary to the investigations of the previous chapter on the form of the Engel curve. The much greater regularity of the data here, however, allows of briefer and more conclusive investigations.

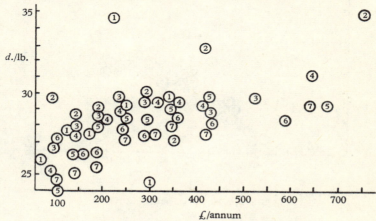

Fig. 11. Average prices paid for tea by British working-class households, 1938.

8.31. VARIATIONS IN THE PRICE PAID FOR TEA

It is convenient to begin by presenting in Fig. 11 a scatter diagram, based on the working-class budgets, of the average price paid for tea against the income of the household. The household size as measured by the number of persons is indicated against each point. From this figure a number of observations emerge. The first is the comparatively wide variation in the prices, a fact on which in earlier chapters it has been possible to speculate only on theoretical grounds. Most of the prices lie within a range of 5d., between 2s. 1d. and 2s. 6d. per pound, though there are points lying outside this range some of which can no doubt be attributed to errors of measurement. In substance, however, there can be little doubt as to the quantitative significance of quality variations in this example.

The second point to notice is that not only do qualities vary with income, but household size also has a systematic influence. At a given income, households of smaller size buy more expensive varieties of tea.

8.32. A SEMI-LOGARITHMIC RELATIONSHIP

The fact that income and household size have inverse effects on quality leads to the adoption of a procedure akin to the homogeneity hypothesis introduced in §7.4 above. In this case the average price paid is plotted against income per person, and as can be seen from Fig. 12 this allows substantially for the effects of household size. It is important to notice not only that the scatter of the points is considerably reduced by this transformation, but also that points referring to households of different sizes now lie randomly about the regression line.

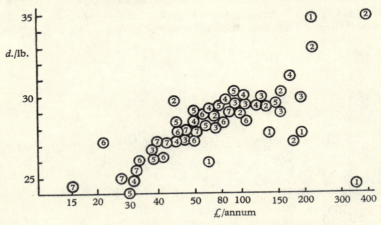

Fig. 12. Average prices paid for tea and logarithm of total expenditure per person in British working-class households, 1938.

The degree of variation in the dependent variable in the quality equation is smaller than that in a typical Engel curve, with the result that it was much easier to find an algebraic function to represent the data. On the basis of a study of Dutch budgets† a semi-logarithmic relation

$$p = \alpha + \beta \log v_0/n \qquad (8.3)$$

was adopted. The investigations are presented in a paper by the authors published in *Économie Appliquée* (1952), and it is not necessary to repeat the argument here. For the present purposes, in addition to the example of tea given above, it is hoped that one further diagram should suffice to demonstrate the *prima facie* adequacy of (8.3) as a description of quality variations.

8.33. AN INDEX OF THE QUALITY OF ALL FOOD

For this the quality of all food for which quantity information was available has been calculated as an index number, weighting the

† See *Huishoudrekeningen*, II, pp. 40–2.

quantities purchased by mean and actual prices to give a 'Laspeyres' index of quality variations.

$$P_i = \frac{\Sigma q_0 p_i}{\Sigma q_0 p_0},\qquad(8.4)$$

where the summation extends over the commodities, the suffix o indicating the mean value for all households and the suffix i the particular household. This gives a measure of the average quality variations of all food items. It should be remembered, however, that only about three-quarters of the total expenditure on food is covered by the above index

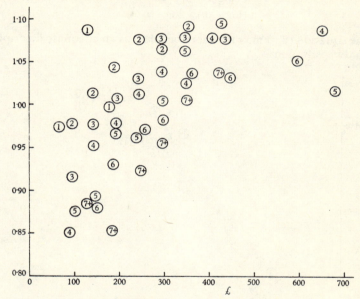

Fig. 13. Quality of all food and total expenditure in British working-class households, 1938.

number, and it may well be that quality variations are even more pronounced for the remaining quarter for which no quantity information was collected.

For some purposes, and this will be seen more clearly in the following chapters, the index number (8.4) provides a measure on which it is possible to base comparisons of standards of living of households in different circumstances, for it attempts to isolate the quality element in consumption from the quantity element. The latter depends on the specific needs and the composition of the household and cannot accordingly be directly used as a measure of welfare or the standard of living. It is therefore worth demonstrating the regularity of the behaviour of this index both when plotted against household income as in Fig. 13 and against the logarithm of income per person as in Fig. 14.

K

The degree of variation both with respect to income and with respect to household size is quite marked. An evaluation of the parameters of (8.3) for the quality index yields

$$p = 0.54 + 0.26(\pm 0.01) \log v_0/n, \tag{8.5}$$

with a correlation coefficient of 0.92. The linearity of the scatter may be judged from the diagram. From (8.5) the quality elasticity may be derived, at the mean values of the sample, as

$$\frac{d(\log p)}{d(\log v_0/n)} = \frac{0.26}{\log_e 10} = 0.11. \tag{8.6}$$

The equation (8.3) may therefore be taken as an adequate description of quality variations.

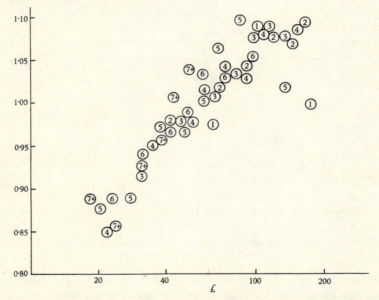

Fig. 14. Quality of all food and logarithm of total expenditure per person in British working-class households, 1938.

8.4. SOME FURTHER INVESTIGATIONS

In this section the formulation of the behaviour of consumers with regard to quality variations will be elaborated in two directions. The first will provide a further test of the adequacy of the algebraic relationship (8.3), and the second will seek to investigate more closely the nature of quality variations as commodity groups are subdivided.

8.41. COVARIANCE ANALYSIS WITH RESPECT TO HOUSEHOLD SIZE

First, it may be noted that (8.3) can be written as

$$p = (\alpha - \beta \log n) + \beta \log v_0, \tag{8.7}$$

so that if this equation is fitted separately to households of each size group an estimate should be obtained of the same coefficient β. On the other hand, the constant term in the equation should vary systematically with household size. This was investigated for the data on tea depicted in Fig. 12 above. Since the data were only available as classified in the fifty-four groups (as explained in §3.4), some of the individual equations are rather unreliable. This is especially true of the equations for households of size one and two for which the correlation coefficient in only 0·2. The results of the calculations are given in Table 22.

TABLE 22. REGRESSION OF PRICE OF TEA ON TOTAL HOUSE-HOLD EXPENDITURE FOR DIFFERENT HOUSEHOLD SIZES

Household size	Equation	Correlation coefficient	Number of groups	Number of households
1	$p = 0·66 - 0·076 \log v_0$	$-0·22$	6	35
2	$p = 0·39 + 0·019 \log v_0$	0·23	8	494
3	$p = 0·19 + 0·072 \log v_0$	0·89	8	629
4	$p = 0·12 + 0·090 \log v_0$	0·96	8	487
5	$p = 0·11 + 0·090 \log v_0$	0·86	8	285
6	$p = 0·18 + 0·067 \log v_0$	0·82	8	138
$\geqslant 7$	$p = 0·05 + 0·101 \log v_0$	0·94	8	153

While there appear to be differences between the estimates the question arises whether, in view of the differing degrees of reliability associated with these estimates, the differences should be judged as significant. A simple comparison of only two of the equations by themselves would not be an adequate test, since it may be only when viewed as a whole are the differences significant; the question can, however, be answered satisfactorily by an analysis of covariance. This proceeds as follows.

An estimate of the residual variability of the data may be obtained by considering the composite sums of squares of the residuals about the individual regression lines. This estimate will be based on $(54 - 14)$ degrees of freedom, since seven regression lines have been fitted, each with two parameters. Another estimate of the residual variability of the data may be obtained by fitting lines with the same slope (but not, of course, with the same intercept) to each household size, the slope being estimated by pooling the covariances of all household sizes. The estimate of the residual variability based on the sum of squares of deviations about these lines will be based on $(54 - 8)$ degrees of freedom, since eight parameters (seven constants and one regression slope) have been fitted to the data.

The difference between these two sums of squares provides a third estimate, based on 6 degrees of freedom, which is independent of the first estimate, and these may therefore be compared by the variance ratio test. The analysis is set out in Table 23.

TABLE 23. ANALYSIS OF COVARIANCE FOR
QUALITY OF TEA

Variations due to	Degrees of freedom	Sums of squares	Quotient
Deviations from individual regressions	40	0·3146	0·00786
Differences between regressions	6	0·0407	0·00679
Deviations from pooled regressions	46	0·3553	0·00772

The ratio 0·00786/0·00679 is equal to 1·16. Entering a table of the distribution of the variance ratio, with 40 and 6 degrees of freedom, it is seen that a value as high as this may be obtained by chance very frequently indeed; the value of the variance ratio which is significant at the 20 % level is 1·95.

It might be thought that in view of the large scatterance of the first two household size groups the calculating should be repeated omitting these values. The calculations for this are accordingly set out in Table 24.

TABLE 24. ANALYSIS OF COVARIANCE FOR QUALITY OF TEA,
OMITTING HOUSEHOLDS OF SIZE ONE AND TWO

Variations due to	Degrees of freedom	Sums of squares	Quotient
Deviations from individual regressions	32	0·06520	0·002037
Differences between regressions	4	0·00502	0·001254
Deviations from pooled regressions	36	0·07022	0·001950

While the estimates of the residual variance are in this case smaller, the variance ratio is 1·62, which, again, may be judged to be not significant.

The same slope may therefore be fitted to the equation for each household size. This slope was found to be $\bar{b} = 0·0713$. The constant terms for each household size may then be evaluated. If these are denoted by a_n (for $n = 1, ..., 7$), inspection of (8.4) will show that the values of $a_n + \bar{b} \log n$ should be constant. This is shown to be approximately true by the values given in Table 25.

The above analysis shows that no significant information is lost if consumers' behaviour with regard to quality variations is represented by the single equation (8.3) rather than by a whole set of equations such as in Table 22. It would, of course, be rash to rely merely on the covariance analysis in support of such a conclusion; it should be regarded as an adjunct to the other consideration.

The approach to a problem through the analysis of covariance is one that can usefully be adopted in analysing many of the problems treated in this monograph by other possibly more curt and less rigorous methods. The above may therefore serve as an example of the way in which the applicability of an equation may be subject to a statistical test.†

TABLE 25. AVERAGE HEIGHT OF THE QUALITY EQUATIONS FOR TEA

Household size (n)	a_n	$a_n + \bar{b} \log n$
1	0·388	0·431
2	0·417	0·482
3	0·405	0·482
4	0·401	0·487
5	0·392	0·485
6	0·380	0·479
≥7	0·369	0·479

8.42. VARIATIONS IN THE QUALITY OF THE VARIETIES OF A COMMODITY

The second subject to be considered in this section is the way in which quality changes take place in the consumers' budget. While in theory a sufficiently refined schedule of expenditures should show items as being bought at the same price by all income groups, it may be questioned whether the required degree of refinement can be achieved in practice.

To cast some light on this matter an examination was made of the results of the more detailed collection of budgets in Holland already referred to above‡ with regard to expenditure on three food items: fruit, vegetables and cheese. The first of these items was subdivided into seven major varieties,§ and the other two were each subdivided into six major varieties; the average quantity purchased and the average price paid was given for seven income groups. Inspection of the data showed that the average price paid for each of the varieties rose regularly through the income range (on occasion the prices rose rather more regularly than did the average quantity purchased). In the case of fruit, for example, the quality elasticity for all fruit was 0·19, while the quality elasticities for the individual varieties were as follows: cooking apples and pears, 0·19; eating apples and pears, 0·30; citrus fruits, 0·15; stone fruits, 0·17; berries, 0·16; bananas, 0·05; dried fruits (raisins, figs and dates), 0·21. The rise in the average price paid for fruit cannot therefore be attributed merely to a shift towards the more expensive varieties when these are only distinguished according to broad characteristics.

† For another application of the analysis of covariance to family budget data, see Stuvel and James (1950).

‡ The data are from *Huishoudrekeningen*, vol. II, pp. 68 et seq.

§ Forty-four minor varieties were also distinguished; there is ample scope here for further analysis.

The next question to be answered was whether, as income increased, in addition to the purchase of better qualities of each variety there was also a significant shift towards the purchase of the more expensive varieties of a commodity. To take once again the example of fruit, the cheapest variety in terms of cost per unit is cooking apples and pears; the most expensive variety is dried fruits (the order of expensiveness of the other varieties is as given in the last paragraph). The order is the same at the top and the bottom income group and may be compared with the order of the varieties based on the proportionate increase in consumption between the bottom and top income groups. If, as income rose, in addition to buying better qualities of each variety, consumers also shifted towards more expensive varieties, this should be shown by a positive correlation between the two orderings.

The method of rank correlation is an adequate tool for this purpose, and Kendall's τ was computed which, surprisingly, gave a negative value of -0.05. The value is, of course, not significant: a table of the distribution of τ shows that such a value occurs with a probability of 50 % when the true value of the correlation is zero.

As far as fruit is concerned, therefore, changes in quality take place in the individual varieties, and there is no additional shift towards the more expensive varieties.

TABLE 26. RANK CORRELATION BETWEEN INCREASE IN CON-
SUMPTION AND EXPENSIVENESS OF VARIETIES, DUTCH
HOUSEHOLDS, 1935–6

Commodity	τ	P
Fruit	-0.05	0.50
Vegetables	$+0.33$	0.24
Cheese	$+0.47$	<0.001

Such a conclusion can have no general validity, since it must be recognized that many varieties of a commodity are inferior with respect to income and some are distinct 'luxury' varieties. The importance of the conclusion for the present argument, however, is to show that in order to obtain schedules of items that are homogeneous with respect to price a very much finer classification than usually found will be required.

The corresponding correlations for the six varieties of vegetables and the six varieties of cheese were computed, and the results are set out in Table 26. The third column, headed P, gives the probability of finding a value of τ as high as that in the second column if the true value of τ is zero.

In the case of cheese and vegetables it can be seen that there is a shift towards the more expensive varieties as income rises, but as is shown by the case of fruit, no general law can be formulated.

8.5. COMBINATION WITH THE ENGEL CURVE

If the average price paid for a commodity rises with the standard of living of the household, the quantity bought will rise less rapidly than the expenditure on the commodity. It is useful to illustrate this as in Fig. 15, which shows both the expenditure on bacon and ham and the quantity bought as varying with income per person.

The observations marked on the diagram are averages of about two hundred households and are obtained from the working-class data by amalgamating groups which have approximately equal values of income per person.

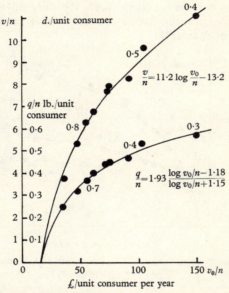

Fig. 15. Expenditure and quantity Engel curves for bacon and ham, based on British working-class households, 1938.

In the case of foodstuffs the combination of the expenditure and quality equations leads to a particularly attractive formulation for the quantity equation. As has been seen in Chapter 7 the Engel curve for foodstuffs is well represented by the semi-logarithmic equation

$$v_i/n = \alpha_i + \beta_i \log v_0/n. \tag{8.8}$$

If the corresponding equation describing price variations is

$$p_i = \gamma_i + \delta_i \log v_0/n, \tag{8.9}$$

it follows from the identity $v_i = p_i q_i$ that the equation describing quantity variations is

$$\frac{q_i}{n} = \frac{\alpha_i + \beta_i \log v_0/n}{\gamma_i + \delta_i \log v_0/n}, \tag{8.10}$$

which is more conveniently written as

$$\frac{q_i}{n} = A_i \frac{B_i + \log v_0/n}{C_i + \log v_0/n}, \tag{8.11}$$

where A_i, B_i and C_i are respectively equal to β_i/δ_i, α_i/β_i and γ_i/δ_i. From (8.11) it can be seen that the quantity equation has an asymptotic level equal to A_i, but this is not true of the expenditure equation. As can be seen from the diagram there are, however, no observations for this commodity which are in the vicinity of the asymptotic level and accordingly no great confidence can be placed in the calculated value.

A similar diagram could, of course, be drawn even if the Engel curve did not have the convenient form (8.8): the only difference would be that the implied expression for the quantity curve might be of a more complicated form than (8.11).

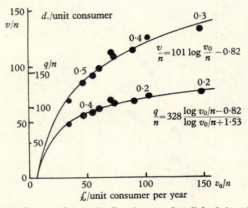

Fig. 16. Expenditure and quantity Engel curves for all food, based on British working-class households, 1938.

The elasticity has been marked at a number of points along both curves, and this diagram may therefore serve to emphasize some conclusions of this and the previous chapter. These are: (*a*) that the income elasticity of expenditure on foodstuffs decreases with income and is inversely proportional to the level of income; (*b*) the elasticity of quantity bought is less than the elasticity of expenditure at any given income level; and (*c*) as income rises there is an increasing 'gap' between the increase in expenditure on the commodity and the increase in the quantity bought.

Finally, having shown in Fig. 14 above the values of the index of the average quality of all foods, there are shown in Fig. 16 the expenditure and quantity Engel curves for all food, where quantity is measured as an index with a mean value of 100. Again, only about three-quarters of all expenditure on foodstuffs is covered since quantity information is not available for the remainder.

8.6. QUALITY ELASTICITIES BASED ON THE BRITISH BUDGETS

Quantity information is given in Part III only for some thirty items of food apart from some fuel items which are of no great interest in this connexion and for tobacco and cigarettes for which the information is unreliable. The information is only available for the working-class collection.

The elasticities presented in Table 27 differ from the corresponding expenditure elasticities given in the previous chapter in that they are here, in effect, evaluated at the average values of income per person for the sample and not at the average value for the population. Since the elasticities are small this is of negligible importance, for if the form (8.3) holds then the variation in the elasticity due to a change in the income level may be measured by considering the elasticity of the elasticity; thus from (8.3)

$$\epsilon_i = \frac{v_0}{p_i}\frac{dp_i}{dv_0} = \frac{\beta_i}{p_i} \tag{8.12}$$

and

$$\frac{v_0}{\epsilon_i}\frac{d\epsilon}{dv_0} = -\frac{v_0}{\epsilon_i}\frac{\beta_i}{p_i^2}\frac{dp_i}{dv_0} = -\frac{v_0}{\epsilon_i}\frac{\beta_i}{p_i^2}\frac{\beta_i}{v_0} = -\epsilon_i, \tag{8.13}$$

assuming that natural logarithms are used in (8.3). In words, the elasticity of the elasticity is equal to the negative of the elasticity. Hence only if the elasticity is large will it be sensitive to variations in the income level. For small elasticities it will also be true that the estimate at the mean income is relatively insensitive to the form of the regression equation adopted in the calculations.

On grounds of convenience, associated with the availability of an appropriate programme for the electronic computer, the elasticities in Table 27 have been computed from a double logarithmic formula. The standard errors which follow the coefficients after the sign $\pm$ have therefore been calculated in the conventional manner. Some experimental calculations show that if an estimate is required which is applicable to the mean income of the population in 1938, it is generally more than sufficient to reduce the second decimal place by a unit. No estimates are given for oatmeal, sugar and coffee, since the standard errors exceeded the values of the elasticities.

An inspection of Table 27 gives quantitative expression to facts which, no doubt, are well known. First, quality variations are of importance in meat and fish items, where they form a considerable proportion of the total variation in expenditure on these commodities. In the nature of the case there must always be considerable variation in the varieties of these commodities that are available on the market. Secondly, the item summarily termed 'cake mixture' is an agglomeration of a number of related products sold generally under trade-marks (Part III may be consulted for a more precise description of the items covered), and the scope for quality variations is shown by the high value of the elasticity.

Thirdly, for the remainder of the items the effect of quality variations is on the whole significant and always positive. In magnitude, however, their importance is not as great, being generally less than a fifth.

Had data been available for non-food items the effect of quality variations would probably be seen to be greater, but the absence of data is no doubt only a reflexion of the difficulty of defining a homogeneous commodity when quality variations are large.

TABLE 27. QUALITY ELASTICITIES BASED ON THE BRITISH WORKING-CLASS BUDGET COLLECTION

No.	Item	Quality elasticity	No.	Item	Quality elasticity
C1	Flour	0·18±0·02	E5	Jam	0·25±0·07
C2	Cake mixture	0·33±0·10	F1	Apples	0·14±0·02
C4	Rice	0·07±0·04	F2	Oranges	0·13±0·02
C6	Bread	0·04±0·01	F3	Bananas	0·03±0·02
C7	Biscuits	0·23±0·03	G1	Potatoes	0·13±0·02
D1	Milk, fresh	0·09±0·01	G4	Onions	0·02±0·02
D2	Milk, skimmed	0·23±0·16	G5	Dried legumes	0·05±0·04
D3	Milk, condensed	0·02±0·03	H1	Fish, fresh	0·29±0·03
D6	Butter	0·01±0·01	H3	Fish, dried	0·25±0·06
D7	Margarine	0·07±0·01	I1	Beef, fresh	0·18±0·03
D8	Lard	0·02±0·01	I2	Beef, frozen	0·20±0·03
D9	Cheese	0·05±0·02	I3	Mutton, fresh	0·28±0·04
D10	Eggs	0·07±0·01	I4	Mutton, frozen	0·21±0·04
D11	Suet	0·08±0·03	I5	Pork	0·13±0·03
E1	Tea	0·06±0·01	I6	Bacon	0·13±0·01
E3	Cocoa	0·02±0·02	I7	Sausages	0·28±0·03

International comparisons of quality elasticities[†] emphasize the relativity of the measure to the nature of the market. Thus in Holland where many varieties of cheese are commonly bought the quality elasticity for cheese is 0·20, while in Britain it is only 0·05, reflecting the predominance of the Cheddar variety. Again, the greater varieties of tea drunk in India (the green tea frequently indulged in there is practically unknown in this country) may well account for a quality elasticity of 0·25 as against 0·06 in Britain.

† For further details see Houthakker and Prais (1952, pp. 76–7).

CHAPTER 9

HOUSEHOLD COMPOSITION AND UNIT-CONSUMER SCALES

9.1. INTRODUCTION

9.11. THE OBJECT OF THIS CHAPTER

The object of this chapter is to investigate the effects of household composition on consumption patterns. By 'household composition' is here meant the age and sex of the members of the household, though the method adopted can be applied to analyse the differential effects of blue-eyed from green-eyed persons and, more practically, the effects of occupation by regarding manual and sedentary workers as different types of persons. From the point of view adopted in previous chapters, the analysis of the effects of household composition arises as a refinement of the analysis of the effects of household size on consumption and as such would eventually lead to more accurate estimates of income elasticities and the like. In particular, in basing analyses of demand on time series of aggregate consumption, our results would be of use in correcting for possible changes in the age structure of the population.

But there is another point of view from which the analysis of household composition is of altogether a more crucial significance, and that is in considering the standard of living of households of different composition. The standard of living may be a tenuous concept, but judgements involving it are unavoidable in rationalizing, for example, policies on the level of allowances for children for income-tax purposes. The same topic was discussed by the recent Royal Commission on Population in whose deliberations the 'cost of a child', or the effect of an additional child on the standard of living of the household, played a considerable role.

In consequence, the implications of the method and results of this chapter for economic policy require the careful appraisal which must, however, lie outside the scope of this volume. The developments both in the theoretical and numerical analysis of the effects of household composition presented in this chapter have resulted from what is—elliptically—termed an objective approach to the problem. The question asked in this study is, 'How in fact does household composition influence consumption patterns?', rather than 'How should consumption be affected by composition?', which is a question often asked by nutritionists. In other words, this chapter investigates how a household, after having given whatever degree of consideration its members think appropriate to the various calls on the household's purse, eventually arranges its expenditure, and how that arrangement varies with the composition of the household. It is a record of the behaviour of the households and not a prescription as to their optimum behaviour.

9.12. A BRIEF SURVEY OF THE LITERATURE

The method of measuring household size by scales of equivalent-adults, man-values or unit-consumers (which is the terminology adopted here) consists in regarding a child, say, as equivalent to a fraction of a man. This method was already used by Engel who labelled the unit a *quet*, after the Belgian statistician Quetelet (*in piam memoriam*) who had so much influenced his attitude to quantitative research in his youth. The main problem is, of course, what are the appropriate fractions for each type of person and how they are to be determined.

Very many scales have been proposed, and there is a considerable literature and a variety of opinions on the subject. Some hold that the phenomena are too complicated to be treated by the simple device of a scale of equivalences and conclude that the problem is more or less insoluble, as Allen (1942), or that it requires a much more intensive investigation in which the device of a scale of equivalences is unnecessary and possibly misleading.†

The view adopted here is essentially that expressed by Sydenstricker and King (1921) in a fundamental paper on 'The measurement of the relative economic status of families'. In this paper many of the problems of principle and practice enountered in this work were expounded and given a satisfactory treatment. The paper was, however, almost entirely ignored in the subsequent literature, possibly due to the obscurity of expression inherent in a literary exposition of a slightly mathematical topic. For a thorough analysis of the reasons for this display of bad manners by posterity the reader should consult the paper by Ogburn (1931).‡

The discussion in this chapter will be in the following order. In the second section the theory of scales of equivalences is expounded and the main results are given in two theorems. Within this theoretical framework it is possible to review concisely some other approaches to the problem of measuring household composition, and this is done in the third section. The fourth section presents the main features of the method adopted here which required an iterative type of treatment of a non-linear equation. The results are given in the fifth section, and some summary conclusions are drawn in the final section.§

† See, for example, the view expressed by Mottram and Graham in Hutchinson's *Food and the Principles of Dietetics* (10th edition, 1948, p. 40).

‡ The method was independently revived by us, and it is with regret that we must admit that the contribution of Sydenstricker and King only came to our notice after the main features of the method had been worked out. Another attempt to revive the method has recently been made by Friedman (1952).

§ An excellent survey of economic consumption scales is given by Woodbury (1944); this paper brings together a number of estimates based on various methods and is a useful starting point for the student.

9.2. THE THEORY OF SCALES OF EQUIVALENCES

9.21. A RÉSUMÉ OF THE EFFECTS OF HOUSEHOLD SIZE

In analysing the differential effect of adding a person of a particular type to the household it is necessary to distinguish two stages in the calculation. There is, first, the question of how an increase merely in the number of persons in the household would affect consumption, all persons being of the same standard type. Once this has been determined it is possible to go to the second stage and ask how the addition of the person of the particular type would compare with that of a person of the standard type.

A provisional answer has been given to the first question in §7.42, where it was shown that if the 'homogeneity hypothesis' holds the different results could be classified according to the income elasticity of demand for the commodity. In particular, for commodities that are luxuries (income elasticity greater than unity) consumption will decline with an increase in household size. The implications of the earlier results are summarized in Table 28, and they should be kept in mind in assessing the approaches to be discussed below. In the case of luxuries, an analysis based merely on a regression of consumption on the numbers of the various types of persons in the households would give meaningless results; the types of persons that tended to occur in large households, such as children, would tend to have a negative coefficient associated with them.

TABLE 28. EFFECT OF AN INCREASE IN HOUSEHOLD SIZE ON CONSUMPTION

(Increase, + ; decrease, −)

Effect on	Inferior goods	Necessaries	Luxuries
Household consumption	+	+	−
Consumption per person	+	−	−

9.22. A FORMULATION OF SPECIFIC AND INCOME EFFECTS

The results given in Table 28 may be derived from the general equation of the Engel curve:

$$v_i/n = f_i(v_0/n), \tag{9.1}$$

where v_i represents the expenditure in the ith commodity, v_0 is the income of, and n is the number of persons in the household. If t types of persons are distinguished then, in refining this formulation, the dependent variable on the left-hand side should become expenditure per unit-consumer, where the number of unit-consumers is measured on the scale appropriate to the particular commodity considered. Thus if the commodity were women's clothing the scale would give unit weights to the number of women but zeros for the other types of person; in the case of foodstuffs it is to be expected that no coefficient will be zero, though some, for example, for young children, may be very small. Denoting by κ_{it} the value of the tth type of person on the unit-consumer scale for the ith commodity, and by n_t the number of persons of type t, the number of unit-consumers in the household is given by' $\sum\limits_{t=1}^{t} \kappa_{it} n_t$, or more simply by $\kappa_{iT} n_T$, where summation is to be understood over repeated capital suffixes (repeated lower-case suffixes are to be understood in the usual way). Accordingly the dependent variable is $v_i/\kappa_{iT} n_T$.

In this formulation, therefore, a different scale of unit-consumers is distinguished for each commodity, and the scale for the ith commodity may be termed the ith specific scale. It is to be expected that the scales will be similar for commodities that have physically similar characteristics, so that it will not be necessary in practice to distinguish a scale for each commodity, but it is important to do so at the conceptual stage.†

Equation (9.1) shows how expenditure on a particular commodity is determined by the income level or standard of living of the household as measured by the income available per person in the household. In the refined formulation this becomes income per unit-consumer, with the number of unit-consumers measured on an income scale which is independent of the commodity considered. The income scale postulated here is related to the specific scales—the precise relationship will shortly be discussed—but for particular commodities may be quite different. To take again the example of women's clothing, on this formulation the Engel curve would have as dependent variable, expenditure on clothing per woman in the household, and as the determining variable, something that may not be very different from income per person.‡

Denoting by κ_{0t} the value of the tth person on the income scale, the formulation of the Engel curve thus becomes

$$v_i/\kappa_{iT} n_T = f_i(v_0/\kappa_{0T} n_T). \tag{9.2}$$

9.23. THE EFFECTS OF A CHANGE IN HOUSEHOLD COMPOSITION

On the basis of this formulation the effect on the consumption of the ith commodity of the addition of a particular type of person to the household, say the tth type, can be derived in the form of a theorem. The result of this theorem is that the effect is approximately proportional to the difference between the value on the specific scale κ_{it}, and the product of the income elasticity for the commodity and the value on the income scale, $\eta_i \kappa_{0t}$. The precise result is demonstrated as follows.

† Many of the earlier arguments against the use of equivalence scales are really only against the use of a single scale for all commodities, with which arguments the present exposition is, of course, in sympathy.

‡ In the formulation of Friedman (1952) the income scale is always set equal to the specific scale for each commodity considered. This leads to obvious conceptual difficulties which he recognizes; see p. 19 of his article.

Note first that the income elasticity for the commodity is

$$\eta_i = \frac{v_0 \partial v_i}{v_i \partial v_0} = \frac{v_0}{v_i} \frac{\kappa_{iT} n_T}{\kappa_{0T} n_T} f_i', \tag{9.3}$$

where f_i' is the differential of f_i. Next, on differentiating v_i with respect to n_t there results

$$\frac{\partial v_i}{\partial n_t} = \kappa_{it} f_i - \kappa_{0t} v_0 \frac{\kappa_{iT} n_T}{(\kappa_{0T} n_T)^2} f_i'. \tag{9.4}$$

On substituting for f from (9.2) and for f' from (9.3), and dividing by v_i to give the proportionate change in consumption, the last expression simplifies to

$$\frac{1}{v_i} \frac{\partial v_i}{\partial n_t} = \frac{\kappa_{it}}{\kappa_{iT} n_T} - \frac{\kappa_{0t} \eta_i}{\kappa_{0T} n_T},$$

that is,

$$\frac{1}{v_i} \frac{\partial v_i}{\partial n_t} = \left(\kappa_{it} - \kappa_{0t} \eta_i \frac{\kappa_{iT} n_T}{\kappa_{0T} n_T} \right) \frac{1}{\kappa_{iT} n_T}. \tag{9.5}$$

The expression $\kappa_{iT} n_T / \kappa_{0T} n_T$ is the ratio of the number of unit consumers on the specific scale to the number on the income scale which will generally (but not always) be about unity, and the approximate statement of the theorem given above then follows. This piece of algebra should not be regarded as a precise statement of what happens,[†] but rather as an aid in the conceptual differentiation of the 'specific effect' of adding an extra person to the household from the 'income effect'.

9.24. THE RELATION BETWEEN INCOME AND SPECIFIC SCALES

The relationship between the income scale and the specific scales for each commodity must next be established. On an intuitive level the specific scales may be regarded as measuring the relative requirements of different types of persons for the various commodities, and judgements on the standard of living of households of different composition must in some way be based on a process of averaging the requirements for the various commodities. The relationship implied by the formulation (9.2) may be derived by taking into account the 'adding-up' proposition that income is always the sum of the expenditures.

This implies, first, that if income changes by a small amount dv_0, it will be absorbed by the consequent changes in expenditures so that

$$\sum_i \frac{\partial v_i}{\partial v_0} = 1. \tag{9.6}$$

Applying this to (9.2) there results

$$\sum_i \frac{\partial v_i}{\partial v_0} = \frac{f_I' \kappa_{IT} n_T}{\kappa_{0T} n_T} = 1, \tag{9.7}$$

where the capital I's and T's indicate summation of both other commodities and types of persons.

[†] This would be true even if the more realistic finite difference operators had been used; these lead to essentially the same results.

Secondly, it implies that if income is unchanged but household composition alters, then the resulting changes in expenditures must sum to zero. Hence, summing (9.4) over all items of expenditure gives

$$\sum_i \frac{\partial v_i}{\partial n_t} = \kappa_{It} f_I - \kappa_{0t} v_0 \frac{f_I' \kappa_{IT} n_T}{(\kappa_{0T} n_T)^2} = 0. \tag{9.8}$$

Using (9.7) this simplifies to

$$\kappa_{It} f_I - \frac{\kappa_{0t} v_0}{\kappa_{0T} n_T} = 0, \tag{9.9}$$

and on substituting for f_i from (9.2) an expression in κ_{0t} may be derived, thus

$$\kappa_{0t} = \sum_i \left(\kappa_{it} \frac{v_i}{v_0} \frac{\kappa_{0T} n_T}{\kappa_{iT} n_T} \right). \tag{9.10}$$

This shows the income scale as a weighted average of the specific scales, with weights approximately proportional to the expenditures on the commodities, the approximation depending again on the fact that $\kappa_{0T} n_T / \kappa_{iT} n_T$ is approximately equal to unity. A more rigorous interpretation of (9.10) is as follows: given a household in which there are no persons of type t, then the addition of a person of that type with specific coefficients κ_{it} ($i = 1, 2, \ldots$) is required to have an income coefficient given by the weighted average (9.10). These weights are, of course, influenced by the addition of that person, so no exact and simple expression is possible for the relationship between income and specific coefficients for finite changes in household size. As before, the algebra should be regarded as a convenient way of summarizing a state of affairs that may be expected to hold approximately in the real world.

9.25. COMPENSATED CHANGES IN INCOME AND HOUSEHOLD COMPOSITION

In discussing the applications below one further derivation is required. The total change in the consumption of the ith commodity resulting from a change in household income of dv_0 and of an increase of dn_t in the tth type of person is given by

$$dv_i = \frac{\partial v_i}{\partial v_0} dv_0 + \frac{\partial v_i}{\partial n_t} dn_t, \tag{9.11}$$

which on using (9.5) may be written as

$$dv_i = \frac{v_i}{v_0} \eta_i dv_0 + v_i \left(\frac{\kappa_{it}}{\kappa_{iT} n_T} - \frac{\kappa_{0t} \eta_i}{\kappa_{0T} n_T} \right) dn_t. \tag{9.12}$$

From this there may be derived an expression for the change in income which would exactly 'compensate' for the change in household composition in the sense that it would leave the total consumption of the ith commodity unchanged. Thus, if $dv_i = 0$ there results from (9.12)

$$dv_0 = \left\{ \frac{\kappa_{0t}}{\kappa_{0T} n_T} v_0 - \frac{\kappa_{it}}{\kappa_{iT} n_T} \frac{v_0}{\eta_i} \right\} dn_t. \qquad (9.13)$$

It is seen that the magnitude of this compensating change in income in general depends on the income elasticity and the specific scale of the commodity considered, as well as on the income scale.

The above theorems, presented here in the general manner, summarize the simple theory which underlies the work of this chapter. To bring out the empirical significance of the equations it is useful to examine some alternative approaches to the treatment of household composition and to examine their differences from that adopted here.

9.3. OTHER APPROACHES TO MEASURES OF HOUSEHOLD COMPOSITION

Before surveying other approaches to this problem a comment may not be out of place on the linguistic ponderousness of the theory set out in the last section. This is unfortunate but seems to be unavoidable. Sydenstricker and King, whose approach, as has already been said, is similar to that adopted here, attempted to by-pass the inconvenience of having to refer to 'the number of unit-consumers measured on the scale for a particular commodity' by developing the 'ammain' and 'fammain' terminology. The number of fammains in a household is the number of unit-consumers measured on the specific scale for food, fammain standing for 'food for adult male maintenance'; similarly, there would be cammains for clothing, and so on. The ammains correspond to our income scale. The use of a special terminology has here been avoided at the cost of some extra words.

9.31. THE COST OF CHILDREN

There are three main alternative approaches that have been adopted in previous studies of household composition. The first is that adopted by Nicholson (1949) and Henderson (1949) in their investigations to measure the cost of a child. Their procedure was to choose some 'standard' commodity such as tobacco, the characteristic of which was that its consumption depended only on the standard of living of the household and not otherwise on the number of children. Then the income was found at which the consumption in a household of, say, two adults and a child was the same as that in a household of only two adults, with a given income. In terms of the diagram (Fig. 17), AA' is the Engel curve for households of two adults, and BB' is that for households of two adults and a child; BB' lies below AA' indicating that the same quantity of the commodity is not bought till a higher income is reached. Considering the income M_0 at which v_i of the standard commodity is brought by the two-person household, the same quantity is not bought by the household with a child till the income M_1 is reached. $M_1 - M_0$ is therefore considered the income necessary to 'compensate' the household for the cost of the child.

In terms of the concepts of the last section this method attempts to estimate the income scale on the assumption that the specific scale is known; referring to (9.13) the assumption is that κ_{it}, the coefficient for the child on the specific scale, is zero, so that only the effects due to the income scale are isolated. Thus, the expression (9.13) reduces to

$$\frac{1}{v_0}\frac{dv_0}{dn_t} = \frac{\kappa_{0t}}{\kappa_{0T}n_T},\qquad(9.14)$$

and provides the basis for this method.

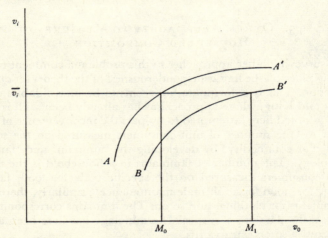

Fig. 17. The standard commodity method for determining the cost of a child.

The 'standard' commodities that have been used in applications of this method are: (a) expenditure on adult clothing: (b) expenditure on drink and tobacco; (c) excess income, that is, the income left after the deduction of the household's expenditure on items considered as necessaries; and (d) savings, which is the limit of (c).

The applications have not, however, proved very successful, and a number of reasons for this may be suggested. There is, first, the greater unreliability of the information for the kind of commodities that can be used as 'standard' commodities. Secondly, the assumption that the children's coefficient is zero may not hold true sufficiently precisely (the father who is driven to drink by his wife and children is the text-book example). Thirdly, the available information is not used in an efficient manner if the two Engel curves are determined separately from the data.[†]

† See Kemsley (1952, p. 198) for an extensive analysis of this kind of difficulty.

9.32. AN APPROACH IGNORING INCOME EFFECTS

The second method to be considered here is based on a regression of consumption against household composition, ignoring entirely the effects of income. The method is generally only applied to necessaries. It is obviously inapplicable to luxuries, since an increase in household size is accompanied by a lower expenditure on the commodity so that types of persons which tend to occur in larger households will tend to receive a negative coefficient.

If the income elasticity for the commodity is zero, or approximately so, this method may be regarded as a satisfactory way of estimating the specific scale for the commodity. For, with this assumption, the last term of (9.5) vanishes and the expression reduces to

$$\frac{1}{v_i}\frac{\partial v_i}{\partial n_t} = \frac{\kappa_{it}}{\kappa_{iT}n_T}. \tag{9.15}$$

If the income elasticity is positive, (9.5) shows that this method will tend to underestimate the scale, the degree of underestimate being proportional to the income elasticity for the commodity.

The importance of the method from the point of view of this chapter is that its applications have shown the possibility of obtaining coefficients within reasonable margins of error which may be assessed statistically, as in the recent paper by Kemsley (1952). He considers expenditure on all food and, separately, expenditure on bread as varying with household composition. Since the income elasticity for bread is close to zero this method should yield good estimates for its specific scale; but for all food, with an elasticity of about a half, it is to be expected that this method will yield coefficients that are on the low side.[†]

9.33. NUTRITIONAL SCALES

Finally, there are the various scales of nutritional requirements based on some standard of optimum health. In their simple form they generally ignore the possibility of complementarity among the various nutritional elements and cannot be regarded as reflecting the average pattern of consumption.[‡] While they may be approximately equal to specific scales they should not be used in economic contexts without explicit justification.

9.4. UNIT-CONSUMER SCALES BASED ON BEHAVIOUR EQUATIONS

A valid analysis of the effects of household composition can, it is apparent, only be carried out if both income and specific effects are

[†] This method has also been used by Quenouille (1950); the methods of Clements (1940) and Williams and Hanson (1939) are similar in some ways though not based on least squares.

[‡] For some cautionary words on the use of nutritional scales see Hutchison (1948, chapter II, especially p. 41); the possibility that nutritional elements—as at present distinguished—may be complementary is brought out by the remark that '*protein when divorced from carbohydrate in the diet is of no use in repairing the wear and tear of body protein*' (Hutchison, p. 95, italics in original).

explicitly taken into account. An equation describing the behaviour of consumers such as (9.2) must lie at the basis of the analysis; the scales may then be estimated from observations of the actual behaviour of households of different compositions.

9.41. THE DIFFICULTIES ARISING FROM NON-LINEARITY

The difficulties which arise in this procedure result from the essential non-linearity of the phenomena investigated. Household composition enters into the determination of consumption patterns in two ways, and it is not possible to linearize the formulation without discarding the essence of the problem. Thus, even if the form of f in (9.2) were linear so that the equation reduced to

$$v_i/\kappa_{iT} n_T = \alpha_i + \beta_i v_0/\kappa_{0T} n_T, \tag{9.16}$$

that is, to

$$v_i = \alpha_i \kappa_{iT} n_T + \beta_i v_0 (\kappa_{iT} n_T/\kappa_{0T} n_T), \tag{9.17}$$

the formulation of the effects of household composition would still be non-linear. Only with the help of the further assumption that the term $\kappa_{iT} n_T/\kappa_{0T} n_T$ may be neglected, since it is of the order of unity, is it possible to arrive at a linear formulation.† But while this kind of argument is useful in leading to an appreciation of the basis of a theory it may be doubted whether it is justified in statistical applications.

The non-linearity of the function would not lead to such difficulties were it not for necessity of utilizing very many observations in order to obtain estimates to a sufficient degree of accuracy. In estimating income elasticities it may be satisfactory if estimates can be obtained which are, say, three times their standard errors; but there would be little gain from the present analysis unless the coefficients are estimated to a much higher degree of accuracy so that, for example, the difference between a coefficient of 0·8 and 0·9 could be judged as significant. Non-linearity and the large number of observations required lead to extremely complicated calculations, which only become practicable if some suitable method of grouping can be devised.

9.42. THE PRINCIPLES OF THE METHOD ADOPTED

The method in fact adopted may now be outlined. It is based on the assumption that if a good guess can be made for the income scale it should be possible to obtain satisfactory estimates of the specific scales. As far as the principle of this procedure is concerned the guess is not an ultimate restriction on the method; for once all the scales, or a sufficient and representative selection of them, have been estimated it will be possible to derive an estimate of the income scale by weighting them as in (9.10) above. In practice, since we have not obtained estimates for all the scales it has not been possible to adopt this procedure and the reliability of the estimates given below is therefore impaired by this assumption.

† This is the method advocated by Friedman (1952).

Denoting by m the value of income per unit-consumer (on the assumed income scale), (9.2) may be written as

$$v_i/\kappa_{iT}n_T = f_i(m),\tag{9.18}$$

which may be transformed to

$$v_i/f_i(m) = \kappa_{i1}n_1 + \ldots + \kappa_{it}n_t.\tag{9.19}$$

The parameters $\kappa_{i1}, \ldots, \kappa_{it}$ can thus be estimated by taking the regression of the composite variable v_i/f_i on the variables n_1 to n_t.

The equation (9.19) is the basis of the estimates to be presented below. The method and assumptions are, of course, neither as elegant nor as straightforward as those involved in treating a linear problem. It is, however, better to attack a non-linear problem with a crude tool than to distort the problem into a linear form.

Two alternative assumptions were made about the function f_i having regard to the results of Chapter 7. These were that the form was, first, semi-logarithmic; thus

$$f_i = \alpha_i + \beta_i \log m$$

$$= \beta_i(\gamma_i + \log m),\tag{9.20}$$

where $\gamma_i = \alpha_i/\beta_i$. The second assumption was that f_i was of the constant elasticity form

$$f_i = A_i m^{\eta_i}.\tag{9.21}$$

These are two parameter forms and, when combined with (9.19), one of the parameters may be regarded as a non-essential scale parameter to be merged with the κ_{it}, since it is only the ratios of the κ_{it} that are of interest. Thus the alternative regression forms become

$$v_i/(\gamma_i + \log m) = \alpha_i \kappa_{iT} n_T \tag{9.22}$$

and

$$v_i m^{-\eta_i} = A_i \kappa_{iT} n_T.\tag{9.23}$$

The left-hand sides of these expressions now involve only one parameter which enters non-linearly, the other parameters on the right-hand side being linear. The method of estimation then proceeds as follows: (a) take some value of γ_i or η_i, (b) calculate the value of the variable on the left-hand side of (9.22) or (9.23), (c) calculate the correlation between this variable and the n_i, and (d) repeat systematically for different values of γ_i or η_i.

In this way there may be obtained a relationship between the correlation coefficient and the values of γ_i or η_i. Those values of κ_{it} are chosen which correspond to the maximum value of this function.

It will have been noted that the criterion is in terms of maximizing the correlation coefficient and not in terms of minimizing the residual sum of squares. In the linear case the two criteria lead, of course, to identical results, but here since the variance of the left-hand side changes with the value of the parameter γ_i or η_i, it is inadequate merely to consider the absolute value of the residual sum of squares. By dividing by the variance of the left-hand side a correction is made for this changing variance, and this is equivalent to considering the correlation coefficient.

Before going on to consider the results of the above procedure some attention is given to the practical aspects of the computations involved and the possibilities of using alternative estimation procedures. The reader not interested in these topics may proceed at once to §9.5.

9.43. THE COMPUTATIONAL PROCEDURES

The combined use of punched-card equipment† and the EDSAC made practicable an extremely involved computation which would otherwise have been prohibitive in cost.

On referring to Chapter 5, the reader will note that the least-squares estimator (5.2) of the parameters κ_{it} require two kinds of sums of cross-products. The first kind is that involved in calculating the sum of cross-products of the determining variables and is simply $\Sigma n_i n_j$, where the summation extends over the observations. The values of the variables n_i, the number of persons of each type in each household, were available on punched-cards, and the requisite cross-products were computed without much difficulty using the method of progressive digiting.

This provided the moment matrix of independent variables the inverse of which was at once found on the EDSAC. Using the notation of Chapter 5 this will be denoted by $(\mathbf{X'X})^{-1}$.

The second kind of sum of cross-products required is that between the dependent variable and each of the determining variables which provide the elements of the vector $\mathbf{X'y}$. In this case the sums of cross-products are of the form $\Sigma n_i v_i / f_i$, as is apparent on referring to (9.19) (the scale-factor adjustment may be ignored for the purposes of this discussion). These could not be calculated in the same manner both because the functions f_i were not available on punched-cards, and because the functions changed at each iteration. The method adopted was therefore to divide the observations into groups for which the function f_i, that is, the variable m, was approximately constant. The function f_i represents the expected expenditure per household on the commodity and is a smooth function of income. Hence no great inaccuracy is introduced if the required sums are estimated from expressions of the type

$$S f_i^{-1} \Sigma n_i v_i, \qquad (9.24)$$

where Σ represents the summation over observations within each group for which m is approximately constant, and S represents the summation over groups.

If there are g such 'income' groups and t types of person, the cross-products $\Sigma n_i v_i$ can be arranged in a matrix $\mathbf{Z}$ of order $t \times g$. If the vector, of length g, with elements f_i^{-1} is denoted by $\mathbf{h}$, the required sums of cross-products are given by

$$\mathbf{X'y} \simeq \mathbf{Zh}. \qquad (9.25)$$

† For constructive advice and help on the punched-card computations referred to in this ection we are considerably indebted to J. E. Fothergill of the Social Survey.

The advantage of this device is that the matrix $\mathbf{Z}$ involves only simple cross-products of variables available on punched-cards and could therefore be computed on punched-card machines once and for all. The subsequent multiplication by $\mathbf{h}$ was then completed by EDSAC.

Ten 'income' groups were distinguished as follows ('income' being measured as total expenditure per person per week):

Income range	Average income	Number of households
$< 13s.$	$10s.\ 4d.$	249
$13s.$ to $15s.\ 6d.$	$14s.\ 5d.$	181
$15s.\ 6d.$ to $18s.$	$16s.\ 9d.$	196
$18s.$ to $21s.$	$19s.\ 6d.$	247
$21s.$ to $24s.$	$22s.\ 6d.$	243
$24s.$ to $27s.$	$25s.\ 6d.$	230
$27s.$ to $31s.$	$28s.\ 9d.$	222
$31s.$ to $35s.\ 6d.$	$33s.\ 1d.$	204
$35s.\ 6d.$ to $42s.$	$38s.\ 7d.$	187
$> 42s.$	$54s.\ 2d.$	249

For each calculation the following numerical information was stored in the EDSAC: the matrices $(\mathbf{X'X})^{-1}$ and $\mathbf{Z}$, the vector of values of m, and the initial value of γ_i or η_i and the interval of interation. The programme was constructed with the help of a number of sub-routines for the multiplication of matrices, for the evaluation of the function f_i, and for iteration for the maximum of the correlation coefficient. The calculations were carried out in floating point form to preserve accuracy.

The order of the computation is then straightforward. The vector $\mathbf{h}$ is first calculated, then $\mathbf{X'y}$ by (9.25), and then the regression coefficients by (5.2). The residual sum of squares is given by

$$\mathbf{e'e} = \mathbf{y'y} - \mathbf{b'X'y}, \tag{9.26}$$

and the squares of the correlation coefficient was calculated from

$$R^2 = \mathbf{b'X'y}/\mathbf{y'y}. \tag{9.27}$$

The iteration for the maximum was carried out in the simplest possible manner so as to economize in storage space for the programme. In the case of (9.22), in addition to storing an initial value of γ_i, say $\gamma_i^{(0)}$, there was also chosen an initial interval, say $\delta^{(0)}$. If the correlation coefficient increased, as compared with the last iteration, the next value of γ_i was taken to be $\gamma_i^{(0)} + \delta^{(0)}$. This continued till the correlation coefficient decreased, when the value of the interval was halved and its sign changed so that $\delta^{(1)} = -\tfrac{1}{2}\delta^{(0)}$. This procedure assures convergence.†

In the case of (9.23) the problem is slightly more complicated, since the ordinary method of evaluating the power $m^{-\eta_i}$ would have required routines for the taking of logarithms and anti-logarithms. The method adopted avoided this by storing an initial *vector* (of order g) of values

† The iterative process has an advantage over calculus methods in that local maxima can be avoided by a proper choice of the initial interval; convergence can then be assured to the maximum maximorum.

$m^{-\eta_i^{(0)}}$ and in addition a *vector* of values $m^{\delta^{(0)}}$. As before the values of the elasticity can then be increased by $\delta^{(0)}$ by multiplying corresponding elements of the two vectors. When the correlation coefficient decreased the new values of the multipliers were found as the vector

$$m^{\delta^{(1)}} = m^{-\frac{1}{2}\delta^{(0)}} = 1/\sqrt{m^{\delta^{(0)}}}.$$

This process thus only required a square-root routine. The convergence of the method is illustrated by the results given in Fig. 18.

Each iteration took about a minute of machine computing time, and the results were printed out at the end of each iteration. The computation was stopped after the value of the elasticity was within a range of approximately 0·005 of the best estimate.

9.44. POSSIBLE ALTERNATIVE METHODS

The method just outlined is comparatively lengthy and is not altogether satisfactory in view of the several approximations that it involves. It is therefore worth setting on record two alternative methods which, while they appeared to be promising, in fact turned out to be less satisfactory than the above method.

The first alternative is based on an extension of the theoretical framework to take into account the effects of household composition on quality variations as considered in Chapter 8. If it can be assumed that the specific scale for the quantity of a commodity is the same as that for the expenditure on the commodity, the specific effects will cancel out in the determination of the price paid for the commodity, considered as the ratio of expenditure to quantity. The basic quality equation (8.3) thus becomes

$$p = \alpha + \beta \log v_0/\kappa_{0T} n_T, \tag{9.28}$$

so that the income scale can be isolated directly in a comparatively simple manner.

The residual variance of (9.28) is, however, considerable in comparison to the original variance, and in order to obtain satisfactory estimates by this method it is necessary to consider some index of quality variations, as, for example, that given by (8.4). Since the information available on the punched-cards was limited to expenditure and quantity for the individual commodities there would have been required a very large amount of computation in order to evaluate such an index; this was therefore not thought to be an economical way of attacking the problem.

The second alternative requiring consideration is that based on the use of the grouped data as given in the tables in Part III. It has been seen that the grouped data have been used with advantage in calculations given in the previous two chapters, and it may be thought that this would also be possible here. This was in fact attempted in an exploratory approach to this problem. The argument of §5.4 showed that the use of grouped data led to unbiased estimates, but it was found that the variance of the estimates was in fact considerably increased by the grouping.

Grouping the data by household size and working with the averaged values meant that there were a larger number of types of persons in the 'averaged' households than there were in the individual households. The correlations between the determining variables, that is, between the types of persons, as computed from the grouped data is therefore very much greater than when computed from the original data. The determinant of $(\mathbf{X'GX})$ is therefore small and the variances of the estimates accordingly large.

Next, the compromise procedure was attempted of estimating $(\mathbf{X'X})$ from the original data, since these were available on punched-cards, but to estimate the cross-products of $\mathbf{X'y}$ from the grouped data. This is, in effect, the method given by the estimator (5.35). The bias of this estimator, as given by the matrix $\mathbf{K}$ of (5.36) is, however, considerable with this method of grouping. The average value of the diagonal elements of $\mathbf{K}$ was found to be 0·24 instead of unity, as would be the case if the grouping was unbiased. This means, roughly, that this estimator provides estimates which are weighted averages of all the parameters, but on the average only 24 % of the weight is allocated to the true parameter of which the regression coefficient purports to be an estimate.†

The method of grouping adopted in Part III may therefore be judged to be useless for the purpose of analysing the effects of household composition. But this should not be taken to imply that no method of grouping is possible. J. A. C. Brown‡ has shown that by grouping the data in terms of household types, defined so as to be of constant composition as far as concerns the classes of person which are distinguished in the analysis, it is possible to obtain reliable estimates of specific scales. The reader should refer to his paper for the possibilities of this method.

9.5. THE RESULTS OF THE PRESENT ANALYSIS

9.51. THE VARIABLES

The method of analysis explained in the last section has been applied to the data of the working-class inquiry, making use of the observations for 2200 households. Eight types of person were distinguished in the

† In an exploratory analysis of the data, estimates were obtained of the specific scales using this biased estimator and, further, an income scale was estimated from a transformation of the quality equation (9.28) also using this estimator. The results seemed to indicate that none of the coefficients was significantly different from unity. It was this surprising result which led to the investigation of the theoretical properties of this grouped estimator which have been set out in Chapter 5. These unit values nevertheless influenced our choice of the income scale for the investigations reported below in this chapter, but in view of the present results it would now seem likely that this assumption of equal values is somewhat extreme for the younger children.

These exploratory results were reported in a paper by Prais read to the 14th European Meeting of the Econometric Society held at Cambridge in August 1952. They are not given here, since the present results have a considerably smaller variance and are obtained by a method which avoids this bias.

‡ In a paper read to the 15th European Meeting of the Econometric Society at Innsbruck, September 1953 and subsequently published in *Econometrica*.

analysis: (1) adult male, (2) adult female, (3) adolescent male (aged 14–17), (4) adolescent female (aged 14–17), (5) child aged 10–13, (6) child aged 5–9, (7) child aged 1–4 and (8) infants under 1 year. There is no reason why further types of person should not be distinguished; there is, indeed, much to be said for treating the husband and wife of the household separately from additional adults. In view of the exploratory nature of the calculations it was thought that the above classification was adequate, since it allowed two comparisons for sex differences besides the age grading. The infant was included in order to provide an *a priori* check on the method as much as for its intrinsic interest.

In calculating the vector of values for m it was assumed that the income scale was given by units so that the value of income per person was an adequate measure of the standard of living. Whilst it was appreciated the specific scales for foodstuffs would show infants at less than unity, it was thought that the scale for household items might well outweigh this. A scale of units seemed to be the most straightforward assumption to make under the circumstances.

The correlations between the eight types of persons are given in the following matrix from which it will be seen that the situation is quite well conditioned. The largest correlation is that between adult males and females, all the remaining coefficients being less than a half:

	Adult male n_1	Adult female n_2	Male 14–17 n_3	Female 14–17 n_4	10–13 n_5	5–9 n_6	1–4 n_7	< 1 n_8
n_1	1	—	—	—	—	—	—	—
n_2	0·837	1	—	—	—	—	—	—
n_3	0·379	0·375	1	—	—	—	—	—
n_4	0·379	0·371	0·191	1	—	—	—	—
n_5	0·444	0·414	0·395	0·417	1	—	—	—
n_6	0·415	0·403	0·264	0·224	0·436	1	—	—
n_7	0·368	0·366	0·143	0·120	0·252	0·434	1	—
n_8	0·232	0·224	0·074	0·111	0·161	0·246	0·344	1

The inverse of the moment matrix, the elements of which are proportional to the variances of the estimates† is as follows:

	Adult male n_1	Adult female n_2	Male 14–17 n_3	Female 14–17 n_4	10–13 n_5	5–9 n_6	1–4 n_7	< 1 n_8
n_1	56	—	—	—	—	—	—	—
n_2	− 40	52	—	—	—	—	—	—
n_3	− 8	− 10	184	—	—	—	—	—
n_4	− 9	− 9	7	193	—	—	—	—
n_5	− 7	0	− 33	− 41	105	—	—	—
n_6	− 4	− 3	− 6	0	− 22	79	—	—
n_7	− 6	− 7	7	10	− 2	− 28	119	—
n_8	− 8	− 4	14	− 8	− 5	− 19	− 78	847

† A scalar transformation has been applied to the matrix which does not affect the present argument: the number of persons was, for each type, the sum of the numbers present in each of the four weeks of the inquiry, and a further factor of 10^6 has been applied. To return to original units the values given should therefore be multiplied by 16×10^{-6}.

It will be seen that the variance of the child coefficient is relatively the greatest, and that most of the covariances are negative, indicating that too high an estimate of one coefficient is accompanied by too low an estimate of another coefficient.

9.52. THE ESTIMATES AND THEIR INTERPRETATION

The main results of this chapter may now be given. They relate to six food groups and to all food (the groups are precisely defined on p. 177). The scales have been estimated according to both the formulation (9.22) and (9.23), since it seemed desirable to see how sensitive the estimates of the specific scales were to changes in assumptions about the form of the Engel curve. The results for the semi-logarithmic formulation, which are to be preferred on the showing of Chapter 7, are given in Table 29, and the results for the constant elasticity form in Table 30.

TABLE 29. SPECIFIC SCALES FOR FOODSTUFFS BASED ON SEMI-LOGARITHMIC ENGEL CURVES

	Farina-ceous	Dairy	Vege-tables	Fruit	Fish	Meat	All food
1. Adult male	1	1	1	1	1	1	1
2. Adult female	0·85	0·97	0·91	1·22	0·91	0·70	0·88
3. Male 14–17	1·01	0·87	1·03	0·65	0·68	0·55	0·81
4. Female 14–17	0·73	0·71	0·72	0·68	0·59	0·48	0·65
5. 10–13	0·89	0·75	0·87	0·66	0·84	0·54	0·71
6. 5–9	0·65	0·58	0·78	0·65	0·41	0·35	0·57
7. 1–4	0·55	0·63	0·75	0·59	0·43	0·30	0·52
8. <1	0·39	0·83	0·36	−0·36	0	0·09	0·35
9. Elasticity	0·27	0·40	0·48	0·68	0·53	0·47	0·46
10. R^2	0·929	0·947	0·869	0·766	0·704	0·932	0·984
11. Standard error	0·05	0·05	0·08	0·11	0·12	0·04	0·02

TABLE 30. SPECIFIC SCALES FOR FOODSTUFFS BASED ON CONSTANT ELASTICITY ENGEL CURVES

	Farina-ceous	Dairy	Vege-tables	Fruit	Fish	Meat	All food
1. Adult male	1	1	1	1	1	1	1
2. Adult female	0·84	0·96	0·89	1·18	0·89	0·68	0·86
3. Male 14–17	1·01	0·85	1·05	0·70	0·71	0·54	0·82
4. Female 14–17	0·73	0·69	0·73	0·70	0·62	0·47	0·65
5. 10–13	0·88	0·69	0·85	0·59	0·83	0·48	0·69
6. 5–9	0·64	0·54	0·77	0·60	0·39	0·31	0·55
7. 1–4	0·54	0·58	0·74	0·56	0·43	0·26	0·51
8. <1	0·38	0·75	0·33	−0·42	−0·03	0·05	0·32
9. Elasticity	0·29	0·41	0·57	0·88	0·66	0·52	0·53
10. R^2	0·929	0·945	0·869	0·764	0·703	0·930	0·983
11. Standard error	0·05	0·05	0·08	0·11	0·12	0·04	0·02

Before examining the detailed results of these tables, two remarks are necessary. The first is that the results given are those of the values of the scales near the maximum point. As far as could be seen there was nowhere any indication of the existence of any extremal values aside from the main maximum. An impression of the nature of the iterative process may be gained from Fig. 18, which shows the values of R^2 and η for all food on the constant-elasticity formulation, the numbers indicating the order followed by the machine. Some of the points near the maximum are calculated more than once, as shown by having more than one number attached to the point; this is due to the elementary nature of the process.

The second remark is concerned with the interpretation of the scales as estimated by this method. The present analysis separates out the total effect on a household's consumption resulting from the addition

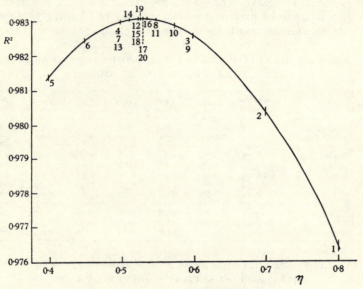

Fig. 18. The convergence of the iterative procedure.

of an extra person, but this may not always be due solely to the consumption of that person himself. For example, the addition of a child to the household will lead to an increase in expenditure on children's clothing, but it may also lead to an increased expenditure on mother's aprons and the like. This method attributes such increases in ancillary expenditures by other members of the household to the particular member added.

Whether this is a desirable property of the estimates or not depends on the purposes for which they are required. For nutritional studies which are necessarily based on the consumption of individual members of the household, this is clearly not a desirable feature, though where the magnitude of such ancillary expenditures may be expected to be small it will not affect the successful application of the method, as in the study by Clements (1940). For purposes of economic policy, on the other hand, it would seem that the inclusion of ancillary expenditures is generally desirable. When the total requirements of a child are therefore assessed by this method, they will, for example, take account of all the expenditure on clothing that it may occasion.

The results for the various commodities may now be considered, noting first that the results of the two tables are very similar. What differences there are affect the income elasticities for the commodities—which are always higher according to the constant elasticity estimate—rather than the coefficients which are the interest of this chapter. The agreement between these estimates and those given in Table 10 (p. 94) of Chapter 7 may be judged as satisfactory in view of the variability of the latter.

Secondly, the adult male is here seen to account generally for the largest proportionate expenditure on foodstuffs. This might have been expected, since the estimates are based on the working-class inquiry in which a large proportion of the households had male manual workers. The difference for expenditure on meat is particularly large.

Thirdly, the difference between the sexes is to be noted also in the adolescent group, aged 14–17, in which the male has a consistently higher coefficient than the female. Indeed, for vegetables and farinaceous foods the male adolescent has a higher coefficient than the adult male, but this difference cannot be judged as significant.

Fourthly, the coefficients for children decrease smoothly with age. The coefficients for the infant under 1 should not be taken too seriously, since the ancillary effect is particularly large here. The great quantity of milk he appears to be drinking no doubt goes largely to his mother, and the negative coefficient for fruit may only mean that the mother with an infant eats less fruit than otherwise; since she is shown to have a large coefficient of 1·2, this would only be reduced to 0·8 on the arrival of the infant. The infant's coefficients for fish and meat, on the other hand, seem to be realistically low.

There are no doubt may other features of these results that will occur to the reader. It would have been desirable to make some comparisons with earlier investigations, but this is only possible directly for the scale for all food, since the individual scales published by nutritionists refer to nutritional elements rather than to food groups. The main characteristic of our scale for all food is that it gives, on the whole, a higher weight for young children than do most other scales. Children under 1 on the Amsterdam scale, for example, are given a coefficient of 0·15, and those between 1 and 5 have an average coefficient of 0·35;† these may be compared, respectively, with our coefficients in table 29 of 0·35 and 0·52.

† See, for example, *Huishoudrekeningen*, I, p. 14.

9.53. THE RELIABILITY OF THE ESTIMATES

Finally, it is necessary to comment on the reliability of the estimates and the degree of confidence that may be placed on them. Estimates may be subject to error both on account of fluctuations due to the statistical element in dealing with a sample of observations and on account of the possible errors in the basic assumptions. In econometric work the statistical error is generally large because of the paucity of observations; even two thousand observations are not necessarily sufficient to provide estimates which are sufficiently accurate for all purposes.

The matrix of the correlations between the types of persons and the inverse of the moment matrix, which provides the variances of the estimates, have already been given. The variances of the coefficients may be derived from the latter by the usual formula for the variance of a ratio given by

$$\sigma_x^2 = x^2[\sigma_u^2/u^2 - 2\sigma_{uv}/uv + \sigma_v^2/v^2], \tag{9.29}$$

where $x = u/v$; in this case the taking of ratios generally doubles the standard error. Row 11 of Tables 29 and 30 gives the standard error of the adult female coefficient calculated in this way; the adult female coefficient for all food in Table 29 is thus to be read as $0\cdot88 \pm 0\cdot02$. The standard errors of the other coefficients are in proportion to those given in row 11, and may be evaluated with the help of (9.29). On the average, the proportions are approximately unity, slightly more for the adolescents and the infant (about $1\cdot2$) and slightly less for the children (about $0\cdot8$).

These sampling errors have been calculated as if (9.22) and (9.23) were ordinary linear equations; since this is not so, the left-hand side depending on an estimated parameter, the standard errors have thus been somewhat underestimated. Nevertheless, as far as the sampling error is concerned there can be little doubt that the first decimal place of the coefficients is well determined; indeed, the regularity of the pattern revealed is such that one is tempted to place some confidence even in the second decimal place.

Rather more serious may be the errors due to the assumptions made about the income scale. If this has been overestimated it will lead to an overestimate of the specific scale by an amount depending on the income elasticity of the commodity, as may be seen from (9.5). The evidence so far available is not, however, sufficient to suggest whether the equal values adopted for the income scale is unrealistic; while for food the costs of an infant may be only a third of that of an adult, it is precisely then that extra expenditure is incurred on prams, baby cots and clothing which may well outweigh the economies achieved in other directions. On account of the high income elasticity for fruit its scale is therefore subject to a greater margin of error than the others.

9.6. SOME CONCLUSIONS

A method has been presented for the analysis of the effects of household composition on consumption which distinguishes 'specific' from 'income' effects, and the analysis has been applied to yield specific scales for six food groups. The conclusions which may be drawn from the analysis and its results are as follows:

(a) The effect of the addition of an extra person to the household on the consumption of a particular commodity depends approximately on the difference between the coefficient of the person on the specific scale for the commodity and the product of the income elasticity and the coefficient on the income scale.

(b) Unless specific and income effects are separated, biased results will in general be obtained in statistical analyses of the data. In particular, unless the income elasticity is zero, an analysis of consumption and household composition which ignores the effect of income may be expected to yield coefficients which are biased downwards.

(c) Using explicit economic behaviour equations it has been possible to obtain estimates of specific scales for foodstuffs which are subject to a moderately small margin of statistical error. The necessity to assume an income scale is a drawback at this stage, but once specific scales are derived also for non-food items it should be possible to improve this step in the argument.

(d) The results show that in the sample investigated the proportion of food consumption to be attributed to females is about 15 % less than that to males. Consumption is shown as consistently lower for younger children than for older, it being about half that of an adult male for children under school age.

(e) Obviously the next step in research along these lines is to obtain comparable estimates for various non-food expenditures; only in this way will it be possible to make the broad comparisons of standards of living which are required in so many aspects of social policy. But the straightforward application of the method of this chapter would be inadequate for most non-food items on account of the existence of economies of scale to a significant extent. To this topic we now turn.

CHAPTER 10

ECONOMIES OF SCALE IN CONSUMPTION

10.1. THE NATURE OF ECONOMIES OF SCALE

The assumption on which the analysis of the previous three chapters has proceeded is that consumption per unit-consumer depends only on the level of income per unit-consumer. This assumption, it is apparent, may require elaboration, if the range of household size investigated is at all large, to take account of the possible existence of economies of scale in consumption. The objects of this chapter are to suggest a formulation of the consumption function which incorporates the effects of economies of scale and then to obtain some estimates of their magnitude. If the formulation of Chapter 7 is regarded as a first approximation, the formulation of this chapter may be regarded as a second approximation.

The concept of economies of scale gives expression to the possibility that, with given levels of income per person, a larger household may be able to attain a higher standard of living than a smaller household. Considered in terms of foodstuffs, economies may arise in the purchasing, storage and preparation of foods. Thus, there may be straightforward discounts for purchasing larger quantities; or it may be that a commodity is only sold in multiples of certain minimum quantities, such as a tin or a packet, which inconveniences the smaller household in that it is required to keep proportionately larger stocks. Again, in a large household there are possibilities of specialization (the housewife preparing the entrée, the daughter preparing the sweet, and the mother-in-law doing all the rest) which while in practice is likely to lead only to the more tasteful preparation of foods, yet may also lead to more economical methods of cooking and the utilization of portions of foodstuffs that are otherwise discarded. The nature and magnitude of these effects are, of course, closely related to the 'technology' of consumption, so that with the development of economical small houses, rapid pressure-cookers, and the like, the disadvantages of small households may today not be so great as before. It is, indeed, quite possible that at a certain stage diseconomies of scale begin, as when the father has a nervous breakdown because of the noise made by all the children when they are together.

In considering non-foods the meaning of economies of scale is slightly more difficult to envisage in a simple manner, since many commodities are only bought for households within given size ranges. Thus it may be that a household will not buy a settee unless there are at least three persons in the household; on the other hand, if there are more than, say, five persons, it will tend to buy a three-piece suite. When considered in broad commodity groups, however, the same phenomena of economies (or diseconomies) of scale can be distinguished as for foodstuffs; indeed, if foodstuffs are also finely divided the concept becomes similarly tenuous.† Perhaps the best example of an economy of scale in non-foods is the 'technical' property that the capacity of pots and pans increases more than in proportion to their price.

The handing on of outgrown clothes from older to younger children in the household may also be regarded as an economy of scale, since the mother could in principle sell the outgrown clothes to a second-hand merchant and buy other clothes for the younger children. The economy is achieved in avoiding the costs of selling and purchasing. It would be possible to analyse this phenomenon in terms of a difference in the coefficients on the unit-consumer scale for first and second children, but since the needs of first and second children are essentially similar it is preferable to recognize explicitly the effects of economies of scale and to treat children of the same age and sex as having the same coefficient on the unit-consumer scale.

In any empirical analysis it is, however, to be expected that there may be some uncertainty as to whether to attribute a given phenomenon to the effects of household composition or to the effects of economies of scale. In principle the issue can always be decided by investigating the comparable phenomenon in households of constant composition but of different sizes.‡

At given levels of income per unit-consumer larger households may have levels of consumption per unit-consumer which differ from those of smaller households, not only because of economies of scale but also because 'tastes' for particular commodities may depend on the size of the household. The most important of these effects are those that are associated with the pleasures of family life; parents, for example, may prefer to watch their children than film stars, with the consequences of increased expenditures on play-pens, toys and armchairs, and decreased expenditures on cinemas, theatres and casual drinks at licensed or unlicensed premises. Analogous differences in expenditure patterns are to be observed for two-person households as compared with single-person households, so that these differences cannot be explained solely by unit-consumer scales. Whether observed differences in consumption are to be interpreted as resulting largely from economies (or diseconomies) of scale or largely from shifts in taste is often a difficult problem, only to be decided by considering the nature of the commodity.

† This is a formal characteristic of all analysis and applies as much to the income-elasticity concept as to the present topic.

‡ That is, households composed of integral multiples of a given constellation of types of persons; a household of four adults and two children is for this purpose to be regarded as having the same composition, but being twice as large, as a household of two adults and one child.

Thus a reduced consumption of potatoes in larger households may be ascribed to an economy of scale resulting from a proportionately smaller quantity being wasted in sticking to the sides of the pot and the like; but the increased consumption of port after dinner may well be ascribed as due to a difference in tastes for port when dining in company.

10.2. A FORMULATION

For simplicity it is convenient to consider first the case in which differences of coefficients on the unit-consumer scales can be ignored either because they are in fact negligible or because attention is confined to households which are of constant composition. At a given level of income per person, if there are economies of scale in the consumption of a particular commodity larger households will tend to have a smaller expenditure per person on that commodity due to those economies. These may be termed the specific economies in the consumption of a particular commodity.

On the other hand, on account of the specific economies achieved in the consumption of all commodities, the larger household will tend to distribute its expenditure according to a standard of life which is higher than that of smaller households with the same level of income per person. On account of this 'income effect' of economies of scale the consumption of larger households is thus raised for goods that are not inferior.

A possible formulation which distinguishes the specific effects is given by an Engel curve of the general form

$$v_i/n^{\theta_i} = f_i(v_0/n^{\theta_0}), \qquad (10.1)$$

where $(1 - \theta_i)$ is the measure of the specific economies of scale for the ith commodity and $(1 - \theta_0)$ is the measure of the income economies of scale. If there are no economies of scale in the consumption of the particular commodity then θ_i is unity; and if there are no economies in the consumption of any commodity then θ_0 is also unity. Economies of scale are represented by values of θ_i and θ_0 less than unity.

The above formulation of specific and income effects is entirely parallel to the similar distinction drawn in the previous chapter in connexion with the analysis of the effects of household composition, and theorems similar to those of §9.2 can easily be derived. It should be noted that the exponential influence of economies of scale adopted in (10.1) is not essential to the distinction between income and specific effects; it is only adopted here for convenience of manipulation.

Two consequences of this formulation require note. The first is that the coefficient θ_0 is a weighted average of the θ_i. The second is that the income and the specific effects of an increase in household size are in general of opposite sign. Thus if a constant elasticity Engel curve were fitted to family-budget data which had the form

$$v_i/n = A(v_0/n)^\beta n^\gamma, \qquad (10.2)$$

when the true curve in consonance with (10.1) were

$$v_i/n^{\theta i} = A(v_0/n^{\theta_0})^\beta, \tag{10.3}$$

then the estimate of β found from (10.2) would provide an estimate of income elasticity, but γ would be a compound coefficient given by

$$\gamma = \beta(1 - \theta_0) - (1 - \theta_i), \tag{10.4}$$

that is, it is equal to the specific effect diminished by the product of the income elasticity and the income effect. This expression may be compared with (9.5) derived in the previous chapter.

Nevertheless, if β and θ_0 are known the regression form (10.2) may provide a good method for estimating θ_i on using (10.4).

The extension of the above formulation to incorporate the effects of changes in household composition leads to the replacement of (10.1) by

$$v_i/(\kappa_{iT}n_T)^{\theta_i} = f_i[v_0/(\kappa_{0T}n_T)^{\theta_0}], \tag{10.5}$$

so that the effects of composition are given a multiplicative formulation, and the effects of economies of scale an exponential formulation.

The analogy with the theory of the previous chapter is also seen in the effects of economies of scale on the quality of the commodities bought. It is natural to suppose that quality is only influenced by the income effects, so that the basic equation for quality becomes

$$p = \alpha + \beta \log [v_0/(\kappa_{0T}n_T)^{\theta_0}]. \tag{10.6}$$

The coefficients $(1 - \theta_i)$ when estimated from data on expenditures and household size will, of course, incorporate the effects of shifts in tastes to or from the particular commodities as household size varies. In their nature, shifts in tastes towards particular commodities tend to be compensated by shifts away from other commodities, with the result that on the average these shifts cancel out; the estimate of the coefficient $(1 - \theta_0)$ may thus be regarded as measuring the average effect of economies of scale. The standard of living of households of different sizes and composition may then be compared on this formulation by the measure $v_0/(\kappa_{0T}n_T)^{\theta_0}$, which may be termed the level of income available per *effective* unit-consumer, the term 'effective' indicating that the number of unit-consumers is to be deflated by the exponent θ_0.

10.3. SOME MEASUREMENTS

An attempt was made to estimate the income effects of economies of scale from the equation

$$p = \alpha + \beta \log v_0/n + \gamma \log n, \tag{10.7}$$

as applied to the quality index for all food given by (8.4).† The result gave an estimate of 0·28 ($\pm$0·02) for β and a value of 0·037 ($\pm$0·02) for γ. On comparing (10.7) with (10.6) it is seen that an estimate of θ_0 is

† n was here taken as the number of persons.

given by $1 - \gamma/\beta$ which is here equal to 0·87, and $(1 - \theta_0)$ which is a measure of the income effects of economies of scale is 0·13. This means that of two households with the same level of income per person, the larger household will, as a result of economies of scale, enjoy a standard of living which is higher by 13 % of the ratio of their sizes; the standard of living is here measured in terms of the quality of the food bought. On account of the possible existence of discounts for bulk purchase it should be noted that this tends to underestimate the 'true' increase in the standard of living.

Estimates for the Engel curves for a number of grouped commodities for the working-class sample were obtained using the regression form (10.2) for non-foods and a corresponding semi-logarithmic form for foods. The parameters are all given in Table 31 in the form of elasticities. Using the above estimate of $(1 - \theta_0)$ and the corresponding income elasticity, an estimate of $(1 - \theta_i)$ was obtained from (10.4), and this is given in the last column of the table.

A number of conclusions may be drawn from this table. The first is that the column headed γ shows that, at given levels of income per person, consumption per person is less in larger households than in smaller households for most commodities. Secondly, the column headed $(1 - \theta_i)$ shows to what extent this is due to specific economies in the consumption of those commodities (the sense of measurement in this column is the reverse of that of the previous column). Thus, in the case of farinaceous foods, the value of γ shows that, at equal levels of income per person, larger households spend approximately 19 % less per person on farinaceous foods than do smaller households. According to this analysis, the value of 19 % is to be attributed to the existence of specific economies of scale of 22 % in the consumption of these foods, and to the income effects of economies of scale of 3 % (being the product of the income elasticity of 0·25 and the value of 0·13 obtained for θ_0 above).

In the case of fruit, a luxury commodity, expenditure per person is larger in larger households, since the income effects more than offset the specific effects of economies of scale. According to this analysis, there are specific economies of 8 % in the consumption of fruit; this is rather smaller than the values obtained for the other foods, but is not surprising in view of the larger proportion of fruit eaten raw.

The table shows, thirdly, that for clothing a similar phenomenon is to be noted. On analysis it appears that the specific economies in the consumption of clothing are negligible with an estimated value of $(1 - \theta_i)$ of -0.01.

Fourthly, for durables there appear to be distinct diseconomies of scale. These are, however, in the nature of an illusion, and the negative value of $(1 - \theta_i)$ in this case is due to the shifts in tastes towards these kinds of commodities as the size of the household increases. This more than offsets whatever economies of scale are in fact achieved, and these are possibly quite as large as the coefficients for rent and fuel (which, it should be noted, may also be influenced by possible shifts in tastes).

TABLE 31. AN ANALYSIS OF ECONOMIES OF SCALE

Commodity	Income elasticity	γ	$1 - \theta_i$
Farinaceous foods	0·25	−0·19	0·22
Dairy products	0·43	−0·10	0·16
Vegetables	0·52	−0·08	0·15
Fruit	1·04	0·05	0·08
Fish	0·70	−0·08	0·17
Meat	0·53	−0·14	0·21
Rent	0·56	−0·60	0·67
Fuel	0·52	−0·43	0·50
Clothes	1·01	0·14	−0·01
Durables	1·98	0·44	−0·18

10.4. SOME IMPLICATIONS

The above analysis is in the nature of a preliminary venture in a new direction and should not be regarded as in any way definitive, especially so since no use has been made of the unit-consumer scales derived in the last chapter. There are, nevertheless, some implications for the analysis presented in the earlier chapters, since the explicit introduction of a factor allowing for economies of scale will affect the estimates of the other parameters of the consumption functions. As a next step, of course, it would be desirable to recalculate the estimates of Table 31 with the unit-consumer scales of Chapter 9.

Consider, first, the estimates of the income elasticities for foodstuffs, comparing the results in Table 31 with those in column 3 of Table 10 (p. 94 above). Economies of scale in foodstuffs are on the whole small, with a value of $(1 - \theta_i)$ of about 0·2, and it is not to be expected that they will greatly influence the estimates of the income elasticity. The direction and magnitude of the influence depends both on the income and the specific effects of economies of scale† as measured by the coefficient γ, so that in the case of fruit the estimate is raised slightly, but for the other foods the estimate is somewhat reduced. Generalizing from this, it would seem that the income elasticities for foodstuffs given in Chapter 7 are somewhat too high, but the degree of overestimate may only be of practical importance in exceptional commodities. For non-foods, on the other hand, it is more difficult to come to any precise conclusion, since both economies of scale and shifts in tastes are rather important.

Secondly, the estimates of the quality elasticities of Chapter 8 are affected according to the formulation (10.6) by the income effects of economies of scale. Since the elasticities are in any case small the effect

† The correlation between household size and income per person, to be expected as negative in general, also enters into the relation. If a constant-elasticity formulation is adopted, the difference between the estimates of the income elasticities, according to whether an estimate of γ is obtained or not, is equal to the product of the value of γ and the elasticity of n with respect to v_0/n. We owe this observation to our colleague, J. A. C. Brown.

of this complication is negligible; for the quality index for all food, the elasticity is increased from 0·26 to 0·28 on introducing a variable to allow for economies of scale.

More important consequences may perhaps be expected for the estimates of the unit-consumer scales, especially for the estimates of the children's coefficients, since children tend to be found in the larger households. Again, the magnitude of γ seems to be the criterion, and while the estimates for foods may be little affected, of the non-foods it is only for clothing that it seems possible to carry out a simple analysis on the lines of Chapter 9. The estimates of the unit-consumer scale obtained from such an analysis (on a constant elasticity formulation) are as follows: adult female, 1·3; adolescent female 1·4; adolescent male, 1·3; child aged 10–13, 1·4; child aged 5–9, 0·7; child aged 1–4, 0·7; and the infant, 0·5 (the standard error of the adult female coefficient is 0·16). To carry out successful analyses of the scales for other non-foods it seems that some elaboration of the procedure of Chapter 9 is essential, and this may require the estimation of both γ and the income elasticity by a modification of the iterative procedure there used.

CHAPTER II

SOCIAL, OCCUPATIONAL AND REGIONAL FACTORS IN CONSUMPTION

11.1. THE RELATION BETWEEN ECONOMIC AND OTHER FACTORS

In the last four chapters an attempt has been made to add some precision to our knowledge of the influences of a few factors on the behaviour of the consumer. The only factors considered have been income, household size and composition; the object of this chapter is to discuss some further factors and, though rather less is known about these, it is hoped that their discussion will set the earlier analyses in a better perspective.

The factors to be considered here are of a generally sociological nature; they are the social class of the household (which the reader may at this stage conceive as he will), the occupations of its earners and the sources of its income, and the geographical region in which the household is situated. Household size and composition are in a sense also social factors, or at any rate non-economic factors, but it has been seen that it is necessary to bring them explicitly into the main analysis in order to make any progress. Whether household size is an economic or a social factor is, however, only a matter of words; the issue is hardly worth developing.

In considering the effects of sociological factors it is necessary to draw once again the distinction between what may here be termed the separate and total effects of a factor. The separate effect of a factor is the effect when only this factor is allowed to vary, and all the other factors are assumed unchanged; the total effect in a particular situation is to be measured by allowing the other factors to take on whatever values they actually have. Thus in investigating the separate effects of social class it would be necessary to compare households of the same income, household size and composition, and the like; but to ascertain the total effect of, say, occupation it would only be necessary to take a representative sample of households whose incomes were derived from that occupation.

In analytic work it is, of course, the separate effects that must be distinguished, as this will always allow the calculation of the total effect to be expected in a particular situation. But in examining complicated situations which require some decision to be made quickly, either by a government department or by a market research agency, it may be that the total effect is of more practical and immediate relevance; for this reason analyses of consumers' expenditures are, for example, often carried out in terms of a 'social-class' concept when the total effect of 'social class', as defined, may be large on account of the accidental distribution of income and household size, but its separate effect may be quite negligible.

The above point has been somewhat laboured, since there seems to be considerable but unnecessary confusion on the interaction between economic and other factors. Some of this can be avoided easily by making clear whether it is the separate or the total effect that is being investigated. In part, however, the difficulty arises from the 'circular' process in which social factors work; thus while a temporary increase in the income of a worker may merely lead to an increase in his expenditure on entertainment, a long-term increase may lead to a change of social class, an increase in education, a change of occupation and income, and even a change of residence to a warmer climate. Again, an increase in the average income of a population may lead to an increase in the birth-rate, and a subsequent decrease in the standard of living. Or it may not. Whether a particular analysis in terms of an economic factor, or any other 'ultimate' factor, is useful must depend on the length of the period considered and the number of subsequent 'feed-backs' through other factors which are taken into consideration.

This point is of particular relevance in considering the effects of social class on consumption habits. For, as already indicated, it may be the case that even over a moderately short period of time, say, a generation, the separate effect of social class is nil, it being entirely a derivative from the long-run income level of the household. An analysis of consumption patterns both in terms of social class and income level would then be equivalent, from the point of view of economics, to an analysis of the effects of long-run and short-run changes in income. A sociologist, however, might explain the same facts in quite different conceptual terms.

It follows that very many analyses indeed have to be carried out before a full understanding is possible of the determinants of consumption patterns. The approaches adopted in analysing different factors may be very different in their nature, since the time period appropriate for the analysis of one factor may be many times that appropriate for another. The different approaches should, however, be regarded as potentially consistent.

The discussion in the next three sections will take up in turn the effects of social class, occupation and region on consumption habits, but it should be clear that no thorough treatment will be possible. All that can be attempted is to make clear the nature of the problems involved and the extent to which they may affect the analyses given in earlier chapters and the conclusions to be drawn from them.

11.2. THE NATURE OF SOCIAL CLASS AND ITS EFFECTS

11.21. CLASS HABITS

Even though the concept of social class is somewhat tenuous it is all too tempting to begin an analysis on the implicit assumption that social-class habits have a significant effect on expenditure patterns. The habits and traditions of the working classes, the professional classes and the landed gentry—as far as the principle is concerned it does not matter how many classes are distinguished—may determine quite rigidly the whole pattern of life of the household in small things as well as in great. Here, for example, are Roy Lewis and Angus Maude writing on *The English Middle Classes*.†

By and large, middle-class homes are distinguished by regularity, order and even ritual; sometimes within a framework so gracious as to represent an almost perfected art of living, sometimes oppressively or meaninglessly, most often somewhere between the two. The young, apart from those who are spoilt, or those enjoying the full glories of self expression for their egos at the hands of 'progressive' parents, are made to conform to a prescribed routine of living, acquiring habits of cleanliness, punctuality, politeness and so forth, necessary to sustain the middle-class standards of life, and hard to acquire without a minimum of the things which make up the middle-class standard—improved housing, domestic service, sufficient food, and a conviction that outward and visible signs connote inward and invisible graces.

The many characteristic habits which affect the expenditure patterns of the social classes require no exposition here; the reader requiring a careful description cannot do better than begin with the book by Lewis and Maude and that by Ferdynand Zweig on *The British Worker*.‡ Consideration must, however, be given here to the extent to which some of these habits may be the result of the normal working of economic factors.

11.22. THE ECONOMIC ORIGINS OF THE HABITS ASCRIBED TO SOCIAL CLASS

Consider first the typical working-class household the economic characteristics of which are that it has a negligible amount of capital at its disposal and the prospect of an uncertain and irregular income stream; the latter, however, may be more characteristic of the inter-war period than it is today. The problem which such a household has to solve is that of establishing habits of expenditure which will allow it to survive in the future as far as it can foresee it. Habits, however, are difficult to establish and even more difficult to change; in particular, it is easier to become accustomed to an increase than to a decrease in the consumption of a particular commodity.

In these circumstances a working-class household will be acting in a perfectly rational manner if it discounts very heavily its expected future income stream and establishes habits of expenditure, at any rate

† Penguin Books (1953, p. 196).
‡ Penguin Books, 1952.

as far as the staple items are concerned, which are appropriate to a lower income level than it may in fact be enjoying; that is, habits which on the whole are similar to those of a household expecting a lower but regular income stream. The excess income is then spent as quickly as possible in some non-habit-forming direction. This kind of motive may in part explain the popularity of television sets in working-class areas immediately after the war. It may also explain why middle-class people typically think that working-class people do not spend their money in a sensible way.

Consider next a characteristic of middle-class households—the existence of a more or less substantial amount of capital. Whether its actual income receipts are regular or not, the middle-class household is able to maintain a stable pattern of living by calling on, or adding to, its capital. Its long-run level of expenditure will be determined by the amount of saving it intends to effect in its lifetime and by its income expectations. Changes in income level can therefore only be expected to affect its pattern of expenditure after a long period.

Another characteristic of some sections of the middle classes is the expectation of a rising income stream throughout the major portion of the life of the household. This is especially true of independent professionals, the lawyers and doctors who are busily building up their practices, and of the salariat who traditionally have an annual increment in their incomes. Once again it is perfectly rational for the young household to stabilize its pattern of expenditure by spending more than its current income at the beginning of its life, entering into mortgage agreements and the like if necessary. Further it will invest in things, such as the education of the children, which it will not really be able to 'afford' for several years to come.

Thus both in the way in which a given total expenditure is financed and in the way in which it is distributed there are typical differences between the social classes which derive from economic factors.

An analogous consideration which may be mentioned here is that a middle-class household forced to contemplate a long-term decline in its income level is quite likely to decide to have fewer children than in the previous generation in an attempt to maintain *per capita* levels of consumption.

11.23. IMPLICATIONS FOR AN ANALYSIS BASED ON FAMILY BUDGETS

Considerations of this sort may to a large extent explain the characteristics commonly ascribed to the influence of social class on consumption. The implications would seem to be as follows:

First, a change in income from one year to the next may have different effects according to the social class of the household. Generally speaking, if the above description is at all realistic, an increase in working-class incomes should have a disproportionate effect on the consumption of luxury or dispensable items; an increase in middle-class incomes, on the other hand, may well be entirely saved either as cash in the bank or in the form of real assets, such as a house or the further education of children.

Secondly, a proper analysis of the effects of social class must be based on 'dynamic' concepts and a knowledge of the past and expected income stream of the household. The amount of capital possessed, perhaps expressed as a multiple of its current income, should also be included among the determinants of the expenditure pattern.

Thirdly, the income-elasticity concept will require elaboration so that a distinction can be drawn between the effects of long-term and short-term changes in income.

Fourthly, it should be noted that on this approach the concept of social class is regarded as being largely a shorthand expression for a particular combination of economic factors. The separate effect of social class after all the economic factors have been taken into account is assumed to be small.

11.24. THE EVIDENCE OF THE TWO INQUIRIES

While this may be the correct way of investigating the effects of social class, the question remains whether it is possible to derive some indication from our two inquiries that have here been termed 'working class' and 'middle class'. As far as the 'middle-class' inquiry is concerned it is clear that it cannot be regarded as representative of the middle classes, since none of the households included derive their income from profits. This inquiry is better regarded as referring to the professional classes, the characteristics of which are that there is security of tenure, a stable income stream while at work, and a pension afterwards.

Nevertheless, there are occasionally substantial differences between the evidence of the two budget collections. The kind of discrepancy to be noted is illustrated in Fig. 19, which shows the expenditure per person on tea against total expenditure per person in the two inquiries. Only the points corresponding to the three total expenditure classes which are the same in both inquiries have been included. The size of the household is shown inside circles for the working-class inquiry, and inside squares for the middle-class inquiry.

It will be seen that on the whole the working-class families spend more on tea at all levels of total expenditure and for all household sizes. Many reasons could be suggested for this: there is, for example, the increased need for drinks by manual workers and, again, the way in which meals are organized in households where the wife either goes out to work or where facilities are limited in other ways. Tea provides a conveniently made and relatively cheap drink.

If there were any reason for thinking that the differences between the results of the inquiries were systematic in a particular way so that, for example, the differences only affected either the height or the slope of the Engel curve (but not both) it would be possible to take this knowledge into account when fitting the curve to both sets of data simultaneously. Thus, if the Engel curve were linear and the effect of

the effect that, even if the same quantities were bought, middle-class households paid an extra percentage over the working-class households.

If, however, both the height of the curve and the slope were expected to be different it would be necessary to treat each of the classes separately. Nevertheless, when only a few observations are available it may be desirable to treat the classes together, making some necessarily arbitrary assumption. The estimate c_i of γ_i gives a summary measure of the difference between the classes. For estimates based on the preliminary analyses of our inquiries the reader should consult the work of Stone (1954, pp. 313 et seq.).

In the present analysis since sufficient information was available, and there seemed to be no good reason for supposing the influence of social class to have the simple effects assumed when a 'dummy' variable is used, it was decided to treat the inquiries separately as has been seen in Chapter 7. A further reason for avoiding a simple social-class factor arises from the danger that a non-linearity in the effect of income may be ascribed to social class, for the two classes only overlap in a portion of the income range.

The differences between the estimates of the income elasticities for the two inquiries given in Table 20 above can be tested for statistical significance. The results are given in Table 32, distinguishing foods from non-foods, and taking a greater middle-class estimate as positive.

TABLE 32. DIFFERENCES BETWEEN THE INCOME ELASTICITIES IN THE TWO INQUIRIES (RATIO OF DIFFERENCE TO ITS STANDARD ERROR)

Difference divided by Standard error	Foods		Non-foods	
	Number of differences	Proportions	Number of differences	Proportions
< -2	7	0·12	24	0·47
-2 to $+2$	37	0·63	21	0·41
> 2	15	0·25	6	0·12
Total	59	1·00	51	1·00

The table shows there are on the whole significant differences between the two samples which reflect either genuine differences in behaviour or inadequate analysis. For non-foods, for which the constant-elasticity form of equation has been used, there is a tendency for lower middle-class elasticities, as shown by the 47 % of cases where the middle-class estimate is less than the working-class estimate by more than two standard errors. On the other hand, while the differences for foodstuffs must also be judged as significant, this tendency, here in the other direction, is not so marked.

Examination of the individual commodities shows that many of the differences occur where the dietary habits of working-class and professional households can be expected to differ. There are tea and coffee, frozen and fresh meat, fish and chips, and meals away from home. Again, with non-foods there are a number of items on which there is hardly any expenditure by one of the samples, such as the laundry item, or wages for domestic help, and for these differences will arise since the use of a constant-elasticity form of curve is clearly inappropriate. On the whole, however, the two sets of estimates agree rather well; what differences there are may well be due to an inadequate formulation of the effects of income rather than to the effects of social class.

11.3. OCCUPATIONAL EFFECTS

11.31. THE SEPARATE EFFECTS OF OCCUPATION

The effects of occupation on consumption habits are in many ways similar to those of social class; indeed, the occupation of the main earner is often taken to be the major determinant of the social class of the household. From the point of view taken here it is, however, important to note that whereas it will generally be the case that the separate effects of social class on consumption are negligible this is not so for the effects of occupation. For manual workers require greater quantities of foods than, and in different proportions to, those required by civil servants; agricultural workers, again, may require special types of clothing. In general these separate effects will only be significant when the items are particularized; the broader the classification the smaller will be the differences to be noted.

While these separate effects may be of some analytical interest it seems that occupational analyses are often carried out in order to determine the total effect of an occupation. The reason is that there are often no reliable figures available of average incomes and standards of living in a particular occupation, so a household survey is used for this purpose.

The main difficulty in analysing the separate effects of an occupation is that it may be correlated with income level and possibly also with the geographical region; but if a sufficient range of variation can be obtained, and this may mean taking broad occupational groupings, it should be possible to overcome this.

11.32. A COMPARISON OF THREE OCCUPATIONAL GROUPS

The differences in the average expenditures of agricultural and industrial households covered by the working-class inquiry have already been given in the earlier analyses.† If our 'middle-class' inquiry is regarded as providing information on the expenditure patterns of a broad occupational group (represented by the civil servants and teachers covered by the inquiry) it is possible to compare the expenditure patterns of three groups. These may be termed: agricultural, industrial, and civil-servants' households.

The average expenditures in these households are given in columns (1), (2) and (3) of Table 33, subdivided according to five main items.

† Ministry of Labour (1940; 1949, p. 33).

Column (2) gives the expenditure in the 2200 households whose main earner was engaged in industry or commerce and who returned annual figures for clothing; annual estimates for clothing are used throughout.

TABLE 33. OCCUPATION AND EXPENDITURE PATTERN

Item	Agri-cultural (1)		Industrial (2)		Civil servant (3)		Industrial households with total expenditure similar to			
							Column (1) (4)		Column (3) (5)	
	s.	d.	s.	d.	s.	d.	s.	d.	s.	d.
Food	27	9	34	4	41	10	24	2	55	6
Rent	4	9	10	10	21	2	8	4	13	9
Fuel	4	11	6	6	10	1	4	11	10	1
Clothing	5	3	8	1	15	6	4	6	17	9
Other items	14	8	28	3	83	7	13	3	83	9
Total	57	4	88	0	172	2	55	2	180	10

The main differences between the occupational groups are clearly due to differences in income, agricultural workers generally having the lowest earnings. It is therefore of some interest to see to what extent it is possible to adjust for the effects of income. This may be most easily achieved by taking the returns for those industrial households which have a total expenditure corresponding as closely as possible to those of the other two occupational groups.

Column (4) of the table accordingly gives the expenditure of those industrial households whose total expenditure is between 50s. and 60s. per week and corresponds with the total expenditure of the households whose main earner was engaged in agriculture. It will be seen that as far as fuel, clothing and other items are concerned the figures in columns (1) and (4) are surprisingly similar. For food there is a small difference of 3s. 7d., that is, the agricultural households spend approximately 15 % more on food than industrial households. In part, if not altogether, this may be attributed to the larger number of persons, 3·79, in the agricultural households as compared with the number, 3·32, in the industrial households here considered.

Column (5) provides a similar comparison for the civil servants on the basis of those industrial households which had a total expenditure of over 140s. per week. Again there is only the discrepancy in expenditure on foods which is rather larger here at about a third, but the difference in household size—4·71 as compared with 3·27—is also larger.

The main difference is, of course, in rent; agricultural workers pay the least and civil servants the most at comparable levels of total expenditure. This, however, is more likely to be due to geographical differences in available housing than to any genuine differences in tastes.

11.4. REGIONAL FACTORS IN CONSUMPTION HABITS

11.41. RENT AND TRANSPORT COSTS

Regional variations in consumption may result from differences in relative prices, especially transport costs and rents, and from differences in tastes conditioned, for example, by climate. These factors affect the net advantages of living in a particular region and, it may be presumed, the consumer takes them into account in choosing his place of living, at any rate, in the long-run. For the kind of problems in connexion with which family budgets are generally investigated, however, a rather shorter period seems appropriate. It is therefore often assumed that expenditure on rent is a predetermined quantity and should be deducted from income received in order to arrive at a better measure of the disposable income available to the consumer to meet his other expenses.

Whether the method just mentioned describes correctly the effects of rent differences or not, it is apparent that in assessing the standard of living in particular areas some adjustment should be made for the level of rents and the like. But for an analysis of the effects of income variations on expenditure such regional variations would not appear to be important. Thus, it was possible to isolate in the working-class inquiry those households living in the London area and to analyse the differences in expenditure patterns with a 'dummy' variable as described in § 11.24 above. The main results† show that London families have a higher expenditure on travelling and on meals away from home and, correspondingly, a lower expenditure on groceries.

11.42. INCOME VARIATIONS

The main danger to be avoided in examining consumption by regions is the attribution of the effects of income differences to taste variations, that is, the confusion of the separate effects of a region with its total effects.

In the working-class inquiry the households were classified according to ten administrative regions and, in §B of Part III, a number of tables have been given classifying expenditures according to these regions and the level of total expenditure per person. This should allow a proper appraisal of the separate effects of regional variations.

The ten regions distinguished are as follows:‡

(1) London: the City of London and Metropolitan Police District.

(2) South-eastern: the parts of the counties of Essex, Hertford, Kent and Surrey outside the Metropolitan Police District, and the counties of Bedford, Berkshire, Buckingham, Cambridge, Huntingdon, Norfolk, Suffolk and Sussex, and the Soke of Peterborough.

(3) South-western: the counties of Cornwall, Devon, Dorset, Gloucester, Hampshire, Oxford, Somerset and Wiltshire.

---

† Given in the paper by Houthakker (1952a, p. 18).
‡ See Ministry of Labour (1949, p. 56).

(4) Midlands: the counties of Derby (except the Buxton, Chapel-en-le-Frith, Glossop, Hadfield and New Mills districts), Hereford, Leicester, Northampton (excluding the Soke of Peterborough), Nottingham, Rutland, Shropshire, Stafford, Warwick and Worcester.

(5) North-eastern: Lincolnshire and Yorkshire (except Cleveland district).

(6) North-western: Lancashire and Cheshire and the Buxton, Chapel-en-le-Frith, Hadfield, New Mills and Glossop districts of Derbyshire.

(7) Northern: the counties of Northumberland, Durham, Cumberland and Westmorland, and the Cleveland district of Yorkshire.

(8) Wales: Wales and Monmouthshire.

(9) Scotland: Scotland.

(10) Northern Ireland: the counties of Antrim, Armagh, Down, Fermanagh, Londonderry and Tyrone.

In addition, we are able to present some hitherto unpublished figures, due to Miss Phyllis Deane, on the relative income levels in these regions in 1938. These have been compiled as follows. It was assumed that the regional variations in income level can, to a first approximation, be attributed to occupational differences in rewards. The distribution of the insured population in each of the regions in 1938 has accordingly been weighted by the average wages paid in the various occupations to give an average wage for each region.

The more detailed analysis made by Miss Deane of the 1948 figures showed that, in addition to the differences due to occupational structure, there could be distinguished a regional factor which can be regarded as having an equi-proportional effect on the earnings of all occupations in each region. Since there were no figures available for 1938 it was assumed that the 1948 values could be used to improve the above first approximation.[†] After multiplying by the number of earners and dividing by the number of persons, the figures of average income per person in the ten regions were found and are given in the third column of Table 34 below.

TABLE 34. INCOME AND EXPENDITURE BY REGIONS IN 1938 (SHILLINGS PER PERSON PER WEEK)

Region	Number of earners per household	Number of persons per household	Income per person	Total expenditure per person
1. London	1·77	3·66	32·2	25·8
2. South-eastern	1·63	3·67	24·3	21·7
3. South-western	1·61	3·66	24·4	21·8
4. Midland	1·83	3·77	27·4	23·5
5. North-eastern	1·70	3·68	25·2	22·2
6. North-western	1·89	3·73	27·5	22·4
7. Northern	1·55	3·69	24·6	21·4
8. Wales	1·52	3·71	24·0	20·9
9. Scotland	1·86	4·02	25·1	22·3
10. Northern Ireland	2·21	4·72	21·1	16·6

† This is the index R_2 given in Miss Deane's (1953) paper, p. 132.

Estimates of total expenditure per person based on the budgets are given in the fourth column. It will be seen that there is a common pattern of regional differences in the last two columns. The average level of the income column is above that of the expenditure column, and this difference is especially marked where there are a comparatively large number of additional earners in the household. It may be inferred that these additional earners are not in full-time employment, and this has probably led to an overestimation of the income figures.

The broad result of a low income level in Ireland and a high income level in London stands out clearly, and this alone should be sufficient to lead to quite considerable (total) differences in the expenditure patterns. The cross-classification adopted in §B of the tables, by region and the level of total expenditure per person, should facilitate any further inquiry into the differences in consumption patterns according to geographical region.

CHAPTER 12

SOME CONCLUSIONS FROM THE INQUIRY

12.1. A SUMMARY OF THE PRINCIPAL RESULTS

This inquiry has been concerned with a wide range of topics, and the many detailed results and estimates that have been derived in its course have been set out in the previous chapters. In this chapter the more central results are drawn together and an attempt is made to indicate the lines along which future research should be directed.

While the inquiry has had a largely quantitative orientation, its central results would seem to be concerned less with the particular numerical estimates that have been obtained than with the tools of analysis that have been developed. These may be reviewed in two parts.

12.11. STATISTICAL AND COMPUTATIONAL TECHNIQUES

First, there are the statistical and computation techniques considered in Chapters 5 and 6. In beginning this study the ideas that we held on problems such as the treatment of non-linear relations, of zero observations in double-logarithmic regressions and the like were rather vague. The ordered exposition and suggested treatment of the problems given in Chapter 5 have, in fact, resulted from a considerable amount of rather less orderly speculation and experimental calculations. A similar pattern of development lies at the back of our remarks on electronic computation in Chapter 6; but the computational and statistical developments should not be regarded as independent. This is most clearly brought out by considering the iterative process used in Chapter 9 and that suggested in §5.32; the development of simple statistical methods is in these cases considerably facilitated by the possibility of solving what amount to non-linear equations by iterative processes with the help of an electronic computer. The problem of treating zeros in double-logarithmic functions can, for example, be avoided by fitting the conceptually simpler constant-elasticity expression on a trial-and-error principle.

In §5.3 a treatment has been given of heteroscedastic error terms in regression analysis which led to the conclusion that for the purpose of fitting Engel curves this complication can largely be neglected; the examination of the problem has, however, led to the suggestion of a treatment which is, as are most of the other matters raised in these two chapters, of general applicability.

12.12. A MODEL OF THE HOUSEHOLD

The second part of our results is connected with the model of the behaviour of the household in response to changes in income level and household composition that has emerged from the investigations of Chapters 7–10. This model relates expenditure per effective unit-consumer on the various commodities to the standard of living of the household as measured by the level of income per effective unit-consumer; in the notation of the previous chapters the fundamental equation is

$$v_i/(\kappa_{iT} n_T)^{\theta_i} = f_i[v_0/(\kappa_{0T} n_T)^{\theta_0}]. \tag{12.1}$$

The conceptual virtues of this equation are that it explicitly distinguishes the specific effects of household composition and economies of scale from their income effects, about each of which something may be known *a priori* or from external sources of information such as nutritional studies. The net effect of the addition of an extra person to the household can be found by compounding these various separate effects taking into account the income elasticity of demand for the commodity; some simplified expressions have been derived for this in Chapter 9. A further advantage of this model is that, as suggested in §7.42, it is possible to draw a distinction between luxuries and necessaries in terms of the change in expenditure on the commodity consequent upon an increase in household size: necessaries are those goods for which there is an increase in expenditure and luxuries are those for which there is a decrease in expenditure. This definition is, under the simplified assumptions of Chapter 7, equivalent to the more usual definition in terms of the magnitude of the income elasticity.

In obtaining estimates of the many parameters of (12.1) the first concern has naturally been to find a suitable function for f_i. The main conclusion to be drawn from the investigations of Chapter 7 is that, while no function had been discovered which is uniformly satisfactory for all commodities, it is nevertheless possible to improve considerably on the linear function used by Allen and Bowley. For foodstuffs a 'semi-logarithmic' relation has been found generally preferable. Its main property is that the income elasticity declines with the income level of the household (instead of asymptotically approaching unity as on the linear formulation). For non-foods a constant elasticity formulation has been adopted, though this is not always quite satisfactory.

The problem of allowing for differences in household composition has been approached since the early studies of Engel with the help of scales of unit-consumers or equivalent-adults. These scales have generally been based on non-economic considerations: the virtue of the approach adopted here in Chapter 9 is that it has been found possible to estimate these scales directly from the data, within our general formulation (12.1), and thus link economic studies of family-budget material with nutritional studies of consumption.

Estimates of the scales have so far been derived only for a number o-broad food groups. The treatment of non-food items is complicated by the possible existence of substantial economies of scale in their consumption and requires the more involved kind of computation suggested in Chapter 10.

12.2. THE IMPLICATIONS FOR FURTHER RESEARCH

As indicated at the beginning of this book, a given piece of research work can hope to fill in only a small portion of any field of knowledge and, almost inevitably, there must remain a wide area in which further research work is immediately possible. There is, it will be apparent, considerable scope in our case for a synthesis of the various developments presented in the previous chapters which should lead directly to improvements in almost all the estimates presented in this book. The most obvious of these required extensions is the simultaneous estimation of unit-consumer scales and coefficients of economies of scale so as to bring together the approaches of Chapters 9 and 10.

Further, by making use of the estimated unit-consumer scales given in Chapter 9 it should be possible to analyse the effects of income variations in other budget studies in a comparatively simple and more precise manner; again, it should be possible to examine the extent of regional variations in consumers' responses to income changes after allowing for differences in household composition.

Apart from the general desirability of a combined estimation procedure there are three remarks which may be relevant for future research. The first is that in the present investigations the analyses for food commodities have consistently been more successful than those for non-foods. To some extent this is, of course, just another way of saying that the demand for food is determined in a more elementary manner than that for non-foods. It therefore seems desirable that future investigations should be more closely directed towards non-food items so that the analyses for these commodities may be raised to a comparable level.

The difference noted between the results for foods and non-foods leads to a second remark. This is related to a general lesson to be learned from the inquiry and is concerned with the problem of the grouping of commodities. In beginning this inquiry it was thought that, in view of the large number of observations that were available, it would be desirable to distinguish as many commodities as possible in all the analyses. This would have been a desirable procedure if the problem had been merely that of finding the correlations between a number of variables specified on a strict *a priori* basis. In fact, as has been seen, it was found better to conduct the inquiry by building a model with a number of new features, and to present our results as investigations of these particular features.

The formulation of the quality equation as one of those features has led to a change in approach to the problem of grouping, and it would now seem more appropriate to begin an analysis by grouping commodities as broadly as possible and only subsequently to carry out analyses on successively closer subdivisions of those groups. Part of the success of the analyses for foodstuffs may perhaps be ascribed to the comparative ease with which it was possible to choose a number of grouped commodities as the correctness of this approach became apparent.

The third remark which follows on the differences between foods and non-foods is in the nature of a further comment on the use of total expenditure as an approximation to the income variable and the investigations of §7.71. For a successful analysis of the demand for many non-foods, such as consumers' durables, it is apparent that this approximation is not altogether adequate; reliable information is desirable in this case on current, past and expected incomes. Its absence has been at any rate part of the reason for our not taking the inquiries into non-foods further than we have done and for the relative over-attention given to foodstuffs.

169

REFERENCES

AITKEN, A. C. (1935). On least squares and linear combinations of observations. *Proc. Roy. Soc. Edin.* **55**, 42.

ALLEN, R. G. D. (1942). Expenditure patterns of families of different sizes. In *Studies in Mathematical Economics and Econometrics* (edited by O. Lange, F. McIntyre and Th. Yntema). Chicago University Press.

ALLEN, R. G. D. and BOWLEY, A. L. (1935). *Family Expenditure.* London: Staples.

BARNA, T. (1945). *Redistribution of Incomes through Public Finance in 1937.* Oxford.

BLACK, G. (1952). Variations in prices paid for food by income level. *J. Farm. Econ.* **34**, 52.

BRADY, D. S. (1938). Variations in family living expenditures. *J. Amer. Statist. Ass.* **33**, 385.

BRADY, D. S. and FRIEDMAN, R. D. (1947). Savings and the income distribution. In *Studies in Income and Wealth*, **10**. New York: N.B.E.R.

BROWN, J. A. C. (1954). The consumption of food in relation to household composition and income. *Econometrica*, **22**, 444.

BROWN, J. A. C., HOUTHAKKER, H. S. and PRAIS, S. J. (1953). Electronic computation in economic statistics. *J. Amer. Statist. Ass.* **48**, 414.

CHAPMAN, A. (1953). *Wages and Salaries in the United Kingdom, 1920–1938.* Cambridge.

CLEMENTS, S. W. (1940). A family coefficient scale developed from the Australian Nutritional Survey. *J. Hyg., Camb.*, **40**, 681.

CRAMER, H. (1946). *Mathematical Methods of Statistics.* Princeton University Press.

CRAWFORD, SIR WILLIAM and H. BROADLEY (1938). *The People's Food.* London.

DEANE, P. (1953). Regional variations in United Kingdom incomes from employment. *J.R. Statist. Soc.* A, **116**, 123.

DUESENBERRY, J. S. (1949). *Income, Savings and the Theory of Consumer Behavior.* Cambridge, Mass.: Harvard University Press.

DUESENBERRY, J. S. and KISTIN, H. (1953). Consumption and final demand. In *Studies in the Structure of the American Economy*, by W. Leontief. Oxford.

DURBIN, J. (1954). Errors in variables. Report of paper read to the Econometric Society. *Econometrica*, **22**, 102.

DURBIN, J. and WATSON, G. S. (1950, 1951). Testing for serial correlation in least-squares regression. *Biometrika*, **37**, 409; **38**, 159.

DWYER, P. S. (1942). Grouping methods. *Ann. Math. Statist.* **13**, 138.

ENGEL, E. (1857). Die Productions- und Consumptions-verhältnisse des Königreichs Sachsen. Reprinted in *ISI Bull.* **9**, Appendix.

ENGEL, E. (1895). Die Lebenskosten Belgischer Arbeiter-Familien Früher und Jetzt. *ISI Bull.* **9**, 1.

FINNEY, D. J. (1951). Subjective judgement in statistical analysis: an experimental study. *J.R. Statist. Soc.* B, **13**, 284.

FRIEDMAN, M. (1937). The use of ranks to avoid the assumption of normality implicit in the analysis of variance. *J. Amer. Statist. Ass.* **32**, 675.

FRIEDMAN, M. (1952). A method of comparing incomes of families differing in composition. In *Studies in Income and Wealth*, **15**. New York: N.B.E.R.

FRISCH, R. (1932). *New Methods of Measuring Marginal Utility.* Tübingen.

GIBRAT, R. (1931). *Les Inégalités Économiques.* Paris.

GOODWIN, R. M. (1949). The multiplier as matrix. *Econ. J.* **59**, 537.

GRAY, P. G. and CORLETT, T. (1950). Sampling for the social survey. *J.R. Statist. Soc.* A, **113**, 150.

HAJNAL, J. and HENDERSON, A. M. (1950). The economic position of the family. *Papers of the Royal Commission on Population*, **5**, 1. London: H.M.S.O.

HANSEN, M. H., HURWITZ, W. N., MARKS, E. S. and MAULDIN, W. P. (1951). Response errors in surveys. *J. Amer. Statist. Ass.* **46**, 147.

HENDERSON, A. (1948). The cost of a family. *Manchester Statist. Soc.* 8 Dec. 1948.

HENDERSON, A. M. (1949). The cost of a family. *R.E. Stud.* **17**, 127.

HENDERSON, A. M. (1949, 1950). The cost of children. *Pop. Stud.* **3**, 130; **4**, 267.

HICKS, J. R. (1939; 2nd ed. 1946). *Value and Capital*. Oxford.

HOFSTEN, E. v. (1952). *Price Indexes and Quality Changes*. Stockholm.

HOUTHAKKER, H. S. (1951). Some calculations on electricity consumption in Great Britain. *J.R. Statist. Soc.* A, **114**, 359.

HOUTHAKKER, H. S. (1952a). The econometrics of family budgets. *J.R. Statist. Soc.* A, **115**, 1.

HOUTHAKKER, H. S. (1952b). La Forme des Courbes d'Engel. *Cahiers du Séminaire d'Econométrie*, **2**, 59. [Publication dated 1953.]

HOUTHAKKER, H. S. (1952c). Compensated changes in quantities and qualities consumed. *R.E. Stud.* **19**, 1.

HOUTHAKKER, H. S. and PRAIS, S. J. (1952). Les variations de qualité dans les budgets de famille. *Écon. Appliq.* **5**, 65.

HOUTHAKKER, H. S. and TOBIN, J. (1952). Estimates of the free demand for rationed foodstuffs. *Econ. J.* **62**, 103.

Huishoudrekeningen van 598 Gezinnen (1937). Centraal Bureau voor de Statistiek. The Hague, 2 vols.

HUTCHISON, R. (1948). *Food and the Principles of Dietetics*, 10th ed. revised by V. H. Mottram and G. Graham. London.

JOHNSON, H. G. (1952). The effects of income-redistribution on aggregate consumption with interdependence of consumers' preferences. *Economica*, **19**, 131.

KEMSLEY, W. F. F. (1952). Estimates of cost of individuals from family data. *Appl. Statist.* **1**, 192.

KENDALL, M. G. (1951). Regression, structure and functional relationship. *Biometrika*, **38**, 11.

KLEIN, L. R. (1951). Estimating patterns of savings behaviour from sample survey data. *Econometrica*, **19**, 438.

KLEIN, L. R. and MORGAN, J. N. (1951). Results of alternative treatments of statistical data. *J. Amer. Statist. Ass.* **46**, 442.

KNEELAND, H. (1939). *Consumer Expenditure in the United States*. Washington: National Resources Committee.

KOOPMANS, T. C. (1951). *Activity Analysis of Production and Allocation*. New York: Wiley; London: Chapman & Hall.

LEWIS, R. and MAUDE, A. (1953). *The English Middle-Classes*. London: Penguin Books.

LYDALL, H. F. (1951). A pilot survey of incomes and savings. *Bull. Oxford Univ. Inst. Statist.* **13**, 257.

MARSHALL, A. (8th ed. 1920). *Principles of Economics*. London: Macmillan.

MASSEY, P. (1942). The expenditure of 1360 middle-class households in 1938. *J.R. Statist. Soc.* A, **105**, 189.

MINISTRY OF FOOD (1951). *The Urban Working-Class Household Diet, 1940 to 1949*. London: H.M.S.O.

MINISTRY OF LABOUR (1949, duplicated). *Weekly Expenditure of Working-Class Households in 1937–38*. Part of the results were given in the *Ministry of Labour Gazette*, December 1940, January and February 1941.

MOOD, A. M. (1950). *Introduction to the Theory of Statistics*. New York: McGraw-Hill.

NICHOLSON, J. L. (1949). Variations in working-class family expenditure. *J.R. Statist. Soc.* **112**, 359.

OGBURN, W. F. (1931). A device for measuring the size of families invented by E. Sydenstricker and W. I. King. In *Methods in Social Science: A Case Book*, edited by S. A. Rice. Chicago University Press.

POLITZ, A. and SIMMONS, W. (1949). An attempt to get the 'Not at Homes' into the sample without callbacks. *J. Amer. Statist. Ass.* **44**, 9.

PRAIS, S. J. (1953). Non-linear estimates of the Engel curves. *R.E. Stud.* **20**, 87.

PRAIS, S. J. and AITCHISON, J. (1954). The treatment of grouped observations. To appear in *ISI Rev.*

QUENOUILLE, M. H. (1950). An application of least squares to family diet surveys. *Econometrica*, **18**, 27.

QUENSEL, C. (1945). Studies of the logarithmic normal curve. *Skand. Aktuar Tidskr.* **28**, 141.

REID, M. G. (1952). Effect of income concept upon expenditure curves of farm families. In *Studies in Income and Wealth*, **15**. New York: N.B.E.R.

ROSS, K. H. (1948). Working-class clothing consumption, 1937–38. *J.R. Statist. Soc.* A, **111**, 145.

ROTHBART, E. (1943). Note on a method of determining equivalent income for families of different composition. Being Appendix IV to *War-time Pattern of Saving and Spending*, by Charles Madge. Cambridge.

SAMUELSON, P. A. (1947). *Foundations of Economic Analysis*. Harvard University Press.

SAMUELSON, P. A. (1950). The problem of integrability in utility theory. *Economica*, **17**, 355.

SCHULTZ, H. (1938). *The Theory and Measurement of Demand*. Chicago.

SHIRRAS, G. F. (1923). *Report into an Enquiry into Working-Class Budgets in Bombay*. Labour Office, Government of Bombay.

STAEHLE, H. (1934). Annual survey of statistical information: family budgets. *Econometrica*, **2**, 349.

STAEHLE, H. (1935). Family budgets—source materials. *Econometrica*, **3**, 106.

STIGLER, G. J. (1954). The early history of empirical studies of consumer behavior. *J.P.E.* **62**, 25.

STONE, R. (1945). The analysis of market demand. *J.R. Statist. Soc.* **108**, 286.

STONE, R. (1951 *a*). The demand for food in the United Kingdom before the war. *Metroeconomica*, **3**, 8.

STONE, R. (1951 *b*). *The Role of Measurement in Economics*. Cambridge.

STONE, R., ROWE, D. A., CORLETT, W. J., HURSTFIELD, R., and POTTER, M. (1954). *The Measurement of Consumers' Expenditure and Behaviour in the United Kingdom, 1920–1938*, **1**. Cambridge.

STUVEL, G. and JAMES, S. F. (1950). Household expenditure on food in Holland. *J.R. Statist. Soc.* A, **113**, 59.

SYDENSTRICKER, E. and KING, W. I. (1921). The measurement of the relative economic status of families. *Quart. Publ. Amer. Statist. Ass.* **17**, 842.

THEIL, H. (1952 *a*). Estimates and their sampling variance of parameters of certain heteroscedastic distributions. *ISI Rev.* **19**, 141.

THEIL, H. (1952 *b*). Qualities, prices and budget enquiries. *R.E. Stud.* **19**, 129.

TINBERGEN, J. (1951). *Econometrics*. London: Allen and Unwin.

TOBIN, J. (1950). A statistical demand function for food in the U.S.A. *J.R. Statist. Soc.* A, **113**, 113.

TOBIN, J. (1951). Relative income, absolute income and saving. In *Money, Trade and Economic Growth* (edited by D. M. Wright and others). New York: Macmillan.

TOBIN, J. and HOUTHAKKER, H. S. (1951). The effects of rationing on demand elasticities. *R.E. Stud.* **18**, 1.

TORNQUIST, L. (1941). Review in *Ekonomisk Tidskrift*, **43**, 216.

UTTING, J. E. G. and COLE, D. (1953). Sample surveys for the social accounts of the household sector. *Bull. Oxford Univ. Inst. Statist.* **15**, 1.

VICKREY, W. (1947). Resource distribution patterns and the classification of families. In *Studies in Income and Wealth*, **10**. New York: N.B.E.R.

WALD, A. (1940). The approximate determination of indifference surfaces by means of Engel curves. *Econometrica*, **8**, 144.

WILLIAMS, F. M. and HANSON, A. C. (1939). *Money Disbursements of Wage Earners and Clerical Workers in Five Cities in the Pacific Region*, 1934–36. Bulletin No. 639 U.S. Bureau of Labor Statistics, Washington.

WILKES, M. V., WHEELER, D. J. and GILL, S. (1951). *Programming for an Electronic Digital Computer*. Cambridge, Mass.: Addison Wesley.

WOLD, H. O. A. (1943–44). A synthesis of pure demand analysis. *Skand. Aktuar Tidskr.* **26**, 85, 220; **27**, 69.

WOLD, H. and JUREEN, L. (1953). *Demand Analysis*. New York: Wiley.

WOODBURY, R. M. (1944). Economic consumption scales and their uses. *J. Amer. Statist. Ass.* **39**, 455.

WORKING, H. (1943). Statistical laws of family expenditure. *J. Amer. Statist. Ass.* **38**, 43.

WORSWICK, G. D. N. and CHAMPERNOWNE, D. G. (1954). A note on the adding-up criterion. *R.E. Stud.* **22**, 57.

YATES, F. (1949). *Sampling Methods for Censuses and Surveys*. London: Griffin.

ZWEIG, F. (1952). *The British Worker*. London: Penguin Books.

PART III
THE DATA

GUIDE TO THE TABLES

The main features of the tables which follow have already been described in §3.4; the object of the following paragraphs is to give an account of a number of details which may be required by those using the tables in further work.

The main set of tables (that is, excluding those in sections B and X) give comparable data for the working-class and middle-class inquiries. The information generally given is the average expenditure in pence per week per household in each group of households (given in the column headed v), and the number of households in that group showing a positive expenditure in at least one of the four weeks of the inquiry (given in the column headed f). The average expenditures, v, are calculated over all the households in the group and not only over those showing a positive expenditure. Hence, in calculating weighted regressions (or weighted averages) the values to be used in weighting the expenditures are those given in column f of table A1; that is, the total numbers of households in the sample should be used as weights, and not merely those showing a positive expenditure.

The grouping of the households is on the two-way basis of total expenditure and household size. The total expenditure grouping runs across the page and is also in units of pence per week per household; thus the first working-class expenditure group covers those households with a total expenditure of less than 500d. per week. The average expenditure by households of various sizes are given down the page, the last row, headed Σ, giving the average for households of all sizes within each expenditure group. The last set of columns, similarly headed Σ, give the average expenditures in each household size group for all values of total expenditure.

For a number of working-class tables information is also given on the quantities bought, the units in which these are measured being given in the top right-hand corner of the tables. Since not so much emphasis was placed on the collection of quantity information as on the expenditure information, it was found that a number of households reported an expenditure on the commodity but not the quantity bought. It was therefore thought advisable to adopt a rather roundabout procedure in calculating the average quantities purchased: the average price paid was first calculated for those households in the group who reported both quantity and expenditure; the average expenditure of all households in the group (including those who were negligent in recording the quantity information) was then divided by that average price to give the estimated average quantity purchased. The average quantity and price so calculated are respectively given in the columns headed q and p. The column headed f still gives the number of households with positive expenditure, and this is in general greater than the numbers reporting positive quantities. The discrepancy in the number is occasionally serious, and no great reliance can then be placed on the quantity and price information. The two total values of f for those commodities with quantity information are as follows:

	Commodity	No. with positive expenditure	No. with positive quantity		Commodity	No. with positive expenditure	No. with positive quantity
C1	Flour	2015	1980	F3	Bananas	1604	1552
C2	Cake mixture	1471	392	G1	Potatoes	2130	2095
C3	Oatmeal	808	552	G4	Onions	1724	1521
C4	Rice	1363	1307	G5	Legumes	1185	825
C7	Biscuits	1654	1487	H1	Fish, fresh	1744	1591
D1	Milk, fresh	2200	2195	H3	Fish, dried	1107	1044
D2	Milk, liquid skim	140	126	I1	Beef and veal, fresh	1926	1894
D3	Milk, condensed	1011	985	I2	Beef, frozen	1429	1362
D6	Butter	2162	2152	I3	Mutton, or lamb, fresh	1432	1153
D7	Margarine	1633	1624				
D8	Lard	1641	1627	I4	Mutton or lamb, frozen	1377	1061
D10	Eggs	2154	2171				
D11	Suet	1622	1482	I5	Pork	1355	1144
E1	Tea	2215	2214	I6	Bacon and ham	2183	2163
E2	Coffee	610	261	I7	Sausages and pies	1928	1736
E3	Cocoa	961	847	K2	Tobacco	821	597
E4	Sugar	2213	2215	K3	Cigarettes	1638	762
E5	Jam and marmalade	1910	1871	M1	Coal	2098	1932
F1	Apples	1835	1792	M2	Coke	166	104
F2	Oranges	1782	1725	M3	Oil	640	597

The number of significant figures to be calculated always presents a problem. The procedure followed here was to give expenditure information on individual commodities to a hundreth of a penny, and other information to three significant figures as far as possible, taking into account the desirability of presenting a uniform number of figures in each table. This is occasionally rather greater than warranted by the inherent accuracy of the figures, but seemed to be desirable in order to make the results useful in subsequent research work.

The use of dashes and zeros to indicate a lack of information or expenditure requires a comment. There are two working-class cells and one middle-class cell in which there were no households in our samples. These have always been indicated by dashes. Zeros have been used elsewhere to indicate that there was no expenditure recorded by any of the households in the group. Occasionally it is found that there is an expenditure on the item by one or two households in the group, but this is so small that when it is averaged over all the households in that group the value is less than the least significant figure. This is indicated by giving the value as 0·00.

It has frequently been found that in view of some inaccuracy in the punched-cards it has been desirable to omit a number of households in the tabulation for a particular commodity. This should not bias the average expenditures in the groups affected since these have always been adjusted for this. But it will be found that on this count some of the tables are not quite comparable in the number of households covered.

Considering next the contents of the tables, it will be seen that they have been divided under a number of heads. Section A gives a description of the samples: the number of households, their total expenditure, and their composition.

Section B gives a number of summary tables, for the working-class inquiry only, classifying household expenditure on a number of grouped commodities by the level of total expenditure per person and by a number of geographical regions. These regions are described in full in Chapter 11, but their short titles may conveniently be repeated here:

1. London	6. North-western
2. South-eastern	7. Northern
3. South-western	8. Wales
4. Midlands	9. Scotland
5. North-eastern	10. Northern Ireland

The average expenditures on the commodities are given for each of these regions at twelve consumption levels, as measured by the level of total expenditure per person. These twelve levels were chosen as follows:

Reference number	Total expenditure per person per week		Number of households
	Range	Average	
1	Less than 10s.	8s. 0d.	99
2	10s. to 13s.	11s. 8d.	150
3	13s. to 15s. 6d.	14s. 5d.	181
4	15s. 6d. to 18s.	16s. 9d.	196
5	18s. to 21s.	19s. 6d.	247
6	21s. to 24s.	22s. 6d.	243
7	24s. to 27s.	25s. 6d.	230
8	27s. to 31s.	28s. 9d.	222
9	31s. to 35s. 6d.	33s. 1d.	204
10	35s. 6d. to 42s.	38s. 7d.	187
11	42s. to 52s.	46s. 7d.	149
12	52s. and over	65s. 5d.	100

These tables may be found useful in exploratory analyses in further research work. The grouped commodities given are among those that have been used in a number of analyses in Chapters 7 and 9, and it is convenient to give here their composition (the code names for the commodities are to be found in the index to the tables given below):

Farinaceous foods	C1 to C8
Dairy products	D1 to D9
Fruit	F1 to F6
Vegetables	G1 to G6
Fish	H1 to H4 and J2
Meat	I1 to I10
Rent	L1 and L2
Fuel	M1 to M6, M8 and M10
Household durables	O3 to O9
Literary activities	P1 to P4
Vice	K1 to K4, and Q1 to Q3.

Section C to section J of the tables give the expenditures on the principal items of food; section L gives expenditure on rents, etc.; section M gives the expenditures on fuel, etc.; section N gives the expenditure on clothing derived from the annual inquiry,† and the remaining sections give the other expenditures in what is hoped will appear to the reader as a not too illogical order.

Section X, finally, gives certain supplementary tables which may be of use in further analyses. These give, in the main, some further information on household compositions and some further tables for the middle-class inquiry relating to commodities which have already been included in the 'all other expenditures' table T 10.

† The estimates for the middle class are based on the sub-sample of 703 households who supplied annual returns as described in § 3.23, p. 29 above. The composition of these households is given in tables X 7 (a) to (d). Estimates of clothing expenditure by the complete sample of 1361 households during the four weeks of the major inquiry are given in tables X 8 (a) to (f).

CONTENTS OF THE TABLES*

A. Description of the samples

B. Certain summary tables classified by the level of total expenditure per person and by region (working class only)

C. Farinaceous foods

* In this impression the tables included are only those in sections A and B (see the Preface to this second impression, p. xxi above). The full list of tables included in the first impression has nevertheless been repeated here for the benefit of research students and others who may be interested in the detail available there.

O

D. Dairy products and fats

D1 Milk—fresh, whole (including milk at school, office, factory, etc.)
D2 Milk—liquid skimmed (including butter-milk)
D3 Milk—condensed (full-cream or skimmed)
D4 Dried milk and milk preparations (including Allenburys, Cow-and-Gate, Glaxo, Ovaltine, Bournvita, malted milk, Horlicks, etc.)
D5 Cream
D6 Butter
D7 Margarine
D8 Lard (including compound lard)
D9 Cheese
D10 Eggs
D11 Suet, dripping and other cooking fats

E. Beverages and sucrose foods

E1 Tea
E2 Coffee and coffee essence
E3 Cocoa and cocoa essence
E4 Sugar
E5 Jam and marmalade (including jelly used as jam)
E6 Syrup, treacle, honey
E7 Sweets, chocolates, ice-cream, lemonade powder, etc.

F. Fruit

F1 Apples
F2 Oranges
F3 Bananas
F4 Other fresh fruit
F5 Dried fruits—currants, raisins, sultanas, prunes, dates, figs, fruit salad, etc.
F6 Tinned and bottled fruits

G. Vegetables

G1 Potatoes (fresh)
G2 Green vegetables and fresh legumes (including cabbage, broccoli, cauliflower, sprouts, greens, spinach, kale, parsley, lettuce, celery, cress, beans and peas)
G3 Root vegetables (including carrots, parsnips, swedes, turnips, artichokes, beetroot, radishes, cucumber, marrows and tomatoes)
G4 Onions, leeks, and shallots
G5 Dried legumes (including lentils, split peas, dried peas, butter beans, haricot beans, peasemeal, pease pudding, potato crisps)
G6 Tinned and bottled vegetables (including tinned tomatoes and tomato puree)

H. Fish

H1 Fish—fresh (including herrings, cod, haddock, hake, plaice, and other fresh fish)
H2 Fish—shell (including crab, lobster, shrimps, winkles, mussels, cockles, whelks, etc.)

H3   Fish—dried and cured (including haddock, bloaters, kippers, etc.)
H4   Fish—tinned (including salmon, sardines, crab, lobster, etc., and fish paste)

I. Meat

I1   Beef and veal (joints, cuts, etc., and mince)—home produce
I2   Beef and veal (joints, cuts, etc., and mince)—imported
I3   Mutton or lamb (joints, cuts, etc., and mince)—home produce
I4   Mutton or lamb (joints, cuts, etc., and mince)—imported
I5   Pork (joints, cuts, etc.)
I6   Bacon and ham—cooked and uncooked (including gammon)
I7   Sausages and meat pies
I8   Tinned and potted meats (including corned beef)
I9   Other meat (including kidney, liver, pluck, fry, heart, head, sweet-breads, brain, chitterlings, tripe, cowheel, brawn, etc.)
I10   Rabbits, poultry, game, etc.

J. Sundry foods

J1   Malt and cod liver oil, etc. (including halibut liver oil, Haliborange, Virol, etc.)
J2   Fried fish and chips
J3   Other food (including meat extracts—Bovril, Marmite, etc.—soups, sauces, chutney, pickles, salad oil, vinegar, salt, pepper, mustard, yeast)
J4   Meals at school
J5   Other food at school
J6   Meals away from home (except at school)—dinners
J7   Meals away from home (except at school)—other meals

K. Drink and tobacco

K1   Drink (alcoholic and soft)
K2   Tobacco
K3   Cigarettes
K4   Tobacco and cigarettes not distinguished

L. Rent

L1   Average weekly payments for rent, rates, and water charges (less any rent received for rooms sublet)
L2   Average weekly payments in respect of purchase instalments, ground rent, rates and water charges (less any rent for rooms sublet)
L3   Average rent (or house purchase instalment, etc.) paid per room and net number of rooms occupied

M. Fuel

M1   Coal
M2   Coke
M3   Oil
M4   Other fuel and light (including firewood, candles, matches, etc., but not gas or electricity)

M5   Gas slot meter: expenditure for gas per week
M6   Gas other meter: expenditure for gas per week
M7   Expenditure on gas fittings etc., per week
M8   Houses with slot meter: expenditure for electric current per week
M9   Houses with slot meter: additional expenditure on electric fittings, etc.,
        per week
M10   Houses with other meter: expenditure for electric current per week
M11   Houses with other meter: expenditure on electric fittings, etc., per
        week

N. Clothing

N1   Men's clothing (annual estimate)
N2   Women's clothing and materials (annual estimate)
N3   Children's clothing and materials (annual estimate)
N4   Clothing repairs, cleaning and dyeing (including cost of dyes pur-
        chased) (annual estimate)
N5   Boots and shoes (annual estimate)
N6   Repairs to boots and shoes (annual estimate)

O. Household items

O1   Soap (including soap flakes)
O2   Soda, polishes and cleaning materials
O3   Ironmongery, cutlery, tools, etc.
O4   Household brushes and brooms
O5   Crockery and glassware
O6   Drapery and haberdashery
O7   Furniture
O8   Carpets, floorcloth, mats, etc.
O9   Other utensils, furnishing and household equipment

P. Literary activities

P1   Education and music lessons (not instruction in sports, games and
        dancing)
P2   Newspapers, magazines and periodicals
P3   Books, stationery, pens, pencils, etc.
P4   Postages, telephones and telegrams

Q. Amusements

Q1   Cinemas
Q2   Theatres, music halls, concerts, dances and other entertainments
        (except sports and games)
Q3   Admission charges to watch sports, games, etc.

R. Travel

R1   Rail, season or contract (travel to and from work)
R2   Rail, workmen's cheap fares (travel to and from work)
R3   Rail, other fares (travel to and from work)
R4   Bus, tram, coach, etc. (travel to and from work)
R5   Rail fares (not to and from work)
R6   Bus, tram, coach, etc. (not to and from work)

S. Personal expenditures

S1 Doctor, dentist, nurse, midwife, optician, etc.
S2 Medicine, drugs, etc., and medical and surgical appliances (including pharmaceutical preparations)
S3 Chemists' sundries (cosmetics, tooth paste, vaseline, tooth brushes, sponges, etc.)
S4 Hairdressing, haircuts, shaving, manicure, shampooing, etc.

T. Sundry expenditures

T1 Laundry
T2 Wages paid for domestic help
T3 Payments to hospital funds, hospital fees, nursing home charges, etc.
T4 Trade union, friendly society, burial club, etc., subscriptions
T5 Unemployment, National Health and Pensions Insurance
T6 Payments to pension funds, insurance premiums, etc.
T7 Licences (dog, wireless, motor-cycle, etc.)
T8 Food for animals, poultry, birds, etc. (bran, maize, maize-meal, bird-seed, dog biscuits, etc.)
T9 Holiday expenditure in the weeks of the inquiry (including holiday travelling and payment to holiday clubs)
T10 All other expenditure

X. Supplementary tables

X1 Expenditure on food (v_1) and expenditure on non-food (v_2)
X2 Supplementary table on household composition. Working class: (a) number of children, aged 5–9; (b) number of children, aged 10–13. Middle class: (c) number of boys, aged 5–13; (d) number of girls, aged 5–13
X3 Supplementary table on household composition. Working class: (a) number of children, aged 1–4; (b) number of infants under 1. Middle class: (c) number of boys aged 4 and under; (d) number of girls aged 4 and under
X4 Bread: white, brown, wholemeal and rolls (bought by weight)
X5 Cheese (by weight)
X6 Income of head of household: middle class
X7 Middle-class annual inquiry
    (a) Number of households and total expenditure
    (b) Number of men (n_1), and women (n_2), aged over 14
    (c) Number of children aged 1–4 (n_1), and 5–13 (n_2)
X8 Four-weekly expenditure on clothing by middle class
    (a) Men's clothing
    (b) Women's clothing and materials
    (c) Children's clothing and materials
    (d) Clothing repairs, cleaning and dyeing (including cost of dyes purchased)
    (e) Boots and shoes
    (f) Repairs to boots and shoes
X9 Sports, games and other forms of exercise
X10 Motor-cars, motor-cycles and pedal cycles, including vehicle, petrol, oil, etc. (not licences or insurance)
X11 Religion and charity
X12 Decoration of house
X13 Gambling

TABLE A1. NUMBER OF HOUSEHOLDS AND TOTAL EXPENDITURE

WORKING CLASS

V	<500		500–750		750–1000		1000–1250		1250–1500		1500–1750		1750–2250		>2250		Σ	
n	f	v	f	v	f	v	f	v	f	v	f	v	f	v	f	v	f	v
1	16	303·9	11	597·3	5	817·5	1	1024·3	1	1445·3	1	1616·8	—	—	—	—	35	560·2
2	35	427·9	142	641·7	168	866·5	86	1108·1	37	1363·6	17	1616·2	6	1928·6	3	3484·0	494	899·4
3	16	429·0	131	651·7	213	879·0	131	1112·1	72	1355·8	36	1607·0	24	1950·0	4	2420·6	627	1016·1
4	12	410·9	91	663·6	142	884·2	107	1114·6	58	1354·6	31	1611·5	25	1919·6	21	2991·5	487	1128·3
5	7	470·5	52	638·6	61	877·9	55	1114·5	53	1365·4	28	1598·8	18	1969·7	11	3131·0	285	1187·3
6	3	459·8	14	641·6	31	864·1	34	1119·0	14	1365·4	20	1621·3	13	2007·5	9	2732·8	138	1270·6
7+	2	460·6	18	636·7	30	855·1	37	1148·3	33	1367·4	16	1614·9	13	1939·0	4	2958·6	153	1232·2
Σ	91	409·1	459	647·2	650	874·5	451	1115·5	268	1360·8	149	1610·3	99	1950·7	52	2869·3	2219	1060·3

MIDDLE CLASS

V	<1250		1250–1500		1500–1750		1750–2250		2250–3000		3000–3750		>3750		Σ	
n	f	v	f	v	f	v	f	v	f	v	f	v	f	v	f	v
1	18	977·3	11	1387·5	4	1633·5	10	1981·7	4	2505·7	2	3331·8	—	—	49	1548·8
2	65	1065·6	70	1365·9	50	1620·9	74	1976·1	51	2592·4	18	3325·8	17	5258·6	345	1952·5
3	46	1093·2	84	1380·9	71	1641·3	100	1992·1	75	2565·2	35	3364·8	31	4787·5	442	2128·0
4	27	1106·6	47	1398·7	54	1628·1	86	1976·9	67	2588·3	32	3395·7	37	5213·0	350	2367·1
5	4	1132·7	13	1363·4	15	1664·7	36	1965·7	20	2601·0	16	3401·6	22	4952·8	126	2646·0
6+	2	1213·5	5	1389·1	6	1636·2	12	1964·2	11	2516·1	7	3230·7	6	5585·1	49	2582·9
Σ	162	1073·9	230	1379·5	200	1634·1	318	1979·9	228	2577·8	110	3363·6	113	5072·2	1361	2188·5

TABLE A2. NUMBER OF PERSONS (f_1) AND NUMBER OF WAGE-EARNERS (f_2) IN HOUSEHOLD

WORKING CLASS

V	<500		500–750		750–1000		1000–1250		1250–1500		1500–1750		1750–2250		>2250		Σ	
n	f_1	f_2	f_1	f_2	f_1	f_2	f_1	f_2	f_1	f_2	f_1	f_2	f_1	f_2	f_1	f_2	f_1	f_2
1	1·02	1·00	1·02	1·00	1·00	1·00	1·00	1·00	1·00	1·00	1·00	1·00	—	—	—	—	1·02	1·00
2	2·05	1·18	2·02	1·14	2·04	1·25	2·03	1·36	2·03	1·25	2·05	1·44	2·00	1·46	2·00	1·00	2·03	1·24
3	3·02	1·13	3·00	1·37	3·01	1·42	3·01	1·56	2·99	1·74	3·06	1·68	3·11	1·85	3·19	1·38	3·01	1·50
4	4·00	1·13	4·25	1·28	4·02	1·67	4·03	1·87	4·03	2·25	3·99	2·37	4·06	2·46	4·06	2·48	4·02	1·82
5	5·04	1·24	5·01	1·40	5·00	1·48	5·01	1·92	5·00	2·61	5·03	2·79	4·99	3·02	4·98	3·14	5·00	2·04
6	6·00	1·17	6·00	1·34	6·02	1·91	6·02	2·47	5·95	3·57	6·00	3·54	5·98	3·81	6·16	4·16	6·01	2·70
7+	9·13	1·63	7·49	1·47	9·08	2·64	8·49	3·40	8·24	3·76	8·13	3·91	9·31	5·44	7·88	5·25	8·46	3·35
Σ	2·81	1·15	3·35	1·28	3·57	1·26	3·98	1·85	4·27	2·30	4·43	2·49	4·81	2·93	4·75	2·97	3·80	1·78

MIDDLE CLASS

V	<1250		1250–1500		1500–1750		1750–2250		2250–3000		3000–3750		>3750		Σ	
n	f_1	f_2	f_1	f_2	f_1	f_2	f_1	f_2	f_1	f_2	f_1	f_2	f_1	f_2	f_1	f_2
1	1·00	1·00	1·02	0·91	1·00	1·00	1·00	1·00	1·00	1·00	1·00	1·00	—	—	1·37	0·98
2	2·00	1·00	2·01	1·08	2·03	1·02	2·02	1·06	2·02	1·11	2·05	1·17	2·06	1·12	2·02	1·06
3	3·01	1·03	3·02	1·07	3·03	1·16	3·02	1·15	3·02	1·33	3·02	1·24	2·99	1·20	3·02	1·16
4	4·01	1·05	4·01	1·21	4·01	1·29	4·04	1·26	4·07	1·34	4·03	1·48	4·08	1·55	4·04	1·31
5	5·06	1·00	5·00	1·13	5·07	1·50	5·01	1·45	4·99	1·35	5·03	2·13	5·06	1·60	5·03	1·51
6+	6·00	1·00	6·20	1·75	6·00	1·79	6·46	1·77	6·16	1·27	6·04	2·32	6·63	1·83	6·25	1·71
Σ	2·63	1·02	3·00	1·11	3·25	1·20	3·35	1·21	3·39	1·28	3·60	1·49	3·80	1·42	3·26	1·22

TABLE A3. NUMBER OF MALES (n_1) AND FEMALES (n_2) OVER 18 YEARS OF AGE

WORKING CLASS

V	<500		500–750		750–1000		1000–1250		1250–1500		1500–1750		1750–2250		>2250		Σ	
n	n_1	n_2	n_1	n_2	n_1	n_2	n_1	n_2	n_1	n_2	n_1	n_2	n_1	n_2	n_1	n_2	n_1	n_2
1	0·375	0·641	0·364	0·659	0·200	0·800	1·000	0	0	1·000	0	1·000	—	—	—	—	0·343	0·671
2	0·943	1·043	0·936	1·057	0·975	1·034	0·980	1·038	1·000	1·000	0·897	1·176	0·833	1·167	1·000	1·000	0·962	1·048
3	0·875	1·250	1·079	1·087	1·123	1·167	1·103	1·194	1·246	1·268	1·336	1·393	1·326	1·304	1·125	1·000	1·137	1·186
4	0·979	1·229	1·071	1·095	1·234	1·163	1·381	1·252	1·496	1·407	1·371	1·532	1·385	1·827	1·786	1·762	1·298	1·283
5	1·000	1·000	1·090	1·038	1·111	1·159	1·350	1·377	1·462	1·575	1·768	1·786	1·528	1·931	2·781	2·273	1·331	1·403
6	1·000	1·000	1·071	1·071	1·142	1·142	1·321	1·286	1·732	1·839	2·063	1·788	2·115	2·462	3·625	2·344	1·560	1·529
7+	1·000	1·000	1·028	1·111	1·250	1·375	1·542	1·639	1·970	1·712	2·016	1·891	2·462	2·596		2·438	1·692	1·661
Σ	0·843	1·027	1·015	1·064	1·107	1·136	1·227	1·240	1·420	1·406	1·537	1·576	1·601	1·869	2·010	1·930	1·211	1·251

MIDDLE CLASS

V	<1250		1250–1500		1500–1750		1750–2250		2250–3000		3000–3750		>3750		Σ	
n	n_1	n_2	n_1	n_2	n_1	n_2	n_1	n_2	n_1	n_2	n_1	n_2	n_1	n_2	n_1	n_2
1	0	1·000	0·091	0·932	0	1·000	0·100	0·900	0·250	0·750	0	1·000	—	—	0·061	0·944
2	0·908	1·088	0·886	1·114	0·910	1·105	0·865	1·139	0·819	1·196	0·583	1·417	0·662	1·397	0·852	1·155
3	0·989	1·114	1·003	1·158	1·007	1·194	1·020	1·215	1·034	1·372	1·036	1·321	1·113	1·339	1·019	1·231
4	1·019	1·056	1·021	1·213	1·074	1·204	1·145	1·169	1·138	1·287	1·320	1·508	1·264	1·486	1·135	1·259
5	1·000	1·000	1·000	1·231	1·167	1·400	1·028	1·444	1·188	1·463	1·469	1·859	1·341	2·193	1·177	1·589
6+	1·125	2·000	1·200	1·200	1·500	1·167	1·250	1·458	1·159	1·205	1·607	1·893	1·000	2·833	1·270	1·592
Σ	0·853	1·090	0·932	1·150	1·008	1·185	0·998	1·210	1·022	1·296	1·125	1·500	1·133	1·642	0·996	1·255

TABLE A4. NUMBER OF MALES (n_3) AND FEMALES (n_4) AGED 14–17

WORKING CLASS

V	<500		500–750		750–1000		1000–1250		1250–1500		1500–1750		1750–2250		>2250		Σ	
n	n_3	n_4	n_3	n_4	n_3	n_4	n_3	n_4	n_3	n_4	n_3	n_4	n_3	n_4	n_3	n_4	n_3	n_4
1	0	0	0	0	0	0	0	0	0	0	0	0	—	—	—	—	0	0
2	0·021	0·021	0·005	0·002	0·001	0·007	0·062	0·109	0·060	0·148	0·014	0·029	0·033	0·141	0	0·250	0·004	0·005
3	0·063	0·047	0·073	0·056	0·082	0·062	0·236	0·159	0·263	0·237	0·266	0·242	0·173	0·192	0·095	0·095	0·067	0·082
4	0·063	0	0·079	0·136	0·098	0·192	0·332	0·200	0·590	0·274	0·321	0·384	0·417	0·278	0·250	0·386	0·158	0·173
5	0	0·143	0·146	0·137	0·187	0·286	0·436	0·679	0·589	0·554	0·488	0·588	0·500	0·308	0·281	0·125	0·306	0·249
6	1·000	0·500	0·071	0·196	0·483	0·242	0·958	0·618	0·879	0·477	0·328	1·031	0·808	0·846	0·250	0·813	0·420	0·436
7+		0·500	0·347	0·167	0·458	0·733											0·673	0·623
Σ	0·049	0·055	0·071	0·072	0·110	0·136	0·224	0·195	0·294	0·233	0·221	0·321	0·301	0·285	0·160	0·230	0·166	0·165

MIDDLE CLASS

V	<1250		1250–1500		1500–1750		1750–2250		2250–3000		3000–3750		>3750		Σ	
n	n_3	n_4	n_3	n_4	n_3	n_4	n_3	n_4	n_3	n_4	n_3	n_4	n_3	n_4	n_3	n_4
1	0	0	0	0	0	0	0	0	0	0	0	0	—	—	0	0
2	0	0·004	0	0·004	0	0	0	0	0	0	0·014	0	0	0	0·001	0·001
3	0·011	0	0·068	0·048	0·046	0·060	0·090	0·125	0·125	0·152	0·086	0·114	0·048	0·145	0·073	0·092
4	0·037	0·083	0·197	0·027	0·236	0·231	0·215	0·189	0·205	0·205	0·172	0·313	0·250	0·264	0·200	0·188
5	0·375	0·188	0·500	0·115	0·217	0·250	0·222	0·264	0·238	0·313	0·391	0·344	0·136	0·352	0·200	0·278
6+		0		0·600	0·167	0·500	0·500	0·667	0·568	0·227	0·214	0·821	0·333	0·333	0·408	0·495
Σ	0·014	0·020	0·076	0·118	0·101	0·118	0·131	0·145	0·150	0·149	0·150	0·230	0·139	0·212	0·109	0·122

TABLE A5. NUMBER OF CHILDREN AGED 5–13 (n_5) AND UNDER 5 (n_6)

WORKING CLASS

V	<500		500–750		750–1000		1000–1250		1250–1500		1500–1750		1750–2250		>2250		Σ	
n	n_5	n_6	n_5	n_6	n_5	n_6	n_5	n_6	n_5	n_6	n_5	n_6	n_5	n_6	n_5	n_6	n_5	n_6
1	0·014	0	0	0	0	0	0	0	0	0	0	0	—	—	—	—	0	0
2	0·406	0	0·007	0·0125	0·059	0·010	0	0·006	0	0·027	0	0·029	0·196	0·087	0·500	0·313	0·005	0·011
3	0·751	0·375	0·375	0·331	0·299	0·282	0·282	0·256	0·134	0·137	0·204	0·057	0·307	0·163	0·262	0·060	0·289	0·253
4	1·750	0·958	0·964	0·682	0·890	0·436	0·644	0·340	0·437	0·178	0·484	0·097	0·709	0·139	0·205	0·068	0·707	0·391
5	3·000	1·143	1·562	1·047	1·635	0·627	1·214	0·528	0·858	0·241	0·733	0·036	0·596	0·036	0·625	0	1·201	0·517
6	4·125	0·500	2·269	0·982	2·058	0·958	1·793	0·521	1·018	0·232	1·025	0·050	1·308	0	0·750	0	1·588	0·485
7+		1·500	3·389	1·472	3·034	1·308	2·590	0·688	2·341	0·583	2·125	0·703		0·212			2·532	0·834
Σ	0·500	0·330	0·696	0·444	0·685	0·354	0·727	0·317	0·643	0·211	0·662	0·127	0·505	0·116	0·355	0·065	0·666	0·314

MIDDLE CLASS

V	<1250		1250–1500		1500–1750		1750–2250		2250–3000		3000–3750		>3750		Σ	
n	n_5	n_6	n_5	n_6	n_5	n_6	n_5	n_6	n_5	n_6	n_5	n_6	n_5	n_6	n_5	n_6
1	0	0	0	0	0	0	0	0	0	0	0	0	—	—	0	0
2	0·266	0	0	0·007	0	0·005	0	0·003	0·005	0	0·042	0	0·218	0·129	0·007	0·003
3	0·981	0·625	0·307	0·435	0·366	0·359	0·350	0·218	0·247	0·095	0·264	0·200	0·709	0·108	0·301	0·295
4	2·375	0·833	0·984	0·569	0·889	0·375	0·904	0·419	0·929	0·299	0·547	0·172	0·909	0·091	0·870	0·386
5	2·500	0·500	1·692	0·962	1·400	0·633	1·590	0·465	1·588	0·200	0·844	0·125	1·458	0·667	1·389	0·387
6+		0	2·100	0·600	2·375	0·292	2·042	0·542	2·023	0·977	1·214	0·286			1·913	0·571
Σ	0·329	0·329	0·454	0·345	0·548	0·286	0·615	0·256	0·594	0·184	0·450	0·150	0·546	0·124	0·521	0·252

NOTE. Tables B1–B22 are regional survey tables (working class only) classified by 10 regions (vertically) and 12 total expenditure per person groups (horizontally). For definitions of the regions and the expenditure groups, see p. 177.

TABLE B1. NUMBER OF HOUSEHOLDS

	1	2	3	4	5	6	7	8	9	10	11	12	Σ
1	6	14	17	25	29	41	36	33	39	28	27	30	325
2	6	18	21	14	23	31	28	17	20	22	10	3	213
3	9	13	16	22	28	20	21	22	19	13	11	11	205
4	17	13	25	28	30	32	33	34	29	31	31	17	320
5	11	19	25	17	22	14	28	34	24	25	15	7	241
6	13	23	22	29	48	34	30	28	29	27	21	16	320
7	4	14	11	17	17	19	16	17	10	7	8	4	144
8	6	7	13	13	13	15	14	10	10	8	6	1	116
9	13	18	22	26	24	27	19	20	18	23	20	10	240
10	14	11	9	5	13	10	5	7	6	3	—	1	84
Σ	99	150	181	196	247	243	230	222	204	187	149	100	2208

TABLE B2. TOTAL EXPENDITURE PER PERSON

	1	2	3	4	5	6	7	8	9	10	11	12	Σ
1	95·00	140·71	172·94	198·40	228·97	263·17	301·11	343·33	392·82	460·36	552·96	761·33	356·98
2	95·00	136·11	169·52	200·00	229·13	265·48	301·79	335·88	391·00	459·09	551·00	743·33	294·37
3	97·78	137·69	166·88	193·64	227·14	265·50	302·38	341·82	391·05	463·85	534·55	735·45	305·22
4	96·47	135·38	168·40	195·36	232·00	265·00	299·70	339·12	394·48	458·06	534·84	844·71	334·81
5	87·27	133·68	171·60	195·29	228·18	268·57	302·14	342·06	389·17	453·20	554·00	758·57	308·17
6	93·08	136·96	161·82	196·21	229·17	262·94	302·67	343·93	391·38	450·00	556·19	766·88	311·59
7	90·00	137·14	168·18	197·06	227·06	265·26	301·25	338·24	392·00	455·71	545·00	762·50	287·99
8	83·33	132·86	164·62	191·54	230·00	266·00	297·86	342·00	391·00	458·75	561·67	760·00	278·79
9	102·31	132·78	168·38	195·38	232·92	264·81	301·58	334·50	393·89	458·70	545·50	889·00	312·92
10	85·71	135·45	168·89	194·00	229·23	260·00	308·00	338·57	403·33	486·67	—	650·00	228·57
Σ	93·13	135·93	168·18	195·87	229·43	264·57	301·43	340·45	392·35	457·59	551·34	784·50	312·74

Table B3. Total household expenditure

	1	2	3	4	5	6	7	8	9	10	11	12	Σ
1	770·58	899·32	925·10	916·94	986·16	1039·06	1159·02	1252·54	1283·30	1204·00	1406·71	1559·69	1165·09
2	615·04	748·40	803·89	794·95	866·90	1013·22	936·69	943·16	1091·43	1397·44	1404·70	2562·92	1000·42
3	604·83	748·25	860·78	848·08	843·24	984·46	1130·90	1039·70	1078·29	1300·71	1528·75	1863·36	1029·82
4	669·59	882·48	822·81	835·14	916·57	1000·60	1102·85	1148·28	1165·69	1253·71	1370·27	2104·40	1102·14
5	655·86	731·04	827·88	839·24	836·44	1004·55	1049·32	954·52	1032·64	1244·87	1361·15	2275·39	1006·72
6	605·50	779·04	870·76	956·21	886·31	995·45	1082·98	1119·88	1164·79	1147·66	1407·95	1807·66	1050·52
7	643·75	666·27	729·05	830·00	824·88	960·42	910·77	952·38	976·73	1333·54	1959·59	2483·56	984·09
8	500·17	697·50	809·17	769·23	906·33	1090·82	889·48	1010·43	1378·78	1232·13	1324·13	760·00	960·81
9	682·29	843·49	934·73	1015·13	1027·42	1036·17	1193·62	1228·89	1079·25	1273·78	1744·39	2173·05	1151·01
10	579·21	880·86	1101·11	892·70	1001·23	950·20	685·80	1030·68	1164·83	1345·75	—	2655·25	940·66
Σ	634·15	787·68	860·87	882·95	907·16	1006·57	1056·95	1086·40	1150·50	1255·59	1475·28	1906·82	1061·03

Table B4. Total number of persons

	1	2	3	4	5	6	7	8	9	10	11	12	Σ
1	7·63	6·18	5·19	4·51	4·22	3·88	3·76	3·58	3·24	2·60	2·55	2·10	3·69
2	6·25	5·26	4·58	3·87	3·68	3·74	3·05	2·78	2·76	3·01	2·50	3·33	3·63
3	6·00	5·31	5·02	4·27	3·61	3·44	3·68	2·99	2·71	2·77	2·80	2·55	3·69
4	6·74	6·37	4·79	4·13	3·85	3·69	3·61	3·34	2·90	2·70	2·45	2·29	3·69
5	7·25	5·26	4·70	4·24	3·56	3·68	3·39	2·73	2·61	2·71	2·42	3·00	3·63
6	6·37	5·55	5·16	4·76	3·79	3·71	3·53	3·21	2·94	2·52	2·49	2·36	3·78
7	7·19	4·75	4·20	4·10	3·53	3·54	2·95	2·76	2·45	2·86	3·53	3·25	3·60
8	5·88	5·14	4·73	3·88	3·81	4·02	2·96	2·90	3·48	2·66	2·33	1·00	3·75
9	6·40	6·10	5·47	5·05	4·31	3·87	3·91	3·59	2·71	2·74	3·14	2·63	4·16
10	6·48	6·27	6·39	4·50	4·27	3·60	2·20	3·00	2·83	2·75	—	4·00	4·67
Σ	6·59	5·61	4·98	4·39	3·85	3·73	3·45	3·14	2·89	2·71	2·64	2·43	3·78

Table B5. Number of males over 18

	1	2	3	4	5	6	7	8	9	10	11	12	Σ
1	1·00	1·07	1·31	1·27	1·29	1·19	1·33	1·31	1·12	1·07	1·22	0·87	1·19
2	1·00	1·29	1·12	1·07	1·34	1·26	1·30	1·26	1·13	1·22	1·05	1·00	1·21
3	1·11	1·23	1·17	1·22	1·19	1·33	1·21	1·25	1·05	1·23	1·25	1·05	1·20
4	1·06	1·08	1·04	1·23	1·25	1·23	1·47	1·27	1·06	1·12	1·11	1·24	1·19
5	1·11	1·17	1·21	1·31	1·16	1·50	1·19	1·07	1·13	1·19	1·15	1·18	1·18
6	1·02	1·11	1·22	1·12	1·24	1·27	1·47	1·16	1·10	1·11	0·96	0·97	1·17
7	1·00	1·07	1·00	1·22	1·34	1·32	1·23	1·10	1·05	1·29	1·88	1·00	1·22
8	1·00	1·29	1·15	1·50	1·25	1·65	1·18	1·15	0·68	1·44	1·17	0	1·33
9	1·17	1·36	1·47	1·24	1·20	1·36	1·39	1·34	1·14	1·15	1·15	1·13	1·27
10	1·13	1·55	1·61	1·80	1·21	1·15	0·80	1·21	0·83	1·08	—	2·00	1·26
Σ	1·08	1·21	1·22	1·25	1·24	1·30	1·32	1·22	1·12	1·16	1·17	1·03	1·21

Table B6. Number of females over 18

	1	2	3	4	5	6	7	8	9	10	11	12	Σ
1	1·17	1·30	1·12	1·06	1·17	1·32	1·44	1·36	1·39	1·30	1·18	1·17	1·27
2	1·00	1·13	1·15	1·21	1·22	1·19	1·16	1·24	1·08	1·37	1·28	2·33	1·21
3	1·00	1·29	1·08	1·24	1·12	1·15	1·05	1·42	1·07	1·37	1·18	1·00	1·17
4	1·13	1·54	1·18	1·16	1·39	1·20	1·45	1·38	1·22	1·35	1·00	1·06	1·26
5	1·14	1·24	1·18	1·18	1·28	1·34	1·32	1·21	1·00	1·12	1·20	1·29	1·20
6	1·38	1·29	1·24	1·36	1·23	1·29	1·13	1·23	1·21	1·15	1·38	1·14	1·25
7	1·00	1·00	1·00	1·06	1·01	1·14	1·14	1·26	1·00	1·18	1·44	2·00	1·14
8	1·17	1·07	1·33	1·08	1·13	1·20	1·11	1·13	1·33	1·06	1·17	1·00	1·16
9	1·10	1·13	1·40	1·35	1·52	1·36	1·38	1·36	1·40	1·48	1·55	1·15	1·37
10	1·32	1·55	2·17	1·20	1·90	1·85	1·40	1·14	1·50	1·33	—	1·00	1·59
Σ	1·17	1·25	1·24	1·20	1·28	1·28	1·27	1·30	1·21	1·28	1·24	1·20	1·25

Table B7. Number of males aged 14–17

	1	2	3	4	5	6	7	8	9	10	11	12	Σ
1	0·33	0·23	0·37	0·18	0·13	0·19	0·17	0·20	0·19	0	0	0	0·15
2	0·33	0·54	0·20	0·23	0·27	0·34	0·05	0	0·10	0·15	0·05	0	0·20
3	0·11	0·31	0·36	0·23	0·16	0·29	0·21	0·05	0·05	0·08	0	0	0·16
4	0·22	0·56	0·24	0·14	0·10	0·40	0·06	0·18	0·12	0·03	0·02	0·11	0·16
5	0·30	0·26	0·28	0·43	0·18	0·23	0·10	0·09	0·11	0·07	0	0	0·17
6	0·19	0·21	0·26	0·32	0·19	0·26	0·06	0·20	0·11	0	0·05	0	0·16
7	0·38	0·21	0·09	0·18	0	0·26	0·06	0·06	0·10	0	0·09	0	0·12
8	0·25	0·46	0·40	0·04	0·25	0·28	0·18	0·03	0	0	0·14	0	0·18
9	0·40	0·28	0·14	0·27	0·19	0·19	0·28	0·03	0·04	0·02	—	0·50	0·17
10	0·25	0·34	0·86	0·05	0·29	0·05	0	0·21	0·21	0			0·27
Σ	0·27	0·33	0·29	0·22	0·17	0·26	0·12	0·11	0·11	0·04	0·04	0·01	0·17

Table B8. Number of females aged 14–17

	1	2	3	4	5	6	7	8	9	10	11	12	Σ
1	0·25	0·21	0·28	0·14	0·24	0·12	0·13	0·28	0·18	0·08	0·03	0·01	0·15
2	0·21	0·18	0·27	0·21	0·10	0·05	0·06	0·04	0·11	0·09	0·03	0	0·11
3	0·44	0·06	0·53	0·25	0·23	0	0·23	0·05	0·01	0	0·18	0·27	0·18
4	0·31	0·48	0·16	0·21	0·23	0·06	0·17	0·12	0·09	0·10	0	0	0·14
5	0·48	0·37	0·30	0·15	0·05	0·07	0·19	0·03	0·04	0·18	0·07	0	0·15
6	0·33	0·30	0·25	0·36	0·11	0·16	0·27	0·16	0·20	0·15	0	0·06	0·19
7	0·25	0·16	0·09	0·13	0·29	0·09	0·11	0·22	0	0	0·09	0	0·14
8	0·08	0·36	0·23	0·15	0·13	0·32	0·14	0	0·15	0·03	0	0	0·16
9	0·17	0·33	0·28	0·45	0·34	0·18	0·14	0·11	0	0·04	0·05	0·15	0·20
10	0·45	0·55	0·28	0·40	0·44	0·25	0	0·14	0	0	—	0	0·31
Σ	0·32	0·29	0·27	0·25	0·20	0·12	0·16	0·12	0·10	0·09	0·04	0·06	0·17

Table B9. Number of children aged 10–13

	1	2	3	4	5	6	7	8	9	10	11	12	Σ
1	1·21	0·79	0·68	0·62	0·44	0·33	0·16	0·16	0·16	0·04	0	0·02	0·28
2	1·13	0·81	0·52	0·37	0·33	0·23	0·10	0·06	0·10	0·09	0·10	0	0·29
3	0·86	0·75	0·58	0·35	0·29	0·16	0·50	0·05	0·25	0	0·18	0	0·31
4	1·04	0·69	0·44	0·37	0·33	0·41	0·17	0·10	0·17	0	0·06	0	0·27
5	1·16	0·75	0·66	0·72	0·19	0·20	0·11	0·06	0·14	0·11	0	0·14	0·31
6	0·85	0·92	0·69	0·50	0·35	0·26	0·14	0·14	0·09	0·04	0·10	0·13	0·32
7	1·56	0·82	0·57	0·44	0·24	0·13	0·13	0·06	0·10	0	0·03	0·25	0·30
8	1·17	0·79	0·58	0·15	0·71	0·45	0·29	0	0	0·13	0	0	0·37
9	1·13	0·74	0·85	0·60	0·42	0·21	0·16	0·15	0·06	0·04	0·14	0·10	0·37
10	0·79	0·77	0·67	0·55	0·04	0·10	0	0	0·21	0	—	0·50	0·37
Σ	1·03	0·79	0·62	0·48	0·34	0·27	0·18	0·09	0·13	0·05	0·07	0·06	0·31

Table B10. Number of children aged 5–9

	1	2	3	4	5	6	7	8	9	10	11	12	Σ
1	2·21	1·68	0·71	0·66	0·45	0·30	0·28	0·14	0·09	0·05	0·04	0	0·34
2	1·33	0·89	0·65	0·55	0·26	0·35	0·13	0	0·18	0·05	0	0	0·33
3	1·03	0·50	0·53	0·64	0·40	0·14	0·29	0·14	0·21	0·02	0·09	0·09	0·32
4	1·65	1·04	0·94	0·49	0·27	0·17	0·13	0·11	0·16	0·03	0	0	0·34
5	1·82	0·92	0·64	0·28	0·27	0·12	0·38	0·09	0·08	0·04	0·09	0·14	0·35
6	1·52	0·88	1·00	0·48	0·45	0·25	0·32	0·23	0·07	0·06	0	0·06	0·40
7	1·25	0·79	0·91	0·46	0·29	0·37	0	0·06	0·10	0·25	0	0	0·34
8	1·13	0·29	0·38	0·42	0·12	0·07	0·07	0	0·20	0	0	0	0·21
9	1·21	1·14	1·00	0·48	0·52	0·29	0·30	0·21	0·06	0	0·08	0·03	0·43
10	1·46	1·05	0·58	0·10	0·23	0·10	0	0	0·08	0	—	0	0·50
Σ	1·48	0·95	0·76	0·49	0·36	0·24	0·22	0·12	0·12	0·04	0·04	0·03	0·36

Table B11. Number of children aged 1–4

	1	2	3	4	5	6	7	8	9	10	11	12	Σ
1	1·17	0·79	0·59	0·47	0·41	0·37	0·17	0·13	0·08	0·04	0·01	0	0·25
2	1·00	0·35	0·63	0·21	0·11	0·23	0·20	0·18	0·08	0·05	0	0	0·23
3	1·33	0·85	0·73	0·27	0·19	0·21	0·06	0·05	0·05	0·06	0	0·11	0·27
4	1·09	0·71	0·65	0·42	0·17	0·13	0·17	0·15	0·04	0·04	0·14	0·14	0·26
5	1·07	0·49	0·37	0·09	0·39	0·21	0·07	0·15	0·08	0·02	0	0	0·22
6	0·79	0·74	0·47	0·56	0·21	0·18	0·11	0·09	0·08	0·07	0	0	0·25
7	1·38	0·61	0·39	0·56	0·32	0·18	0·25	0	0·10	0	0	0	0·29
8	1·04	0·71	0·58	0·40	0·15	0	0·18	0·60	0·13	0·07	0	0	0·29
9	0·96	0·92	0·32	0·64	0·13	0·19	0	0·33	0	0	0·04	0	0·30
10	0·91	0·39	0·22	0·10	0·15	0	0	0·29	0	0·33	—	0	0·29
Σ	1·04	0·65	0·51	0·42	0·23	0·20	0·13	0·16	0·07	0·03	0·04	0·03	0·26

Table B12. Number of children aged under 1

	1	2	3	4	5	6	7	8	9	10	11	12	Σ
1	0·29	0·11	0·15	0·11	0·08	0·06	0·07	0·01	0·02	0·01	0·07	0·02	0·06
2	0·25	0·08	0·02	0	0·07	0·10	0·04	0	0·02	0·02	0	0	0·04
3	0·11	0·33	0·03	0·08	0·04	0·16	0·13	0·02	0·01	0·02	0·03	0·02	0·07
4	0·24	0·27	0·14	0·11	0·09	0·09	0	0·04	0·03	0·02	0	0	0·07
5	0·18	0·07	0·06	0·09	0·03	0	0·04	0	0·03	0	0	0	0·04
6	0·29	0·10	0·03	0·05	0	0·04	0·03	0	0·08	0·07	0	0	0·04
7	0·38	0·09	0·16	0·06	0·03	0·05	0·03	0	0	0	0	0·08	0·05
8	0·04	0·18	0·08	0·13	0·06	0·08	0·07	0·06	0·01	0	0	0	0·06
9	0·25	0·21	0·01	0·02	0	0·10	0	0	0	0	—	0	0·07
10	0·18	0·09	0	0·30	0	0·10	0	0	0	0	0	0	0·07
Σ	0·22	0·14	0·07	0·08	0·04	0·07	0·04	0·02	0·03	0·01	0·02	0·02	0·06

Table B13. Expenditure on all food

	1	2	3	4	5	6	7	8	9	10	11	12	Σ
1	378·83	406·00	403·41	371·12	401·48	422·44	448·92	478·94	447·77	428·50	437·04	406·17	426·06
2	302·17	365·11	364·81	361·00	379·83	411·55	376·39	379·94	377·50	451·59	391·00	553·33	388·01
3	304·00	370·15	414·44	413·45	366·71	372·80	454·00	402·50	388·11	455·31	459·91	482·64	405·12
4	353·76	465·15	383·48	380·54	402·63	417·59	471·67	473·00	396·17	419·16	386·39	408·41	414·99
5	335·36	350·63	396·52	389·18	348·95	438·43	399·46	363·94	367·33	406·16	429·27	538·00	387·67
6	275·54	367·04	401·14	406·59	387·33	422·00	427·13	403·54	415·66	398·00	456·05	432·88	403·11
7	356·75	323·57	355·45	373·06	389·41	422·53	378·88	389·71	360·20	433·86	536·63	586·75	394·60
8	287·67	361·00	403·69	371·00	414·08	504·67	370·71	393·90	460·50	454·13	463·17	225·00	410·76
9	377·92	427·28	441·55	460·12	449·54	454·89	508·63	481·75	394·44	438·78	511·45	472·50	453·32
10	332·43	454·73	594·11	375·20	470·69	397·60	271·00	438·00	382·67	435·00	—	799·00	426·13
Σ	331·59	386·46	407·15	395·38	396·38	424·85	426·39	424·05	403·67	426·81	443·38	448·85	411·43

Table B14. Farinaceous foods

	1	2	3	4	5	6	7	8	9	10	11	12	Σ
1	89·67	80·71	69·71	55·84	54·90	58·24	58·78	60·52	61·82	49·36	50·15	41·87	57·68
2	73·67	67·33	69·95	62·21	56·04	64·19	56·46	57·06	58·45	62·45	58·10	82·33	61·95
3	70·33	74·62	77·00	80·91	67·86	62·60	58·52	57·55	57·89	68·92	64·27	72·36	69·18
4	77·35	98·38	68·80	62·82	65·20	65·31	67·18	64·24	55·03	54·52	49·74	51·82	63·22
5	75·09	58·95	62·24	62·24	54·82	63·43	53·11	52·68	61·67	57·36	54·80	72·29	58·81
6	69·00	81·96	80·32	73·21	63·54	66·24	68·23	67·93	59·41	59·81	60·57	54·44	66·89
7	87·25	53·57	57·55	64·71	64·71	60·74	62·00	63·53	63·80	64·00	76·13	68·75	63·56
8	66·50	73·43	78·85	61·46	65·85	77·13	57·93	54·90	68·50	79·00	63·83	24·00	67·53
9	91·38	99·67	97·64	94·04	88·83	81·96	93·42	85·10	71·22	79·35	82·85	75·90	87·17
10	88·50	99·91	144·22	97·40	92·00	85·60	46·00	75·43	74·17	71·00	—	166·00	92·35
Σ	79·05	78·35	77·53	70·63	65·90	66·83	64·80	62·92	61·42	61·55	59·91	57·81	66·84

Table B15. Dairy produce

	1	2	3	4	5	6	7	8	9	10	11	12	Σ
1	75·83	80·21	87·18	80·96	88·79	95·73	96·03	92·18	84·44	80·68	84·04	68·63	86·04
2	64·67	86·78	89·19	84·21	91·65	94·06	81·50	83·06	84·95	96·86	82·10	113·00	87·84
3	75·44	92·85	102·88	99·55	85·29	84·00	102·76	93·82	88·05	108·62	99·64	92·55	93·71
4	79·88	111·00	89·00	84·75	90·87	89·03	99·88	92·56	88·03	87·48	71·39	73·41	87·95
5	63·55	69·68	82·92	79·65	72·05	87·07	78·11	70·38	68·67	68·88	69·93	78·86	73·88
6	53·69	78·22	84·32	89·72	83·71	88·71	92·63	88·11	85·10	77·85	77·10	81·00	83·50
7	50·75	64·14	72·73	75·35	74·35	82·42	76·75	76·00	63·30	79·29	90·13	105·25	75·43
8	75·83	88·57	96·46	89·46	92·15	117·93	82·93	86·80	106·80	94·50	86·83	45·00	93·78
9	81·54	94·06	97·45	105·77	87·71	100·78	96·11	94·20	73·83	75·04	96·60	83·90	91·70
10	87·79	101·64	140·00	85·80	109·31	86·70	57·60	93·57	88·50	98·67	—	165·00	98·32
Σ	72·97	85·25	91·78	88·49	86·59	92·71	89·83	86·59	82·82	83·80	82·15	79·82	86·30

Table B16. Fruit

	1	2	3	4	5	6	7	8	9	10	11	12	Σ
1	10·33	14·21	18·71	16·72	19·03	24·02	27·44	27·45	25·49	27·32	27·11	26·77	23·76
2	9·17	14·06	18·10	19·79	18·04	22·42	21·39	22·71	24·10	32·32	28·80	44·00	21·94
3	10·00	12·92	19·31	17·86	16·14	14·90	26·95	21·23	21·63	27·54	30·00	36·64	20·71
4	8·06	11·15	16·28	17·50	20·33	20·00	26·33	24·82	21·10	25·65	21·94	32·06	21·17
5	6·36	15·05	21·48	19·71	20·09	23·57	27·36	17·53	21·17	23·28	25·53	76·57	22·29
6	6·08	13·04	18·59	16·69	20·96	21·41	25·13	22·71	25·38	23·33	30·24	30·38	21·51
7	10·00	15·43	20·64	20·71	19·71	22·21	22·00	24·82	19·30	33·14	44·88	43·75	23·09
8	7·33	13·57	16·23	19·00	18·85	31·13	25·14	26·80	32·10	29·13	49·00	25·00	24·16
9	6·08	9·33	18·82	19·69	25·96	23·04	29·42	28·95	24·00	32·74	34·70	36·00	24·15
10	3·36	10·64	28·00	12·20	20·69	19·50	13·60	20·43	26·00	15·33	—	86·00	17·14
Σ	7·10	12·98	19·14	18·21	20·04	22·15	25·53	23·64	23·75	27·30	29·50	35·51	22·21

Table B17. Vegetables

	1	2	3	4	5	6	7	8	9	10	11	12	Σ
1	38·00	41·43	35·00	34·36	29·93	35·71	38·83	36·67	36·97	35·79	32·33	29·07	35·05
2	20·00	26·72	25·81	20·79	25·17	28·45	21·89	24·18	26·25	30·82	28·10	44·67	26·00
3	17·11	23·46	28·19	29·50	29·61	23·20	30·71	27·45	26·42	24·77	35·91	30·82	27·60
4	28·41	37·00	28·96	29·39	30·37	36·09	37·15	37·41	28·76	31·61	29·87	31·18	32·33
5	25·55	25·21	29·28	28·59	25·95	29·21	31·86	22·32	23·54	31·68	35·67	49·29	28·41
6	22·69	30·22	31·23	29·69	28·60	30·53	27·57	29·61	26·76	27·07	27·71	26·38	28·49
7	18·25	27·29	27·00	26·00	25·24	28·21	26·44	24·47	26·00	27·57	35·88	43·75	26·79
8	20·17	26·14	27·00	26·77	28·69	40·73	23·64	31·00	33·60	30·38	41·17	17·00	29·92
9	26·54	29·39	29·32	31·85	34·83	28·41	36·05	30·95	25·22	25·65	27·55	23·40	29·51
10	25·07	29·82	45·78	24·00	34·54	24·80	14·00	35·71	26·17	28·33	—	53·00	30·04
Σ	24·76	29·62	29·73	29·12	29·22	31·17	30·91	30·09	28·68	30·03	31·39	31·21	29·81

Table B18. Fish

	1	2	3	4	5	6	7	8	9	10	11	12	Σ
1	11·17	11·86	15·41	15·64	20·14	15·61	17·06	21·18	19·33	20·82	21·70	18·07	18·12
2	22·33	14·56	16·38	12·43	11·96	17·94	15·29	12·18	15·55	15·14	11·10	22·67	15·04
3	7·44	11·15	13·06	11·91	13·57	11·45	14·86	20·23	12·89	17·08	11·55	21·82	14·06
4	9·41	18·23	12·24	13·71	13·97	16·00	20·24	20·24	13·76	18·26	18·52	21·76	16·51
5	17·00	11·47	18·20	18·88	17·59	20·43	17·18	24·82	18·33	19·32	20·80	28·86	19·15
6	10·08	13·83	12·77	13·45	15·23	17·12	16·93	16·93	19·38	14·78	24·57	21·75	16·38
7	27·25	12·57	16·82	16·24	16·35	19·37	15·94	14·24	18·10	21·71	23·25	15·75	17·16
8	6·50	8·71	16·00	12·85	22·46	18·20	12·57	15·00	26·00	15·50	19·50	7·00	16·16
9	17·92	14·06	13·18	15·69	13·75	19·00	20·00	23·95	19·11	17·96	22·75	21·50	17·97
10	4·93	8·73	11·33	4·80	14·62	11·00	21·00	9·57	9·50	17·33	—	22·00	10·64
Σ	12·08	12·88	14·60	14·27	15·65	16·74	17·07	19·35	17·42	17·79	20·03	20·77	16·61

Table B19. Meat

	1	2	3	4	5	6	7	8	9	10	11	12	Σ
1	76·50	91·36	91·06	84·00	97·24	99·44	98·94	111·12	108·38	95·93	94·37	77·83	96·33
2	52·67	72·83	73·90	84·29	99·70	93·74	96·18	99·71	86·30	102·55	100·40	85·33	90·08
3	61·22	78·54	90·13	99·41	86·89	95·20	101·71	98·32	96·58	107·31	108·82	113·09	95·16
4	75·76	98·38	94·76	96·89	104·03	105·00	119·09	131·24	105·34	104·90	98·55	104·76	105·20
5	77·55	85·79	92·64	98·24	81·59	102·29	97·71	86·91	87·83	102·64	120·53	103·86	93·76
6	60·92	73·52	85·77	94·17	98·48	100·59	101·57	93·11	99·03	92·15	99·86	101·25	93·68
7	93·75	76·50	89·27	93·41	104·35	114·37	97·94	105·94	91·40	123·57	156·38	155·75	104·06
8	56·00	81·00	86·77	85·62	104·23	124·40	91·21	100·30	108·20	110·25	111·67	21·00	97·41
9	70·31	80·44	97·00	94·23	103·88	102·04	122·53	107·50	88·17	100·70	124·30	109·00	100·63
10	53·71	79·73	104·56	64·40	82·54	83·20	63·60	98·00	84·33	83·00	—	169·00	80·06
Σ	67·03	81·16	99·05	92·11	96·70	101·75	102·58	104·45	97·61	101·36	108·16	98·66	96·65

Table B20. Rent

	1	2	3	4	5	6	7	8	9	10	11	12	Σ
1	170·00	163·57	172·94	178·40	157·59	187·80	182·22	186·67	196·15	179·29	230·37	236·33	189·78
2	85·00	94·44	112·86	126·43	153·91	146·45	128·93	126·47	178·00	222·27	143·00	150·00	143·29
3	100·00	120·77	123·13	100·00	118·21	145·00	138·10	125·45	103·68	176·92	168·18	187·27	130·20
4	95·29	104·62	107·60	100·71	115·33	126·88	104·85	120·88	128·97	138·39	129·35	173·53	120·53
5	122·73	103·16	116·00	122·35	100·00	115·00	123·21	162·35	122·50	138·00	161·33	157·14	128·55
6	103·08	110·43	107·27	133·45	116·87	122·65	113·67	113·21	132·41	132·59	161·43	203·13	126·66
7	80·00	96·43	69·09	106·47	155·88	112·11	89·38	118·82	121·00	141·43	152·50	172·50	115·14
8	68·33	84·29	99·23	100·77	96·92	83·33	138·57	131·00	136·00	111·25	130·00	120·00	107·84
9	63·85	77·22	93·18	91·92	91·67	99·26	106·84	122·50	106·67	119·57	125·00	152·00	102·96
10	47·14	54·55	81·11	56·00	70·00	75·00	82·00	111·43	96·67	183·33	—	50·00	75·00
Σ	90·51	102·33	110·83	117·30	120·28	130·82	126·96	137·07	141·03	153·53	159·87	192·80	130·92

Table B21. Fuel

	I	2	3	4	5	6	7	8	9	10	11	12	Σ
1	81·83	77·14	75·06	76·88	80·76	77·44	83·22	87·12	84·28	77·00	88·22	81·97	81·36
2	56·17	60·44	64·71	67·36	70·70	85·32	63·86	73·88	74·20	86·50	101·00	116·33	74·12
3	57·11	63·31	67·00	68·45	62·25	71·35	64·05	86·45	81·47	69·15	62·91	119·55	72·13
4	66·24	68·08	60·32	68·04	71·33	72·50	78·12	80·56	73·72	99·81	79·65	90·18	76·36
5	65·45	66·84	62·92	59·06	66·77	76·07	72·46	69·91	115·92	78·36	137·47	86·57	78·49
6	56·46	73·78	77·64	79·38	72·15	76·26	83·87	79·14	75·10	103·78	81·38	76·56	78·57
7	66·75	48·79	35·55	55·65	66·41	52·47	59·56	78·47	58·90	82·43	101·88	102·25	63·12
8	45·00	51·57	56·08	59·77	74·23	80·20	66·93	82·30	81·90	106·25	105·17	6·00	72·16
9	61·31	71·61	70·14	63·27	66·50	73·63	69·21	78·95	59·56	66·17	84·95	116·80	71·72
10	57·14	78·00	104·78	92·00	82·15	83·70	93·80	101·86	78·83	124·33	—	133·00	84·85
Σ	61·17	66·89	66·86	68·42	71·02	75·10	73·59	80·24	80·25	86·28	90·40	92·03	75·77

Table B22. Household durables

	I	2	3	4	5	6	7	8	9	10	11	12	Σ
1	6·00	16·43	20·94	25·68	33·66	29·93	24·53	36·03	32·15	25·14	48·22	147·77	40·71
2	11·50	11·28	19·10	12·36	12·43	29·29	21·64	18·82	29·75	83·91	179·90	107·00	35·34
3	5·89	7·00	18·81	14·36	20·36	33·10	39·00	35·50	31·79	77·54	130·18	184·73	42·29
4	9·94	22·46	16·96	13·36	19·63	28·94	28·76	36·09	26·97	38·81	142·39	270·65	49·84
5	18·82	22·68	21·52	16·00	25·27	20·93	36·64	32·97	30·88	46·28	89·53	167·86	36·76
6	5·62	12·78	24·36	24·66	19·71	32·24	17·73	38·29	47·97	41·37	124·38	153·00	40·10
7	5·25	21·21	21·82	22·12	15·24	33·84	37·00	25·35	52·00	90·43	249·88	317·75	50·57
8	18·17	23·86	15·38	26·69	34·85	29·40	23·14	33·20	82·10	117·38	112·67	0	41·46
9	20·54	10·06	19·59	28·08	21·50	30·63	20·05	45·35	41·56	49·91	99·35	330·20	47·60
10	6·86	16·73	7·22	39·80	24·92	17·40	36·20	34·71	134·50	143·33	—	203·00	34·60
Σ	11·11	15·80	19·29	21·14	22·17	29·62	27·36	34·34	40·50	54·47	117·88	197·86	42·34

INDEX

For general headings the reader may find it more convenient to consult the Contents, pp. vii–xi; for individual commodities he should refer to the Contents of the Tables, pp. 179–83.